COMMITTED TO

International treaties are the primary means for codifying global human rights standards. However, nation-states are able to make their own choices in how to legally commit to human rights treaties. A state commits to a treaty through four commitment acts: signature, ratification, accession, and succession. These acts signify diverging legal paths with distinct contexts and mechanisms for rights change reflecting legalization, negotiation, sovereignty, and domestic constraints. How a state moves through these actions determines how, when, and to what extent it will comply with the human rights treaties it commits to. Using legal, archival, and quantitative analysis this important book shows that disentangling legal paths to commitment reveals distinct and significant compliance outcomes. Legal context matters for human rights and has important implications for the conceptualization of treaty commitment, the consideration of non-binding commitment, and an optimistic outlook for the impact of human rights treaties.

AUDREY L. COMSTOCK is an Assistant Professor of Political Science in the School of Social and Behavioral Sciences at Arizona State University. Her research focuses on international law, human rights, and international organizations, including the punishment of peacekeepers accused of sexual exploitation and abuse of civilians.

COMMITTED TO RIGHTS

UN Human Rights Treaties and Legal Paths for Commitment and Compliance

AUDREY L. COMSTOCK

Arizona State University

CAMBRIDGE
UNIVERSITY PRESS

CAMBRIDGE
UNIVERSITY PRESS

Shaftesbury Road, Cambridge CB2 8EA, United Kingdom

One Liberty Plaza, 20th Floor, New York, NY 10006, USA

477 Williamstown Road, Port Melbourne, VIC 3207, Australia

314–321, 3rd Floor, Plot 3, Splendor Forum, Jasola District Centre, New Delhi – 110025, India

103 Penang Road, #05–06/07, Visioncrest Commercial, Singapore 238467

Cambridge University Press is part of Cambridge University Press & Assessment,
a department of the University of Cambridge.

We share the University's mission to contribute to society through the pursuit of
education, learning and research at the highest international levels of excellence.

www.cambridge.org
Information on this title: www.cambridge.org/9781108821582

DOI: 10.1017/9781108908979

First published 2021
First paperback edition 2023

A catalogue record for this publication is available from the British Library

ISBN   978-1-108-83007-2   Hardback
ISBN   978-1-108-82158-2   Paperback

CONTENTS

FIGURES AND TABLES

Figures

Tables

ACKNOWLEDGMENTS

This book developed along its own pathway with the help, direction, feedback, and support from many.

The earliest academic step came during my undergraduate studies at the University at Albany, State University of New York. I thank Rey Koslowski, who guided my honors thesis and humored many, many ratification graphs. I express my thanks to Victor Asal and Tom Walker, who patiently trained young research assistants on important topics of alliances and terrorism and, in doing so, planted the seed of academic interest, causal relationships, and linking data analysis to big problems.

The Government Department at Cornell University trained and treated me well. Matt Evangelista, Peter Katzenstein, and Sarah Kreps provided guidance, countless thoughtful comments, and feedback as my dissertation developed. I recall them always being happy to discuss my latest version at coffee shops across the world during my fellowships and their travels. The International Law/International Relations Colloquium at Cornell, in particular, offered a space of interdisciplinary research and discussion that was invaluable during formative dissertation writing. The ideas and framework for this book would not be possible without these folks.

I thank both the Browne Center for International Politics at the University of Pennsylvania and the Williams Institute at the University of California, Los Angeles (UCLA), where I spent predoctoral fellowship time. The intellectual environment and support (in particular from Kal Raustiala and Asli U. Bâli) were very helpful. I also thank Drexel University for the resources and space that afforded me insightful conversations with Zoltán Búzás, Amelia Hoover Green, Erin Graham, and Joel Oestreich about international law, global governance, and human rights.

The community of scholars at the intersection of international law and international relations has been fantastic and an amazing resource to draw on through conferences, workshops, and friendships. In particular, at the University of Pennsylvania, the Perry World House "Workshop on International Law, Organizations, and Politics" offered an extraordinarily helpful setting with detailed feedback on parts of this book from Duncan Hollis, Beth Simmons, and Zeid Ra'ad al Hussein. Throughout the years, I've received valuable feedback on different iterations of this project from Clifford Bob, Cosette Creamer, Jean Galbraith, Mi Hwa Hong, Mark Pollack, Frances Rosenbluth, Heather Smith-Cannoy, Jana von Stein, Andrea Vilán, and David Zaring. Additionally, I am grateful to Susan M. Sterett for her continued support and inclusion into Law and Society.

At Arizona State University (ASU), I benefited first as a postdoctoral scholar in the School of Politics and Global Studies and School of Social and Behavioral Sciences and then as an assistant professor. I am grateful for the resources, time, and space ASU provided that allowed me to put pen to page. It has been incredible to be a part of ASU's energy, commitment to inclusion, and support for global human rights initiatives while writing this book.

Numerous people at Cambridge University Press have been helpful in shepherding this project along. Thanks go to John Berger, who saw an interesting project, and to Finola O'Sullivan and Marianne Nield, who saw it through to the end. My immense gratitude goes to the two anonymous reviewers for their careful reading, actionable criticisms, and support. The book is unquestionably the better for it. Thanks to Jennifer Quincey for close reading and editing. All errors remain my own.

The final pieces of this book came together during the 2020 coronavirus pandemic. I was privileged to be in isolation, writing at home, while essential personnel around the globe worked to protect and heal. Vulnerable groups like refugees had no option of isolating. The impoverished had no clean water and soap to wash their hands. May this context serve as a reminder of the perpetual importance of protecting human rights and the findings of this book provide some optimism about the potential of international institutions and law to help.

I am extremely grateful to my family – big and small – for their support during this endeavor. To my parents, Barb and Gary Comstock, thank you for always being supportive and instilling a lifelong love of learning. Thanks to my brother, Aaron, the anthropologist, for some healthy sibling rivalry as we both completed PhDs, applied for grants, and wrote up our findings. To my husband Scott: thank you for your unwavering confidence in me and this project. I cannot express how much your love and support mean to me. We are blessed with two sons, Henry and Oliver, who bring joy and excitement to our days. Through them, I see the world anew. Thank you, boys, for the gifts of patience and unconditional love. I am sorry to disappoint you that my sort of book does not have an illustrator, pictures, and jokes – but it's for you nonetheless, and I hope you'll enjoy reading it someday.

ABBREVIATIONS

CAT	Convention against Torture and Other Cruel, Inhuman, or Degrading Treatment or Punishment
CED	International Convention for the Protection of All Persons from Enforced Disappearance
CEDAW	Convention on the Elimination of All Forms of Discrimination against Women
CERD	Convention on the Elimination of All Forms of Racial Discrimination
CMW	International Convention on the Protection of the Rights of All Migrant Workers and Members of Their Families
CRC	Convention on the Rights of the Child
CRPD	Convention on the Rights of Persons with Disabilities
ECHR	European Court of Human Rights
EIF	entry into force
ICC	International Criminal Court
ICCPR	International Covenant on Civil and Political Rights
ICESCR	International Covenant on Economic, Social, and Cultural Rights
ICJ	International Court of Justice
ICTY	International Criminal Tribunal for the former Yugoslavia
IGO	Intergovernmental organizations
NGO	nongovernmental organization
OHCHR	Office of the High Commissioner for Human Rights
UDHR	Universal Declaration of Human Rights
UN	United Nations
US	United States
VCLT	Vienna Convention on the Law of Treaties

1

Introduction

The opening lines of the preamble to the United Nations Charter (1945) established the mission and role of the new international organization, calling it to

> save succeeding generations from the scourge of war, which twice in our lifetime has brought untold sorrow to mankind, and to reaffirm faith in fundamental human rights, in the dignity and worth of the human person, in the equal rights of men and women and of nations large and small, and to establish conditions under which justice and respect for the obligations arising from treaties and other sources of international law can be maintained . . .

With the recent and devastating memory of World Wars I and II fresh in their minds, international leaders sought cooperative means to protect global human rights and to maintain peace. They sought to eliminate the interstate tensions and humanitarian atrocities that ignited immense global wars. When meeting in San Francisco to create the United Nations Charter, states endeavored to establish a more peaceful and just international order through legal means. Their tools were charters, agreements, and treaties to establish norms of behavior on the international plane. Their bold goal was to bind states to uphold these peaceful ideals. Much has happened since the United Nations Charter was written almost seventy-five years ago. Covering twenty-nine issue areas and written in at least six languages, almost six hundred multilateral treaties have been deposited with the UN secretary-general.[1] UN multilateral treaties cover subjects ranging from nuclear weapons and torture to the standardization of international road signs and regulation of state activities on the moon. International treaties cover the many facets of state actions from the subnational to the celestial level.

The increase in treaties negotiated, created, and deposited with the United Nations represents a global commitment to the legalization of norms, standards, and ideas. Even states that are in violation or plan to

[1] "Multilateral Treaties Deposited with the Secretary General," available at https://treaties .un.org/.Pages/Content.aspx?path=DB/MTDSGStatus/pageIntro_en.xml

violate international law still commit to them, and states that oppose particular treaties are still generally involved with the treaty at some point. The United States infamously withdrew support for the Rome Statute of the International Criminal Court, yet it played a large role in treaty negotiations and still has overall cooperated with Court activities.[2] There is an expectation that international law, and in particular treaties, will be used to address important issues of transnational and international concern. While it is not necessarily surprising when liberal democracies readily commit to human rights treaties, nondemocratic states do so as well. Rights-hostile, nondemocratic regimes also identify a need or desire to engage with the international legal system. Democracies, dictatorships, and all states in between recognize how essential it is to participate in the international legal system. Much scholarship has studied how regime type matters for human rights practices, citing the importance of democracy for human rights recognition (Apodaca 2001; Bueno de Mesquita et al. 2005; Davenport 1995, 1999; Moravcsik 2000; Poe and Tate 1994; Poe, Tate, and Keith 1999). Several important works examine how regime type can matter for legal commitment, noting nondemocracies' participation in the international human rights regime either for strategic reasons (e.g., Conrad 2014; Vreeland 2008) or at the urging of other actors (e.g., Spar 1998). In fact, growing research points to authoritarian regimes, and their citizens, engaging more with human rights, democracy, and foreign policy than prior assumptions held (e.g., Brownlee 2007; Gandhi 2008; Gandhi and Lust-Okar 2009). All of these findings underscore the importance of human rights.

This book builds on a growing wave of scholarship that complicates the study of international law and compliance (Finnemore and Toope [2001, 754], e.g., argue for a process-based study of international law that takes variation of domestic politics into account). I draw on the literatures on the domestic/international legal nexus to address a gap in our understanding of how states legally commit to international treaty law (Hillebrecht 2012, 2014; Lupu 2013b; Mitchell and Powell 2011; Powell and Mitchell 2007; Powell and Staton 2009). I argue that the type of commitment states make toward international treaties matters for understanding (1) what, if any, changes they will make in their human rights behavior and (2) when changes are expected to happen. Depending on

---

[2] The United States did not veto, for example, a UN Security Council request that the International Criminal Court (ICC) investigate crimes in Darfur, Sudan.

the domestic and legal definitional contexts within which the commitment actions are made, states take differing approaches toward human rights practices following treaty commitments. Different commitment paths mean different things at different times for different states: though a potentially obvious statement to make, this is a new approach for studying international human rights law. Through a clear examination of types of treaty commitment and the domestic contexts within which commitment happens, I unpack when commitment is likely to signify important positive changes in human rights practices.

Treaties are a clear and public signal of support for international law. Dignitaries sign a treaty amid international fanfare and media coverage. Treaty commitment has been meticulously recorded and archived by international organizations, national governments, nongovernmental organizations (NGOs), and other groups for nearly one hundred years, and in many cases prior centuries, as well. But the treaty commitment signal is not as simple as many scholars present. Simmons, for instance, writes that treaties "set the stage" in international relations (2009, 5). However, states are setting different stages at different times based on *how* they commit to treaty law. The "how" of treaty commitment connects into a variety of domestic and international contexts that are imperative to understand when studying human rights behavior changes. Several noted pieces of scholarship criticize a ratification-dominated approach to understanding international law. For example, nearly two decades ago, Goodman and Jinks critiqued the use of treaty ratification as the "proxy for the formal acceptance of international human rights law" (2003, 173). However, little has been done within international relations to move research away from a ratification focus, and it remains the dominant assessment tool for international relations and legal scholars.

My findings point to the notable differences in rights practices across commitment types to international human rights treaties: states that opted out of treaty negotiations had worse practices after acceding to human rights treaties than their counterparts who did negotiate; states with domestic ratification policies requiring legislative approval used signature as a means to communicate support of human rights treaties earlier than states allowing executive treaty ratification (for *Legislative Approval States*, signature – not ratification – marked the inflection point in rights practices); new states recommitting to treaties via succession improved their rights practices as they signaled to the international community their overall commitment to human rights ideas while confronting growing pressure from NGOs and the United Nations to establish themselves as new, "Westernized" states through human rights norms and law adoption.

Whether legal commitment to international law has the potential to change state behavior is a driving question within international legal and international relations scholarship. Oona Hathaway (2002) famously asked, "Do Human Rights Treaties Make a Difference?" The question of whether international law changes or constrains state behavior has become an existential one for the study of international treaties. A driving critique from the legal community asks, "Is International Law Really Law?" (D'Amato 2010). For activists, practitioners, and politicians, the extent to which committing to international law has an impact on human rights change is an increasingly pressing question. If some legal commitment paths elicit more positive change than others, this is important information for the international community and rights-based groups. Mobilization strategies, campaigns, and media attention may shift accordingly to support any action that is associated with improved rights, and shaming campaigns may target actions used as hollow gestures of commitment to rights.

More broadly, the extent to which international law matters in international relations speaks to the merits of international cooperation within an anarchical system. Commitment to treaties alone demonstrates states' willingness to participate in the international bodies that seek to constrain them; changing behavior after commitment and complying with international laws demonstrates a willingness to sacrifice sovereignty for a greater good. As many scholars note, there is much gray area in between commitment and compliance, and much disagreement about what compliance entails. Without question, international norms, rules, and laws constrain states in new ways and chip away at the anarchical international system. Exploring the efficacy of international human rights law is an important endeavor that deserves more nuanced means to test international cooperation broadly and human rights treaties specifically.

Why International Treaty Law?

When asked to point to the beginning of the modern international system, students of international relations cite a specific year and connect it to a particular set of treaties. The noted Peace of Westphalia comprised two treaties signed a few months apart in 1648, bringing to a close conflicts between Spain and the Netherlands and between the Holy Roman Empire, Germany, France, and Sweden. The Treaty of

Westphalia established state sovereignty for the modern era and demonstrated the existing states' commitment to use treaty law as the language of interstate diplomacy, even with the political pains and delays that accompany treaty negotiation. Negotiating the peace treaties reportedly took five years, with the first six months focused on the order of diplomats' entry into the negotiating room and seating arrangements once entered (Sofer 2013, 29). The Treaty established states as the main actors in the international system and international law as a primary tool for them to conduct international relations.

The international system and international law have both changed since the 1600s. Two world wars shaped the global view on human rights and humanitarian practices. The Cold War shaped conflict and political dynamics in the context of a bipolar system and nuclear threats. Globalization processes and information dissemination have made for a quickly interconnected world. The rise of terrorism, both domestic and international, emphasized non-state actors' capabilities and significance. Despite these and other changes in the last four hundred years, state sovereignty remains a core tenet of international relations. International law continues to thrive.

International law is a broad entity covering many different areas and actions. It comprises thousands of agreements brought together by states, NGOs, businesses, and individuals. Article 2(1)(a) of the Vienna Convention on the Law of Treaties (VCLT) defines a treaty as "an international agreement concluded between States in written form and governed by international law, whether embodied in a single instrument or in two or more related instruments and whatever its particular designation." Some scholars debate the merits of international law and are skeptical about its use as a tool for changing state behavior or even reflecting all state preferences. Hans Morgenthau, for instance, wrote that states "are always anxious to shake off the restraining influence that international law might have upon their foreign policies, to use international law instead for the promotion of their national interests" (1985, 299).

However, international law does offer a codified set of rules against which we can measure the extent to which and conditions under which states alter their behavior. Examining international law is fruitful in assessing when, if ever, states respond to legal guidelines and how changing legal guidelines codify and reflect changing global norms. In this project, I limit the examination to treaty law. This is not to argue that other forms of international law – such as case law, customary international law, and general or natural principles of international law – are trivial areas for study. In fact, important research is beginning to examine the use of international court decisions within domestic courts (e.g., Fikfak 2014; Roberts 2011) and the development of customary international law over time (e.g., Posner and Goldsmith 1999; Wood 2015). Rather, I focus on international treaty law for the following four reasons.

First, treaty law has emerged in the post–World War II period as the dominant form of international law. Thousands of treaties have been created both within and outside of the UN treaty system, in contrast to international case law, which while growing has yet to reach the same volume or frequency. The International Court of Justice, for example, heard 134 cases between 1947 and 2014, while bilateral investment treaties alone totaled 2,181 between 1990 and 2002, according to the United Nations. The narrower area of multilateral treaties deposited with the Secretary-General of the United Nations also out-totaled case law. According to the United Nations, more than six hundred multilateral treaties were deposited between 1948 and 2017.

Second, treaty law requires some involvement of the domestic level to approve law at the international level. This contrasts with customary international law, which through its definition is not based on formal, legal commitment but rather "international custom, as evidence of a general practice accepted as law."[3] Customary international law increasingly functions as a source of international law, but variation in state integration of customary international law results in a lack of uniform commitment standards and timing across states. For example, in defining and exploring customary international law, Lepard (2010) downplays state practices as criteria demonstrating customary international law, and authors D'Amato (1971, 5) and Koskenniemi (2010, 361–362) critique the conceptual use of customary international law based on its inconsistency of rules, applications, and theories. The same broadly applicable yet often less-legalized character of customary international law that makes it appealing to states also makes it more difficult to substantively study, measure, and assess. Given these aspects of customary international law, treaty law offers a more structured type of law for analyzing state behavior and domestic legal involvement.

Third, formalizing the treaty-making process makes for precise records of participation. The United Nations houses hundreds of multilateral treaties deposited with the UN Secretary-General and keeps records of which states committed to what treaties, when, and how. Unlike less-formalized

---

[3] Article 38(1) (b) Statute of the International Court of Justice.

customary international law, which does not have precise points of rights emergence, treaty law offers more concrete times for legal emergence and commitment for study. The UN Office of Legal Affairs Treaty Section provides real-time updates of participatory actions, disseminates this information to member states, and makes it public on their website. Participation in UN multilateral treaties is formal, legalized, and transparent.

Fourth, multilateral treaties by definition involve more than two states, thus enabling us to engage with broader treaty commitment. Even though customary international is conceptually applicable to every state, it becomes more difficult to pinpoint times of emergence and change as well as which states participate, when, and to what extent. Bilateral treaties are legally precise in terms of who participates, when, and how but are limited to two states. A state may make separate bilateral trade agreements with different states. These actions may demonstrate one state's legal preferences but not necessarily reflect the system's preferences overall. International court cases also involve fewer state participants. Often court rulings apply to those states that are members of a certain court. The European Court of Human Rights decisions, for example, would have limited-to-no legal basis for application within the United States or Nigeria. The International Court of Justice takes on cases and rulings between two states and administers advisory opinions. Posner and de Figueiredo (2005) find statistical evidence supporting the charges that International Court of Justice (ICJ) judges are biased in rulings, based on similarities between judges and state participant judicial systems, which states appoint them, wealth, and cultural similarities. The ICC has been criticized for targeting African leaders, in particular, introducing the possibility of regional biases in participation (Kaye 2011; Shamsi 2016). Treaty commitment, alternatively, is voluntary and open to any UN member state, broadening the total number of possible involved states to almost two hundred.

While this book focuses on a specific "home" for international law – the UN treaty framework – elements of these mechanisms are translatable and generalizable across agreements within other international organizations and across other forms of international law. First, although the four commitment types analyzed in this book – ratification, signature, accession, and succession – have precise definitions and requirements within the UN treaty framework, several are used within other international organizational settings. For example, the Council of Europe Convention for the Protection of Human Rights and Fundamental Freedoms (1950) recognizes the four types of commitment. Treaties are used within the International Monetary Fund (IMF) as a formal system of legal agreement. However, within core agreements at the IMF, commitment takes the effect of a definitive signature, a variety of signature that is binding and not subject to ratification (see Article XXXI, section 2 (g) and (4), of the IMF Articles of Agreement). Similarly, the Articles of Agreement of the International Bank for Reconstruction and Development, establishing the World Bank, uses definitive signature as the authoritative commitment form. This legal practice distinguishes these types of agreements from UN agreements, which entail a period of nonbinding commitment. In that respect, the book's findings and arguments differ from the particularities of these legal frameworks. However, although the terminology differs among the international organizations, context and processes do extend across organizations. In the IMF and World Bank, international agreements operate with a period leading up to entry into force (EIF), offering a nonbinding time within which to consider state compliance. Similarly, agreements in these other international organization settings are negotiated by membership.

Second, less-formalized agreements may not seek binding status at all. The nonbinding nature of international agreements, declarations, and conventions aligns with the book's argument that nonbinding signature paves the path toward compliance. The World Medical Association's Declaration of Helsinki is widely considered a successful and nonbinding declaration on public health, subjects, and consent (Bodansky 2015, 162). Within the UN framework, declarations provide important nonbinding agreements reasserting state commitment to issues covering human rights (1948), combating human trafficking (2017), and forming nonbinding foundations to future hard law (e.g., the 1959 Declaration on the Rights of the Child and the 1961 Declaration on the Prohibition of the Use of Nuclear and Thermonuclear Weapons both led to treaties).

Additionally, the domestic processes discussed here – arriving at binding commitment, the power of participating in agreement negotiations, and the role of regime transitions and international legitimation on compliance – are illuminating elements of international commitment and follow-through. These dynamics speak to and extend beyond international treaty law.

Why Human Rights?

International treaty law covers many issue areas, ranging from high-politics topics of nuclear weapons to low-politics topics covering road creation. Each of these areas offers the aforementioned benefits to study by having many participants, clear participation times, and treaties as a frequently used form of international law. This book limits its scope to human rights treaty law. Within this limited scope, the United Nations has created sixteen treaties and eleven Optional Protocols since 1945. A focus on the human rights issue area is of interest for both scholarly and policy reasons.

In the academic context, focusing on human rights offers several distinct advantages. First, the analysis of human rights behavior has vastly expanded in the last twenty years. Projects such as those of Risse, Ropp, and Sikkink (1999) offer extensive case-study analysis through which the authors explore the relationship between international human rights norms and domestic practices. Quantitative analyses such as those conducted by Hathaway (2002), von Stein (2005), Neumayer (2005), Hafner-Burton and Tsutsui (2005), and Zhou (2014) provide a host of statistical tests modeling the linkages between legal commitment and compliance and human rights treaties. Researching in this area allows for comparison across previous findings and for improving understanding by building upon prior findings.

In the policy context, human rights violations continue to be a problem of heightened importance. The plight of refugees, political imprisonment, forced disappearances, and discrimination against vulnerable populations fill the headlines. The Universal Declaration of Human Rights, created in 1948, maintains the world's record for most translated document, translated into more than five hundred languages in the past seventy years (UN 2016). This extensive dissemination of the United Nation's first legal agreement on human rights demonstrates the importance with which human rights are viewed globally. The United Nations and its member states perpetually seek to provide resources for victims of human rights violations, improve on violating states' poor practices, and understand the ways in which global human rights can be improved. The United Nations recognizes the weaknesses in the current treaty body system, acknowledging that only 16 percent of state parties submit reports to treaty bodies on time (Pillay 2012, 8). The United Nations also identifies when noncompliance problems exist, shining light on state violations.

The generalizability of human rights law findings to other issue areas has been a contested topic within academic research. Depending on whom you ask, research on human rights laws can or cannot speak to international law more generally. Legal texts caution about generalizing human rights law to other issue areas (e.g., Dunoff, Ratner, and Wippman 2010). On the one hand, some argue that human rights laws are "window dressing" and that states have no intention of following through with their commitments. On the other hand, human rights as an issue area is arguably a "hard case" to test. Human rights laws are the international community directing states on how to treat their citizens. Subnational groups opposed to treaty ratification frequently rally around the argument that an international organization such as the United Nations has no authority to dictate life in the country. The United States is a prime example, wherein the state is generally compliant with a treaty while confronting domestic opposition to ratification. The UN Convention on the Rights of Persons with Disabilities (CRPD) was based largely on the Americans with Disabilities Act. Domestic groups opposed ratification on the principle of protecting domestic sovereignty against an overbearing United Nations. Nevertheless, the US State Department writes that it "promotes international implementation of the Convention on the Rights of Persons with Disabilities ... linking US experience and technical assistance to interested governments ... [and to be] inclusive of disability rights in key [US] foreign policy areas" (US Department of State, 2017).

Noting conceptual and substantive differences among international treaty areas, some legal scholars argue that legal behavior differs in the area of human rights. For example, reservations may be overrepresented and objections underrepresented. Dunoff, Ratner, and Wippman (2010) suggest that reservations to human rights treaties are frequent, while "most multilateral treaties are ratified with few or no reservations" (436). Scholars explain this pattern through a historic desire to encourage increased participation in human rights treaties by allowing for more reservations. When considering reservations to the Genocide Convention, the ICJ Advisory Opinion wrote that human rights and humanitarian treaties were special issue areas "adopted for a purely humanitarian and civilizing purpose." As such, the ICJ desired that "as many States as possible should participate."[4] Swain highlights Judge Rosalyn Higgins's argument that states care about their own ability to make reservations but care little about other states' reservations when it comes to human rights treaties: "The basic intuition is that states care more about preserving their right to make reservations than they do about their right to object" (2006, 327). While in other treaty areas,

---

[4] Reservations to the Convention on the Prevention and Punishment of the Crime of Genocide, 1951 I. C. J. 15, 24 and discussed in Dunoff, Ratner, and Wippman (2010, 436) and Alston and Goodman (2013, 1081).

increased reservations may elicit increased objections, a state is "reluctant to accept international scrutiny of its owns human rights practices" (Dunoff, Ratner, and Wippman 2010, 437).

Even with these potentially unique attributes of human rights law and state approaches to it, scholars also note the similarities across human rights and related issue areas of environmental law and health law. As Boyle writes, the substantial overlap between human rights and environmental policies has spawned a "greening of human rights law" (2006, 472). Von Stein (2008) argues that flexibility in agreement design matters for climate change law in similar ways that have been argued in the human rights realm (Goodliffe and Hawkins 2006; Hathaway 2003). Young and Levy (1998) argue that international organizations promote norm adoption of environmental regulation, and Mitchell (1994) finds that environmental treaties can affect state behavior. Scholars similarly note the interrelated nature of human rights practices and policy with trade agreement design (Hafner-Burton 2005; Spilker and Böhmelt 2013).

Acknowledging the potential different attitudes states adopt toward human rights law while embracing the overlap with other international legal issue areas, I take the view that core findings from this book are translatable to other areas of international law. As demonstrated through the research on international environmental, trade, and even disarmament law, many of the same domestic factors are important across treaty issue areas. States with legislative requirements for ratification consequently require consensus from many domestic constituencies before advancing to treaty ratification. New states emerging in the international system must address all prior treaty obligations across issue areas. All international agreements are negotiated.

What Treaties?

The United Nations has created sixteen human rights treaties since its formation. It identifies nine of these as "core human rights treaties."[5] Core treaties cover broad concepts of human rights, including political rights, equality between the sexes, rights for children, racial equality, protection against torture, and forced disappearances. Each of the core human rights treaties has a treaty-based body to monitor implementation (the Subcommittee on the Prevention of Torture serves as an additional treaty

---

[5] The United Nations Office of the High Commissioner identifies these as the nine core human rights treaties on www.ohchr.org/EN/ProfessionalInterest/Pages/CoreInstruments.aspx.

body paired with the Committee against Torture to the 1984 Convention against Torture and Other Cruel, Inhuman or Degrading Treatment or Punishment). Outside of the nine core treaties, the other seven cover a range of rights in scenarios from genocide to apartheid in sport and a development fund for indigenous peoples of Latin American and the Caribbean.

Throughout this book, I engage all nine core human rights treaties. I collected data from the United Nations Treaty Collection Database and graph and discuss commitment patterns across these important treaties. Table 1.1 lists the nine treaties, their creation dates, and the counts of signatories and parties to the treaty.[6] In addition to this discussion, I focus particular attention and statistical analysis on two treaties: the International Covenant on Civil and Political Rights (ICCPR) and Convention on the Elimination of All Forms of Discrimination against Women (CEDAW).

The ICCPR was created in 1966 as a broad human rights treaty covering many aspects of civil and political rights, including freedom to assemble, participation in governance, women's rights, and some physical human rights, including freedom from torture. This is an example of a treaty created in response to the end of World War II. Soon after the United Nations's creation, state leaders began pressing for a treaty covering a wide range of human rights. The initial push for the ICCPR treaty came when states wanted a harder articulation of the human rights presented in the Universal Declaration of Human Rights. In 1952, the General Assembly directed that two draft treaties be written: one focused on civil and political rights and the other on social and cultural rights (UNGA Res 543(VI)). An initial draft was completed by 1954, and after a prolonged negotiation process, the General Assembly adopted the ICCPR treaty in 1966 (Res 2200 (XXI)). The ICCPR has wide participation. As of 2020, there are 173 state parties to the treaty. The United Nations views the ICCPR as a successful treaty. In reviewing the ICCPR for the UN Audiovisual Library, Dr. Christian Tomuschat (2008) wrote, "It is at the national level that the ICCPR has exerted its greatest impact. When today anywhere in the world a national constitution is framed, the ICCPR serves as the natural yardstick for the drafting of a section on fundamental rights." The ICCPR also offers an opportunity to examine

---

[6] These data come from the United Nations Treaty Collection Status of Treaties. "Parties" designation counts the total number of states committed to the treaty through legally binding commitment. As discussed extensively in this book, that count includes ratification, accession, and succession.

Table 1.1 *Core UN human rights treaties*

Human rights treaty	Acronym	Creation date	Signatories	Parties
International Convention on the Elimination of All Forms of Racial Discrimination	CERD	December 21, 1965	88	181
International Covenant on Civil and Political Rights	ICCPR	December 16, 1966	74	173
International Covenant on Economic, Social, and Cultural Rights	ICESCR	December 16, 1966	71	170
Convention on the Elimination of All Forms of Discrimination against Women	CEDAW	December 18, 1979	99	189
Convention against Torture and Other Cruel, Inhuman or Degrading Treatment or Punishment	CAT	December 10, 1984	83	166
Convention on the Rights of the Child	CRC	November 20, 1989	140	196
International Convention on the Protection of the Rights of All Migrant Workers and Members of Their Families	CMW	December 18, 1990	39	54

Table 1.1 (*cont.*)

Human rights treaty	Acronym	Creation date	Signatories	Parties
Convention on the Rights of Persons with Disabilities	CRPD	December 13, 2006	162	179
International Convention for the Protection of All Persons from Enforced Disappearance	CED	December 20, 2006	98	60

a broad human rights treaty that provides many country-years for observation and rich information for consideration related to negotiations and commitments. Given the early creation of the ICCPR within the context of human rights treaties (predating the recent wave of state independence from the end of the Cold War), it is one of the few treaties through which we can study succession commitment.

The CEDAW was created after the immediate post–World War II era and focuses on a much narrower set of rights. CEDAW was created in response to continued sex- and gender-based discrimination despite codified condemnation in earlier treaties, such as the ICCPR. As early as 1963, the General Assembly requested a draft declaration on the elimination of discrimination against women (RES 1921 (XVIII)). In 1975, the World Conference of the International Women's Year called upon the Commission on the Status of Women to prepare a draft convention. After several working groups and draft conventions, the CEDAW treaty was created in 1979 and opened for signature in 1980. CEDAW is a specialized treaty covering numerous aspects of women's and gender equality rights (RES 34/180). In particular, CEDAW covers social, political, economic, family, cultural, and civil components of women's rights. As of 2020, 189 states are party to the CEDAW. The United Nations heralds the importance of CEDAW and has labeled the treaty the "international bill of rights for women." My sustained focus on CEDAW offers the advantage of studying (1) a treaty that specifically targets rights protection for a minority group and (2) commitment and rights trends over several decades. The treaty also underwent faster negotiations than the ICCPR, offering a comparison case.

The Argument in Brief

In this book, *commitment* is the formal agreement of states to adhere to the standards, norms, and expectations articulated within international human rights treaties. Commitment is a state-made action and, I argue, imperative for understanding how states *comply*, or meet the standards, norms, and expectations articulated within international human rights treaties. States commit to treaty law in different ways. While ratification commitment has been well studied, I argue that it is important to examine ratification along with other commitment types that thus far have been overlooked or lumped together as one and the same with ratification. Focusing on only ratification limits the study and understanding of state relationships with international treaty law. These actions have different legal definitions dictating which states can commit through them at what point. Many legal definitional issues connect into domestic processes and contexts that are intertwined with a state's capacity, intent, and willingness to commit and comply with human rights law. To more fully understand compliance with human rights law, we must look more closely at commitment itself. Looking closer at the variation in paths to treaty commitment and compliance builds our understanding of international human rights law.

In drawing conclusions about the efficacy of international law, scholars typically rely on assessing state behavior before and after treaty ratification. However, types of commitment other than ratification and even within ratification exist. States have various approaches and requirements that are largely overlooked in the current study of international law. Table 1.2 lists and describes the four primary commitment types that states use with UN international human rights law.[7] This book is organized around the expanded study of these actions as building blocks of different commitment and compliance paths. These actions are mentioned and defined in the VCLT of 1969, the authoritative

---

[7] I thank Duncan Hollis for helpful comments on other, less-used commitments. His *Oxford Guide to Treaties* includes a fifth commitment action–*Approval and/or Acceptance* (2012, 680–81). The United Nations Treaty Glossary describes Acceptance and Approval as "having the same legal effect as ratification … have been used instead of ratification, when at a national level, constitutional law does not require the treaty to be ratified by the head of state." The UN Treaty Collection Status of Treaties does not list any state committing via Acceptance and/or Approval to the nine core human rights treaties.

Table 1.2 *Types of treaty commitment*

Legal status	Action type	Description
Not Binding	*Signature*	Non-legally binding commitment action. States are expected to refrain from acts that would violate the purpose of the treaty after signing.*
Binding	*Ratification*	The action whereby a state consents to be legally bound by the treaty.**
	Accession	The action whereby a state that is not an original party to the treaty consents to be legally bound by a treaty it did not negotiate.***
	Succession	The action of recommitting to treaties that another, preexisting state had already committed to.****

* VCLT 1969 Articles 10 and 18
** VCLT 1969 Article 14
*** VCLT 1969 Article 15
**** Vienna Convention on Succession of States in Respect of Treaties 1978 Article 2(1)(b)

treaty on treaties. Aside from gaining legitimacy from the VCLT context, these actions have continued through state practice and UN normative guidance for almost the entirety of the modern human rights regime. I argue for an expanded study of treaty commitment through an inclusive focus on four categories of treaty commitment. In doing so, I place ratification within the broader context of available mechanisms of commitment and recognize the importance within that context.

The first commitment action for consideration is signature. Signature is the only commitment action that is nonbinding.[8] Signing treaty law is an initial commitment step en route to binding commitment. Almost all social science studies of international human rights law have excluded signature from consideration and analysis.[9] As I argue, this is a fundamental misstep for understanding international cooperation. Ratification is the commitment action following treaty signature. It is legally binding. Scholarship has primarily focused on ratification as synonymous with treaty commitment and as a point after which to measure treaty compliance. However, research demonstrates that nonbinding norms have been extremely influential within the human rights regime and contribute to improved human rights practices through shared expectations, socialization, and shaming mechanisms (e.g., Finnemore and Sikkink 1998; Risse, Ropp, and Sikkink 1999; Sikkink 2018). NGOs and other actors work with treaty ratification (Clark 2001) or around it (Hafner-Burton and Tsutsui 2005). Treaty signature similarly has this power to activate human rights mechanisms. As a nonbinding form of commitment, state signature signifies a state's willingness to recognize and support international standards of human rights behavior. By situating signature as harder than rhetoric and communicative action alone (Risse 2000) but yet to meet the hardest law obligation (Abbott and Snidal 2000), we can theorize how and when nonbinding commitment matters for human rights.

Three principal options, not one, exist within the umbrella of legally binding commitment actions to UN treaty law. Each has important distinguishing characteristics. States that commit via accession are committing to treaties *already negotiated* by other states. Accession states, generally, did not create the law to which they are committing. Accession often signifies that commitment occurred following the formal treaty EIF date. States that commit through succession are committing to treaties that another, preexisting state already committed to; they are *recommitting* to treaties after the emergence of a newly created state. The new state

---

[8] Unless otherwise noted, when discussing signature, I am referring to signature, subject to ratification, which is the dominant practice within UN human rights law, not definitive signature, which *is* binding and the dominant practice within the IMF (without ratification following).

[9] Notable exceptions include Landman (2005) and Cole (2012).

acknowledges the prior state's ratification and assumes the commitment and accompanying obligations with its new legal identity.

Different domestic contexts and mechanisms for changes in human rights practices are connected with these four paths to treaty commitment. Each of the three less-examined commitment actions – signature, accession, and succession – are unique but intertwined with ratification. It is therefore helpful to situate these legal paths against that of ratification. The United Nations views the two-step signature and ratification path as the standard and most common means of treaty commitment. I argue that to understand the steps in the commitment process we must first look to domestic ratification requirements. Over half of the states within the international system have domestic legislative approval requirements to ratify international treaties. This is an additional, and at times arduous, domestic hurdle that the rest of the states do not have to confront when seeking to ratify treaties. I argue that *Legislative Approval States* – states with domestic ratification hurdles – approach nonbinding treaty signature as an important commitment step that the executive can participate in without legislative support. *Legislative Approval States* sign treaties earlier to signal support for human rights treaties. I argue that we should expect a shift in human rights practice following signature, when the head of state is on board, and not first when the treaty is ratified. Ratification can happen years or decades later, when the legislature is finally supportive. The domestic approval contexts shape how states use and emphasize different steps in the signature followed by ratification path to commitment.

States that commit through the action of accession are late to the game. These states are committing to a treaty that has been negotiated and already committed to by other states. This is a distinction that merits closer examining. I argue that states that participate in and experience the complications of treaty negotiation are more committed to and concerned with the product than their counterparts who do not engage with the treaty through negotiation; the process of negotiation is a lengthy one that makes involved states more invested and likely to adhere to the treaty's terms than states that did not participate in and experience the throes of negotiation. Additionally, some treaties only allow states the participatory option of accession if they missed the opportunity to sign and/or ratify by the EIF date. Though this latter criterion is uncommon in human rights treaties and unlikely to be enforced by the UN legal machinery, states generally follow this norm of practice even when it is not specifically articulated within the treaty's guidelines.[10]

While only a handful of states in the modern system commit through succession, the action's distinction from ratification is subtle and important. Succession states are new states that emerged out of preexisting states that had committed to international treaties. Upon state creation, new states are faced with the decision of what to do with the prior state's international legal obligations. The new state recommits to treaties through succession rather than ratification, having already obtained earlier domestic approval for its initial treaty commitment. I argue that newly emerging states are undergoing institutional and political changes that make their time of recommitment unique. International human rights treaty commitment offers an opportunity for succession states to foster legitimacy and communicate human rights norm adherence across the international human rights regime. Given the unique political circumstances and the frequent accompanying processes of democratization facing succession states, it is important to recognize the unique path they take to commit and comply with international human rights law.

The focus on the role of domestic institutional constraints, the negotiation process, regime transition, and international legitimation, paired with the terms of precise type of treaty commitment, produces a more nuanced understanding of the relationship between committing to international human rights law and changes in human rights practices. Perhaps the most important finding in this book is that context matters – specifically, the domestic treaty accessibility, negotiation participation, and legal contexts from which states commit to human rights law. These contexts shape how and when states commit to international human rights treaties. Context informs the legal paths states take for commitment and compliance.

Organization of the Book

This book is organized around four commitment types to international law: signature, ratification, accession, and succession. These different commitment types highlight different domestic contexts and international legal circumstances under which states commit to international human rights treaties. Using large-n quantitative analysis, legal histories,

---

[10] The vast majority of states that acceded to the core human rights treaties did so following EIF.

and case examples, I support my argument that each commitment type should be analyzed separately to identify unique underlying mechanisms of change within each commitment context. Through this inclusive, commitment-based organization, my findings produce encouraging conclusions about human rights commitment's overall contribution to positive human rights changes following most occurrences of treaty commitment.

Chapter 2 begins by unpacking the findings and assumptions of the ratification-centered research on international human rights law. It develops the theoretical approach to legal commitment and compliance advanced throughout the rest of the book. Drawing on the literature from political science, international law, and sociology, this chapter discusses the findings and conclusions drawn by research that centers the conceptual analysis and empirical testing of international legal behavior around the sole action of ratification. I argue that these works have oversimplified the action of commitment and in doing so have oversimplified the process of compliance.

Chapter 3 presents the book's argument that states have divergent paths to commitment and the context of commitment paths matters in explaining how, if, and when compliance will happen. In this chapter, I provide descriptive commitment data across the core human rights treaties to provide insight into the pathways to commitment. I draw hypotheses about the expected relationship between each commitment action and human rights outcomes. Through the description, I present an argument about the four paths of commitment, which I develop throughout the rest of the book.

Chapter 4 focuses on the nonbinding commitment action of signature. I discuss the two-step legal nature of signing and ratifying international treaties and present an original argument about when and why signature is a significant indicator of human rights practices. I argue that nonbinding signature contains a promise of commitment that actors at levels above and below the state use to hold a state accountable to its commitment. I argue that NGOs, other states, and the United Nations do not wait for binding ratification to begin pressuring, shaming, and socializing a signatory state toward compliance. Processes that international relations and legal scholars identify as important following ratification also are important following treaty signature. Additionally, I argue that treaty signature is of heightened importance for *Legislative Approval States*. For these states, signature offers a legally accessible and institutionally simpler means to communicate support for international human rights law, which they use to signal support for treaties earlier than their *Executive Approval State* counterparts. I examine the case of the United States and the historic hurdles confronting ratifying human rights law. Then, I statistically test the effect of signing the ICCPR and CEDAW on human rights behavior. I find a positive and significant relationship between signing treaties and improved human rights practices. I find that *Legislative Approval States* with legislative ratification requirements improve rights earlier than those without such barriers. These findings indicate the importance of examining domestic institutional requirements for ratification.

Chapter 5 examines the commitment action dynamic between accession and ratification. This chapter focuses on the importance of state involvement in treaty negotiations from both socialization and legal approaches. Accession differs from ratification in that states commit through accession after the treaty has already been negotiated and signed by other states. Acceding states, in general, come to the treaty later and were not involved in the lengthy negotiations to construct the laws. I argue that this difference in involvement is an important but overlooked distinction. States that have participated in treaty negotiations are socialized to specific rights standards in focused and prolonged ways that negotiation nonparticipant states are not. I focus on the history of treaty negotiations of the ICCPR and highlight how states involved in negotiations shaped the law's breadth and strength, whereas states not involved in negotiations missed important opportunities to contribute. Then, I quantitatively test accession and ratification for effects on human rights behavior after committing to the ICCPR and CEDAW treaties. I find states that acceded and opted out of treaty negotiations had worse rights practices than those who participated in negotiations and ratified.

Chapter 6 highlights the unique pathway to commitment undertaken by new states within the international system. In this chapter, I focus on the legal commitment act of treaty succession. States commit through succession when new states have emerged and the prior state had already ratified the treaty. The new state is recommitting to human rights treaties. Like ratification, succession is legally binding. Unlike ratification, succession is a concerted and deliberate recommitment to human rights. Succession is only available to new states that have separated from other states with distinct legal identity. Succession is a rare treaty commitment type used by states experiencing a unique identity transformation after or within a democratizing and/or postconflict context. Because of these unique circumstances of recommitment, I argue that succession merits disaggregation from ratification, wherein most scholars categorize it.

I examine the historic case of the Czech Republic and Slovakia and track human rights patterns following succession in the succession states versus ratification states. I illustrate how each new state used succession commitment to advance its international legitimacy and signal its commitment to the international human rights regime. Upon conducting a large-n statistical analysis, I find that states that commit through succession to the ICCPR had significant and positive improvements in human rights practices following commitment. The findings align with these states experiencing unique political and legal contexts and support my call to separate out succession from ratification when analyzing human rights treaty commitment.

The seventh and concluding chapter synthesizes the findings from statistical, case, and legal evidence presented throughout the book to demonstrate that research within international relations and international legal studies has overlooked important underpinnings of legal commitment to human rights treaties. In the conclusion, I revisit ratification and argue that through looking beyond ratification, we can get a clearer picture of what it actually means, constitutes, entails, and signifies for human rights practices. The legal pathways of committing to and complying with treaties are firmly established within the UN legal framework and repeated across issue areas. The legal pathways are particularly illuminating in the human rights issue area where NGOs, rights entrepreneurs, other governments, and moral arguments are all involved in urging states to commit and comply with international law. The findings from this book emphasize the need for socio-legal scholars to unpack the different ways that states approach international law given their domestic political and legal contexts of commitment. The findings also emphasize how many of the legal paths lead to promising results concerning global human rights practices.

2

On Ratification

Rethinking a Ratification-Centered Approach to International Law

Amnesty International "works to promote all the human rights enshrined in the Universal Declaration of Human Rights and other international standards through human rights education programs and campaigning for ratification of human rights treaties."

Amnesty International's mission statement

Amnesty International, Human Rights Watch, and other prominent human rights nongovernmental organizations (NGOs) specifically craft campaigns around treaty ratification. Though their primary focus is on stopping human rights abuses on the ground, the groups also recognize the need to engage the international legal machinery through which human rights abuses are criminalized. The aforementioned quote illustrates the centrality of treaty ratification to Amnesty International:[1] achieving ratification features in its mission statement. Thus far, the dominant international legal focus has been on ratification, and academics have largely followed human rights groups' lead, keeping their eye on binding ratification when studying human rights treaties.

This chapter maps the existing approaches to measuring and conceptualizing treaty commitment; in doing so, it problematizes the ratification-based focus of treaty commitment coming from the human rights activist community and from within academia. In the first section of this chapter, I draw on the fields of political science, international law, and sociology and review the existing literature explaining both compliance with international human rights treaties and why states commit to the laws in the first place. In reviewing this body of work, I critically engage the focus on ratification; argue that these works have overlooked the

---

[1] Amnesty International mission statement as quoted in Morsink (1999, xii). The updated Amnesty International mission statement of 2013 has slightly different wording.

important dynamics, processes, and movement toward change that accompany other commitment types; and review the findings and conclusions from these studies. Paying particular attention to quantitative coding and categorization, I engage with how scholars have conceptualized and defined legal commitment, lay out the actions they did and did not include, and discuss how the resultant focus left a gap in researching treaty commitment more completely. Without studying the larger universe of legal commitment options, the academic understanding of international law excludes the nuances found within international legal practice. I also point to the ratification-centric approach that NGOs and the United Nations have taken when campaigning for human rights treaty commitment and when assessing states in the Universal Periodic Review. The Review lays the foundation to present my argument for extending scholarly focus to other types of treaty commitment, thus uncovering variation in legal paths to commitment and compliance.

What the Academic Literature Tells Us about Treaty Commitment

International relations and international legal scholars have studied many aspects of international law in the post–World War II era. Although he was skeptical of its utility, Hans Morgenthau correctly wrote that "the main instrumentality by which international law is created is the international treaty" ([1948] 1993, 212). In studying the international treaty, scholars delved into insightful consideration of the legalization of treaties and agreements (Abbott and Snidal 2000; Abbott et al. 2000; Goldstein et al. 2000), including their rational design (Koremenos, Lipson, and Snidal 2001). In their pursuit of understanding state behavior related to international treaty law, scholars have determinedly focused on the action of ratification, even when confronted with the occasional biting critique of such a treaty-centered approach (e.g., Finnemore and Toope 2001; Goodman and Jinks 2003). NGOs and rights groups have viewed ratification as a moral and legal goal for states to achieve. Scholars have pragmatically viewed ratification as the sole way to measure commitment and to assess compliance with international treaty law, given its legal standing.

Treaty Talk: Terminology and Word Choice for Commitment

Before jumping into a critical review of the existing scholarship, it is prudent to note that numerous points of my critiques center on the overly broad usage of terminology when referring to treaty commitment. At times, the exceedingly general terminology results in a less accurate depiction of what is actually being studied. While some of the literatures broadly write of "parties to the treaty" or "signing on" to international law, the focus – in terms of conceptual arguments and empirical measurement – has predominantly remained on ratification. This incorrect wording irritates legal practitioners, with such descriptions being labeled "abuse of the term" *signature* (see Aust 2007, 437 n. 47). Aust opines that word choice confusion may stem from politicians: "One also often hears a government minister saying that the state has 'signed up to' a treaty. In English, the expression usually means being bound legally, but not always. So, being a loose term, it should be avoided if at all possible" (2007, 115). The terminology of being a state party to a treaty refers to "a country that has ratified or acceded to that particular treaty, and is therefore legally bound by the provisions in the instrument" (UNICEF n.d.). Aust adds that describing a state as a party to a treaty is reserved for when the treaty has entered into force (2007, 114).

This expanded definition includes binding commitment actions beyond ratification. When writing about signing on, authors are rarely writing about signature but rather about ratification, which occurs after states sign treaties. Beyond linguistic opaqueness, the lack of precision in legal commitment terminology creates a disjuncture between what is conceptually and legally being written and what is being measured, tested, and used to evaluate arguments related to international human rights law. The following discussion delves into what we know from the literature about international law, illustrates how it has centered on ratification, and clarifies some of the language used by prominent studies.

Studying Compliance: Using Ratification as a Critical Point of Departure

Beginning with Keith's (1999) article "The UN International Covenant on Civil and Political Rights: Does It Make a Difference in Human Rights Behavior?" scholars have built quantitative analysis around the questions of when and why states commit to international human rights law and whether or not states comply with the law following commitment. Before this time, as Hathaway notes, "the question of international law compliance fell by the wayside of both international law and international relations scholarship" (2002, 1942). Keith's article has since been cited hundreds of times and motivated expanded quantitative analysis of treaties. Keith sought to understand the changes in state behavior that occur after committing to the International Covenant on Civil and Political Rights (ICCPR) treaty; to measure commitment, she conceptually relied on ratification as the point of commitment. Ratification is "the formal and highly visible commitment that should make the state more willing to improve its performance" (1999, 100). The article dismissed treaty signature as nonbinding and thus an inconsequential act. States that signed but did not yet ratify (or never ratified) were considered nonparticipants of the treaty: "those states that have signed but have never formally ratified the treaty are nonparty states because the treaties are not legally binding upon them" (101). The act of signature was coded as no move toward commitment at all. The analysis groups accession and ratification together as uniform acts of commitment: "In this analysis, states that either have formally ratified or have made accession to the treaty have been coded as states parties to treaty" (101). She finds that state commitment to the ICCPR does not lead to any significant changes in states' human rights practices and concludes that it may be "overly optimistic to expect that being a party to this international covenant will produce an observable impact" (112). The takeaways from this first article on the effect of legal commitment are that nonbinding treaty commitment is inconsequential for study, all binding commitment types are the same, and, when states do commit, no significant effect on human rights practices results.

Building from Keith's original work, scholars expanded on the number of treaties analyzed and on the statistical sophistication through which they tested the effects of committing to human rights treaties. Hathaway sought to "trace relationships between treaty ratification and country practices" (2002, 1939) by asking: "Do human rights treaties make a difference in countries' human rights practices?" (1962). This article expands the study of international human rights law's impact beyond the ICCPR to include additional treaties and protocols. The project included multilateral global treaties created within the UN framework, such as the ICCPR, Convention against Torture and Other Cruel, Inhuman, or Degrading Treatment or Punishment (CAT), Convention on the Elimination of All Forms of Discrimination against Women (CEDAW), and the Genocide Convention, along with prominent regional agreements of the American Torture Convention, African Charter on Human Rights, and the European Convention on Human Rights. Hathaway is laudable for producing the noteworthy study with findings indicating worse human rights practices after legal commitment. She found that "noncompliance seems to be rampant" and that "countries with poor human rights ratings are sometimes more likely to have ratified the relevant treaties than are countries with better ratings" (1935). Additionally, "many countries that ratify human rights treaties, it appears, regularly and predictably violate their voluntarily assumed human rights treaty obligations" (1981). In fact, the study did not find "a single treaty for which ratification seems to be reliably associated with better human rights practices and several for which it appears to be associated with worse practices" (5). This surprising finding and expanded analysis contribute to this study's widespread influence. It has been cited over 2,000 times as of 2020.[2]

Hathaway explicitly anchors research questions founded on commitment and compliance to the action of ratification: "I therefore seek to determine whether there is any evidence indicating that countries' practices are different when they have ratified a given treaty than they would have been expected to be absent ratification" (1965). Interestingly, in the footnotes, Hathaway details important and germane processes unique to states that sought to commit via accession to the European regional agreements. She observes that "accession to the Council [of Europe] therefore may often require countries to enact legislative changes and satisfy experts operating on behalf of the Council that the country meets minimum human rights standards" (2002, 2018 n. 276). This legal and commitment process dimension, while included in the footnotes, is missing from the analysis, argument, and findings.

These early and critical quantitative assessments of the relationship between ratification and human rights compliance shaped other quantitative research. It should be noted that qualitative studies on human rights have, overall, had a more positive outlook and findings about human rights compliance and patterns (Hafner-Burton and Ron 2009). Kathryn Sikkink's recent *Evidence for Hope* (2017) highlights this distinction and reflects on positive rights changes that have been largely dismissed by a generally pessimistic scholarship focused on an ideal of compliance instead of the possible (32). Simmons (2015) posits that works critical of international human rights law do not recognize that "not perfect" practice after treaty commitment is "hardly a damning criticism of law's effects" (106).

In an insightful critique of Hathaway (2002), Goodman and Jinks (2003) assert (among other criticisms) that the work exclusively emphasizes ratification.

---

[2] Google Scholar search.

> Hathaway's focus on ratification as the independent variable is question-
> able. Ratification is not the "magic moment" of acceptance of human
> rights norms. Rather, ratification is a point in the broader process of
> incorporation; and the relative significance of this point will, we would
> expect, vary widely with diverse impacts on measures of compliance. As
> a matter of international law, core treaty obligations attach earlier in the
> incorporation process – that is upon *signature* of the treaty. (173,
> emphasis in original)

The authors argue that the international legal wheels turn prior to treaty
ratification and urge scholars to examine the extent of the treaty law process.
However, the dominant research on international human rights treaty law
did not take Goodman and Jinks's critical assessment fully to heart.

A number of prominent works on compliance with international
human rights treaties point to the importance of domestic groups, civil
society, and associated mobilization processes in bringing compliance to
fruition. Hafner-Burton and Tsutsui (2005) bring consideration of international civil society and advocacy networks into the study of international legal compliance. They argue that there is a "paradox of empty
promises" after states ratify international human rights treaties.
Following the achievement of ratification, states are held less accountable
by the international community and can spiral into worse practices
(1378). Human rights advocates mobilize and improve rights practices
despite the lack of institutional accountability offered via the treaties
(1378). The authors find that "state commitment to the international
human rights legal regime does not automatically translate into government respect for rights" (1395). To come to this conclusion, the authors
focus on ratification as a measure of compliance. Ratification is measured
in two ways. The first is a count of how many of six treaties a state has
ratified. The second is dichotomous coding for each treaty to determine
whether or not a state ratified each treaty. They find that ratification of six
international treaties – the ICCPR, International Covenant on Economic,
Social, and Cultural Rights (ICESCR), CAT, Convention on the
Elimination of All Forms of Racial Discrimination (CERD), CEDAW,
and Convention on the Rights of the Child (CRC) – results in worse
rights practices (1396–1397). Hafner-Burton and Tsutsui do find that the
presence of NGOs contributes to better rights practices, supporting their
argument that treaties alone do not improve rights behavior, but that civil
society can operate after ratification to improve rights. The authors
contribute to the understanding of how NGOs operate within the shadow

of international law but miss an important opportunity to see if and how NGOs begin to mobilize earlier in the international legal process. Given the nature of treaty signature and ratification processes, all of the states of interest in this project had already committed through signature earlier.

Neumayer (2005) makes an argument that human rights treaty effects are conditional on the strength of democracy and the presence of international NGOs. This situates Neumayer's argument within a broader theoretical framework relying on NGO and advocacy networks found within Risse, Ropp, and Sikkink (1999) and Hafner-Burton and Tsutsui (2005). These works recognize an implicit problem in focusing on ratification, as "ratification is more a manifestation of human rights improvement rather than a cause of it."[3] Despite this recognition, Neumayer codes treaty commitment as "whether a country has ratified or acceded to a specific human rights treaty in a given year or not" (20). This coding does recognize that accession is an additional type of treaty commitment, but it does so in a way that bypasses the legal and conceptual differences between commitment types. The study does not separate commitment types for statistical analysis. It examines the ICCPR, the First Optional Protocol to the ICCPR, the CAT, Articles 21 and 22 of the CAT, along with several regional treaties, including the European Convention for the Protection of Human Rights and Fundamental Freedoms, the European Convention for the Prevention of Torture and Inhuman or Degrading Treatment or Punishment, the American Convention on Human Rights, the Inter-American Convention to Prevent and Punish Torture, and the African Charter on Human and People's Rights. In this research, the division in treaty effectiveness rests on regime type: "ratification can be expected to have no effect" in "very autocratic regimes" (1). Neumayer finds that when autocracies ratify the ICCPR, personal integrity rights generally worsen. More democratic states have improved rights practices following ratification (27).

In her extensive and influential work *Mobilizing for Rights*, Simmons (2009) situates the use of international treaties as a tool for mobilizing domestic human rights groups. She examines the ICCPR, ICESCR, CERD, CEDAW, CAT, and CRC treaties, finding differing effects of commitment across them. Consistent with other studies, she found somewhat positive effects of ratifying the ICCPR and notably negative effects of ratifying the CAT.

---

[3] As summarized in Neumayer (2005, 12).

> The major result is the weak but noticeable influence of the ICCPR within
> five years of ratification for all regime types . . ... The unconditional effects
> of ratifying the CAT were, if anything, negative, indicating that it is quite
> common for governments to perform worse on this scale once they have
> ratified the CAT. (305)

This study is notable for its rigorous and expansive analysis of human rights treaties and its finding that human rights law has a more positive influence on human rights outcomes than previously held due to activists' ability to mobilize around the law.

However, this important work misses the opportunity to see how NGOs and other groups mobilize around and after treaty signature. The argument is that state ratification makes human rights treaties visible. Human rights treaty ratification materializes as a point around which groups can mobilize. This could also be the case for signature, but the study does not delve into that question. Related, is signing human rights treaties enough to satisfy some NGOs? Simmons also dismisses any distinction between the legally binding forms of treaty commitment, briefly noting in an appendix that "throughout, 'accession' is coded as 'ratification,' since the legal obligations are generally indistinguishable" (381). *Mobilizing for Rights* does not discuss treaty succession, though it poses an interesting question for rights mobilization: Do NGOs support new states and mobilize for recommitment?

Subsequent work questions how the findings of civil society and NGO influence on human rights play out in nondemocratic states. Hafner-Burton and Tsutsui (2007) focus on repressive government behavior after ratifying international human rights treaties. To their credit, the authors identify the different commitment types when they write that

> our dependent variable, treaty commitment, is a binary variable coded 0 if
> a state i in year t has made no formal commitment to either the CCPR or
> the CAT by ratifying, acceding, or succeeding to the treaties, and 1 if that
> state has committed to either or both treaties. (411)

Despite listing the different commitment types, Hafner-Burton and Tsutsui do not test the actions separately when analyzing for effect of commitment on compliance with the treaties. The article finds that the treaties are least effective in changing the rights behavior of repressive states and that civil society groups' activities did not significantly improve practices.

In addition to domestic human rights activism, scholarship has focused on the role of domestic institutions in implementing international human rights treaties. Powell and Staton (2009) bring domestic courts into consideration when analyzing determinants of human rights compliance and write that "the costs of ratification are lower when judicial systems are ineffective than when they are effective because citizens are unlikely to seek legal redress when courts are unlikely to provide it" (151). While this research remains ratification focused, it does through its argument recognize that ratification is costly in domestic judicial contexts.

The extension of this argument is that ratification is more costly than other types of treaty commitment that are not binding on domestic courts. While Powell and Staton (2009) compare the costs of ratification in democratic versus nondemocratic states, the authors overlook the relevant comparison of committing through signature. Researchers could compare the cost to domestic courts and institutions when states commit but have yet to legally bind themselves to international human rights law. Lupu (2013b) builds on the courts-based explanations of treaty compliance by specifically studying the types of rights abuse and the extent to which evidence is available for domestic courts to prosecute. He examines the ICCPR and argues that evidence is easier to obtain on personal integrity rights violations and more difficult to obtain for civil rights violations. When evidence is more difficult to obtain, it is harder for courts to hold violators accountable. To test this argument, Lupu examines ratification of the ICCPR and finds support for his argument that certain types of rights improve after ratification while others do not. He writes about ratification alone, but his quantitative analysis included accession and succession counts in the totals of ratification. This has been a general practice of quantitative analysis of human rights treaty commitment.[4]

International relations scholars have noted the existence of selection-effect issues influencing when states enter international treaties and have made breakthroughs in addressing these methodological and conceptual issues, as I point out. However, scholars have missed the opportunity to examine signature as a precursor to ratification when thinking about state actions and preferences leading up to treaty ratification. An early discussion

---

[4] For example, Lupu writes that the ICCPR has "been ratified by 167 countries" (2013b, 484). Without explicitly acknowledging this, the author includes accession and succession counts into the ratification variable.

of treaty selection effects revolved around Simmons's (2000) work on commitment to International Monetary Fund (IMF) Articles of Agreement, Article VIII. Addressing international treaty commitment more broadly and beyond international human rights treaties, Simmons and Hopkins (2005) responded to von Stein's (2005) selection-effect critique of earlier treaty research (specifically Simmons 2000). Simmons and Hopkins's rejoinder argues that the core issue is not selection effects but model dependence (624). All of the works relevant to this exchange (Simmons 2000; von Stein 2005; Simmons and Hopkins 2005) use the terminology of "signing onto Article VIII" of the IMF Articles of Agreement (e.g., Simmons and Hopkins 2005, 623). Simmons and Hopkins acknowledge that their grouping of ratification is legally problematic, that "we are here using 'ratification' in its broad political rather than narrow legal sense, although for some countries and issue areas they will be essentially the same" (624, n. 4). Simmons's 2000 article examines legal commitment broadly as to whether or not a "country has accepted Article VIII status" (833). The related articles' cautious language about legal commitment reflects, to some extent, the different legal terminology used by the IMF in comparison with the United Nations. The IMF uses the terminology of "signature" as its only designation for legal commitment (see Article XXXI, Section 2.1a, of the IMF Articles of Agreement).

This difference in semantics is important in comparing these works' findings and discussions to other works examining UN treaties, including this book. The IMF Articles of Agreement make no use of the terms "ratification" or "ratify" in its 136 pages but rather address commitment as "signature." Simmons's (2000), Simmons and Hopkins's (2005), and von Stein's (2005) writing about "signing on" to Article III is analogous to how the rest of the international legal literature writes about ratification. For the IMF and related research, signature is not a first step in a two-step process but rather the ultimate form of legal commitment to the IMF's Articles of Agreement. IMF signature is definitive and not subject to ratification. As a result, the aforementioned scholarship addresses selection into a final commitment (equivalent to ratification) of the IMF agreement, with all authors ultimately arguing that state preferences and practices leading up to commitment are important to factor into selection effects when analyzing compliance.

Building on this call for accounting for selection effects and increased analytical rigor, Hill (2010) employs a matching technique to more accurately compare ratifiers and non-ratifiers and account for domestic and other factors that self-select states into human rights treaty ratification. This study advanced statistical accounting for selection into treaty commitment. Hill separates a treatment group by looking at the "expected value of repression if the treaty were not ratified" (1170). However, the category of ratification excludes some states and observations where some commitment level did occur. Signatories are placed alongside states without any commitment; these country-year observations would be expected to be inherently different from the observations where states did not commit at all. The study thus equates signature country-years with not committing at all. In examining the ICCPR, CAT, and CEDAW, Hill finds that ratifying states had worse practices after ratifying the ICCPR and CAT but improved practices after ratifying the CEDAW. Lupu (2013a) works to address selection effects into treaty commitment and improve on earlier matching techniques by accounting for states' commitment preferences (912). His argument centers around treaty commitment broadly, but his statistical analysis centers squarely on the division between ratification and non-ratification (see 916, 921, table 3). Although he briefly discusses states as "signatories" (918), Lupu is not analyzing signature as a separate point of commitment. The work makes great strides in addressing selection effects into treaty ratification. Nonetheless, it is problematic to frame a study on treaty commitment writ large without examining the different types of commitment and different factors that could explain selection into other non-ratification types of commitment that lead up to ratification.

Along with the above factors influencing treaty compliance, scholars have also looked at the legalization of international agreements, which affects the specificity and depth of not only the terms of the agreement but, as Landman (2005) and Cole (2012) point out, the type of commitment itself. In perhaps the most multilayered approaches to studying international legal commitment thus far, they both conceptualize commitment at different levels of depth. Landman critiques a "lawyer-based approach" wherein "ratification is the true measure of commitment to human rights norms, and therefore a simple dummy variable suffices" (2005, 40). Instead, he creates a three-point variable measuring treaty commitment ranging from 0 – no commitment, 1 – signature, and 2 – ratification. While this coding does not separately test the effect of nonbinding signature as unique from ratification or distinguish accession and succession from ratification coding, it greatly advanced the understanding of commitment depth and human rights treaties. Landman then includes varied coding of treaty reservations to create a "weighted ratification variable, which changes fundamentally the depiction and meaning of the overall pattern of ratifications" (43). Overall, he found a positive relationship between depth of treaty partici-pation and protection of human rights (164).

Similarly, Cole rightly criticizes scholars as tending to "view treaty membership as a binary variable – either a country ratified a treaty or not – that fails to consider different levels of treaty commitment" (2012, 1133). Cole divides commitment into four levels. The first is signature, second is ratification qualified with RUDs (reservations, understandings, and declarations), third is ratification, and fourth is ratification with stronger monitoring and enforcement than required (1137). He finds some support for his argument that the strength of treaty commitment matters; he also finds that committing to additional provisions generally resulted in improved human rights (1161).

Cole made a great contribution to the study of international law commit-ment by moving beyond ratification when considering commitment. However, even with this differentiated approach, he quickly noted some definitional limitations, writing that "for the purposes of this study, ratifica-tion includes accession, which combines signature and ratification into a single act, and succession, whereby a newly established state accepts the treaty obligations of its predecessor" (1138, n. 4). This discussion of acces-sion is a bit ambiguous, since accession does not so much combine signature and ratification as offer a different path to commitment for states not participating in negotiations and that missed the opportunity to sign the treaty. Similarly, Cole implies that accession is an inherently stronger form of commitment to treaties (as discussed on 1140 and 1134). This is not the case. As discussed later in this book, accession differs from ratification based on temporal and involvement factors, not depth dimensions of commit-ment. Both are legally binding, though arrived at differently. Comstock (2020) focuses on the act of signature and argues that groups can mobilize and implement international treaties before ratification occurs.

The tendency to simplify commitment to human rights law happens even when reexamining and updating prior studies. *The Persistent Power of Human Rights* (Risse, Ropp, and Sikkink 2013) updated and reassessed the spiral model of socialization of human rights found in the earlier *Power of Human Rights* (Risse, Ropp, and Sikkink 1999). Both works consider legal commitment broadly: "by 'commitment' we mean that actors accept international human rights as valid and binding for themselves." They further specify that "this usually requires signing up to and/or ratifying international human rights treaties" (2013, 9). The 2013 volume extends its consideration to include non-state actors, a broader definition of human rights to specifically examine women and gender rights, and an expanded temporal consideration when selecting cases (12). The authors, however, miss an opportunity to look at commitment other than binding ratification. Despite their mention of considering commitment as "signing up to" international law, all the conceptual discussion, legal analysis, and quantitative testing (Simmons 2013) use ratification as the point of commitment. Dai (2013) briefly mentions "signature or ratification" but does not further differentiate these actions (86), and Clark (2013) overstates the role that ratification plays, legally. Clark defines commitment as "the ratification of one or two major human rights treaties" (125) and writes that "ratification sets in motion" human rights dialogue (128). Setting aside the issue of the effects of different legally binding commitment action types, this consideration of ratification misses the important commitment and temporal layer that analyzing signature in the study of human rights treaties offers. Signature predates ratification and is a first step toward binding commitment. To better situate normative recognition and a process of compliance, the authors could situate signature within their spiral model. Doing so would allow for examining socialization of human rights norms after nonbinding versus binding commitment and further expanding their study of human rights.

This critical discussion is not meant to question the seminal contribution the aforementioned research made to the area of international human rights law. Rather, I am noting that considering different commitment types and paths has not been on the dominant research agenda in the evolving and expanding study of international human rights law, where many other important areas have developed in both in depth and nuance. For example, recent focus has been on more accurately measuring human rights violations (e.g., Fariss 2014), selection bias (von Stein 2005), and domestic court involvement (e.g., Powell and Staton 2009). Though getting commitment types on the agenda speaks to these areas.

Studying Commitment: Setting Ratification as the Goal

Related, but distinct from the question of treaty compliance, is the question of why states commit to international human rights law in the first place. Increasingly seen as going hand in hand with the compliance literature are works that uniquely study states' decisions to join and commit to international treaty law. This research is frequently linked to the compliance literature and often conducted by the same scholars. It is of little surprise, then, that the commitment literature presents a similarly problematic approach focused only on ratification. Although research questions are often broadly framed by asking why states commit to international law or to human rights law more specifically, the measurements and language almost exclusively denote ratification. Similar to the compliance literature, scholars use terminology loosely, conflating signing with ratifying and ratifying with acceding to international treaties. A notable exception is Simmons's unpublished 2002 working paper, in which she developed a three-point coding of commitment with 0 as no commitment, signature as 1, and ratification as 2. This progressive conceptualization of commitment was not used in subsequent research projects. Simmons sought to explain "degree of commitment" and found that governments characterized as "Left" are more likely to commit to a higher degree and that regional socialization is a significant indicator of commitment.

While most of the scholars studying determinants of treaty commitment rely on explanations and explanatory variables similar to those in works explaining treaty compliance, important work has called for distinguishing these two related but separate questions. Cardenas (2007) made a case for a conceptual separation of commitment and compliance research. She argues that drivers of commitment and compliance are separate. While international pressures lead directly to committing to human rights treaties, international pressures only indirectly effect compliance (12). She also asserts that "domestic institutional configurations define national security threats and empower pro-violation groups, which helps to explain why the preferences of those who support international norms cannot always trump their opponents" (13).

In what is described as the "first systemic study on states' participation in international human rights regimes" (Wotipka and Tsutsui 2008, n. 4), Moravcsik (2000) examined European states' post–World War II commitment to supranational agreements and organizations, framing the question around why states would want to surrender authority and sovereignty to other entities (219). He argues that the main proponents of "reciprocally binding human rights obligations" were "governments of newly established democracies" eschewing NGO-based arguments and great powers–based arguments (220). Great powers, in fact, were reticent. Moravcsik described the British fear of further pushing to incorporate the European Court of Human Rights "once the document was signed" (243). He also points out that democratic states can, somewhat counterintuitively, be the *most* resistant to treaty ratification (245). This reluctance to ratify binding obligations mirrors Hathaway's (2007) finding that states' domestic legal enforcement capabilities affect their likelihood of ratifying human rights treaties. She asks the broad question of "Why do countries commit to human rights?" and subsequently narrows it to the more specific question of how we best explain "state decisions to ratify human rights treaties" (590). The greater the capability to enforce a treaty, the less likely a state is to ratify: "where compliance is most likely, commitment is often most consequential" (613). Hathaway limits the conceptual consideration of commitment to ratification. Given the counts of states and state actions listed in the article, in coding ratification, Hathaway includes the other binding actions of accession and succession under the heading of "ratification." She and Moravcsik both note democracies' tendency to hesitate before ratifying binding international law because they are the states more likely to uphold the treaties. This interesting focus overlooks any nuance with which democracies approach nonbinding commitment treaties as well as variation across binding commitment actions.

Wotipka and Tsutsui (2008) move away from a regime-centered explanation when asking what explains "states' decisions to ratify human rights treaties" (726) and argue that international socialization pressures via coercion, imitation, and normative compliance explain state ratification of human rights treaties (726). They examine seven human rights treaties: CERD, ICESCR, ICCPR, Convention on the Suppression and Punishment of the Crime of Apartheid, CEDAW, CAT, and the CRC. The authors frame their puzzle (i.e., why states commit) around ratification and distinguish treaty ratification as follows: "Unlike declarations, treaties are binding legal documents" that are "much stronger instruments to promote" (726). Wotipka and Tsutsui dichotomously code ratification to mark its presence or absence (739). Although the authors did not note that they included accession and succession into the coding of ratification, their counts of states party indicate that they grouped them together when discussing and measuring ratification (727).[5] They find support for the power of normative pressure in explaining state ratification. States embedded within international society (defined through the number of networks and NGOs) are more likely to ratify (748).

The study also found support for the imitation argument but not for the coercion argument. This work tested how normative and socialization factors influenced treaty commitment but, in limiting the definition of commitment to ratification, the authors overlooked the

---

[5] See Table 1.1 in the Wotipka and Tsutsui (2008) article.

question of how different mechanisms could take hold for different commitment processes. States recommitting via succession as they are undergoing democratization may be more susceptible to certain socialization mechanisms than other states. Additionally, the distinction between accession and ratification identifies states that committed to a treaty they did not create. The authors could have separated these commitment types to test whether states drafting international law became more socialized to it.

Using a spatial modeling approach, Lupu (2016) models state preferences for joining international treaties. Analyzing treaties across subject areas, he finds that trade is the best predictor of committing to treaties. This is particularly interesting, as this finding holds across issue areas not addressing trade and economic topics. Lupu uses the broad and vague language of "joining on" to international treaties and uses data on treaty ratification for the analysis (1228). This is problematic, as different factors and circumstances lead to states committing via ratification versus accession versus succession. In grouping all of these actions together as ratification, Lupu misses some of this nuance. Treaties with strict accession requirements are excluded from the analysis. This exclusion misses the variation occurring in accession commitment (1229). Lupu acknowledges that new states may have different commitment priorities: "new states, in particular, often have many higher priorities than universal treaty ratification" (1241). The study also considers years that states signed but did not ratify to be the same as years that states did not commit at all. As a result, the study models factors explaining the move to binding commitment but not the initial decision to commit.

Other scholars highlight the role of domestic institutions and politics to explain human rights treaty commitment. Sandholtz (2017) explores the important question of how domestic policy on treaty incorporation and international legal supremacy matter for commitment. In measuring commitment, Sandholtz recognizes the three types of binding commitment. However, he groups them together for analysis and does not include nonbinding signature.

> The dependent variables in the analyses that follow derive from the year of ratification, accession, or succession to the Convention against Torture. Though there are technical differences among the three modes of becoming party to a treaty, they all produce the same legal obligations and I use the term "ratification" to cover all three mechanisms. (31)

As a result, how domestic incorporation policy affects timing of signature, or variation across ratification, accession, and succession, remains unclear.

Efrat (2016) argues that legal tradition significantly affects a state's likelihood of joining nonbinding international agreements, demonstrating the strong effect of domestic institutions on international legal behavior. He focuses on UN model commercial legislation that is explicitly nonbinding without the possibility of moving toward binding commitment actions. Looking more specifically at domestic legal doctrine, Elkins, Ginsburg, and Simmons (2013) find that rights presence in domestic constitutions has an interactive effect with treaty ratification that supports improvements in human rights practices. They note that human rights treaty ratification "produces both a direct as well as a mediated influence on domestic respect for human rights via constitutional incorporation" (64). Haftel and Thompson (2013) find that the presence of domestic legislative "veto players" delays treaty ratification. For example, the US Senate has played a detrimental role in treaty ratification (Henkin 1995), resulting in weakened rights commitment and practices (Mayerfeld 2007).

This review highlights how prominent scholars within international relations, sociology, and international law have worked hard (since Keith's first take) on testing the effect of commitment to international human rights treaties on human rights practices. It is also clear that their studies have been problematic in only focusing on ratification when testing the effect of treaty commitment on state behavior. Thus far the approach, excepting Landman (2005) and Cole (2012), has generally been to overlook signature when analyzing international human rights treaty commitment. The dominant approach has been to rely on ratification as the critical point for commitment and compliance behavior. When writing about commitment types, scholars have frequently been vague about what they are measuring, using terms such as "signing on," "joining," "committing," and "ratifying" interchangeably when discussing legal commitment. When measuring commitment, studies used "ratification," and when using "ratification," they actually have been measuring ratification, accession, and succession counts combined, without differentiating these legal commitment types. This leaves us with less certainty about (1) trends and influence of nonbinding signature, (2) the influence of other binding commitment types, and (3) general conclusions about human rights treaty commitment.

Compliance around Ratification

The aforementioned literature review focused on ratification and compliance with international law. This book focuses squarely on legal commitment as it connects with domestic politics and processes. However, it is important to acknowledge the research tackling international human rights that examines human rights practices and normative compliance around ratification or works that in fact eschew the importance of legal commitment. Waves of research on human rights conceptualized human rights compliance *around* or without ratification. For this literature, legal commitment does not constitute a prerequisite for compliance. Bringing international standards and commitments to the local level has been the focus of this area of research, emphasizing national human rights institutions (NHRIs), bottom-up approaches, and the importance of local interpretations. Some scholars find the concept of compliance itself to be inherently problematic. I briefly review these works and make the case for why this book speaks to this literature even with differing approaches to the importance of legalism when studying international human rights.

A notable critique of a legalized approach to international human rights is that processes of commitment and change are not necessarily reflected in, via, or at the time of ratification. Finnemore and Toope (2001) critiqued the legalization approach (Abbott and Snidal 2000) in part due to what they argue was an approach that overlooked the process of law. Hillebrecht similarly argued that "compliance is more than just an outcome, however. It is also a process . . . which invokes multiple actors on the domestic and international levels" (2016, 28). Huneeus argues that although the concept of compliance can be difficult to measure and the causality difficult to ascertain (especially with treaties), compliance with court decisions and judgments has an important legitimating effect on the court itself (2014, 440–442).

Scholars, especially those from anthropological and sociological traditions, emphasize the localization processes associated with human rights change. Merry (2009) embraces the importance of local translation of international human rights focusing on women's rights. Translation and vernacular are important components of rights change, and she is critical of human rights treaty ratification as some countries view ratification as "an end in itself." She argues that "participating in the international human rights regime allows countries to claim civilized status in the present international order, much as ideas of civilization provided the standard for colonized countries during the imperial era" (79). Haglund and Aggarwal (2011) also emphasize a local, bottom-up, approach to human rights norm compliance. However, they acknowledge the role of treaty commitment in formalizing rights obligations. They argue that norms of economic and social rights (ESR) are defended more in poor countries than rich ones (498) and require different tools for analysis than political rights: "translation of ESR from norms to realization is different enough from political and civil rights to require the application of different theoretical and methodological tools" (507). However, the authors argue that ESR are different from other human rights; their "social and economic rights triangle" includes regulation and obligations as two points, mirroring the approach used by other scholars favoring international legal commitments as a means to measure obligation and commitment. International treaties are seen as a "formal mechanism for holding states accountable to international norms" (Kratochvíl 2009).

Other human rights researchers emphasize domestic institutions' role in implementing international rights commitments. The commitments themselves are not sufficient for rights changes; rather, commitment is a "signal" that domestic institutions use to actualize rights compliance. Goodman and Pegram (2011) emphasize the role of NHRIs in actualizing the human rights goals articulated in international treaties. Welch (2017) focuses on NHRI effect in treaty implementation, measuring treaty commitment by coding "whether a country has ratified, acceded or succeeded (here on referred to as ratified) to the CAT" (103). He finds that countries with NHRIs have fewer torture violations. His coding acknowledges different binding types of treaty commitment, but he does not disaggregate them when testing the interactive role of commitment on CAT compliance. While NHRIs can contribute to a "race to the middle," wherein states have few incentives to achieve better human rights standards than the minimums set by NHRIs, the Goodman and Pegram (2011) argue that, more often than not, NHRIs amplify effectiveness of human rights endeavors. Through their unique positioning "at the intersection of international and domestic domains" NHRIs "function as special vehicles for fostering the diffusion of international human rights norms within local settings" (12).

This book offers a means to speak to this literature as well. *Committed to Rights* considers the international human rights regime's legal framing and goals as important elements of state behavior, as constraints on state activity, and key to global human rights. Those scholars who remain skeptical about the role of ratification can look to state behavior with nonbinding signature to study how states change (or not) when those states are under less of a reputational spotlight. Scholars looking for a process-based study of compliance will also find such an approach in this book's consideration of signature and ratification. I do not treat ratification as the pinnacle of commitment and compliance. Scholars emphasizing a localized approach to human rights changes will find that local rights groups embrace different treaty commitment actions for meaning, signaling, and significance via legal mobilization. This is not to say that the research placing less emphasis on legal-based study of human rights will not find differing interpretations or critiques of this volume. Rather, I am saying that I note and incorporate these scholars' concerns in executing this research project.

Ratification Campaigns from Civil Society and the United Nations

Academics are not the only ones focused on the ratification of human rights treaties. NGOs frequently campaign explicitly on the goal of getting states to ratify UN human rights treaties. The United Nations also calls for ratification of human rights treaties during its Universal Periodic Review process. However, both NGO and international governmental organization actors commonly neglect to consider what positive changes can occur leading up to binding legal commitment and make assumptions about the superiority of ratification over other commitment types.

Amnesty International has centered campaigns on ratifying UN treaties. It identified important UN human rights treaties and called explicitly for citizens to encourage their states to ratify.

> The specific rights in the UDHR have been codified into the International Covenant on Economic, Social, and Cultural Rights (ICESCR) and the International Covenant on Civil and Political Rights (ICCPR). A covenant is a treaty which, under the rules of international law, creates legal obligations on all states that ratify it. Similarly, the Convention on the Rights of the Child (CRC) and Convention on the Elimination of All Forms of Discrimination against Women (CEDAW) also are treaties that are binding on the states that ratify them . . . Therefore, citizens worldwide should put pressure on their governments to ratify these treaties and to abide by the obligations they set forth. (1998)

Amnesty International framed its Arms Trade Treaty campaign around three goals: "1. Ratify the Arms Trade Treaty, 2. Create or amend national laws to reflect the rules of the treaty. And 3. Implement those laws effectively" (n.d.a). Because ratification is binding, the group cites ratification, not signing, as its goal. According to the UN Office for Disarmament Affairs, 92 states are party to the Arms Trade Treaty, committing through binding action, while 130 states are signatories to the treaty. In celebrating ratification, Amnesty International overlooked the additional 38 states that had signed but had not yet legally bound themselves to the treaty. Amnesty International also campaigns and targets countries to ratify international human rights treaties. It wrote a report specifically calling for "Saint Lucia to ratify key human rights treaties, to protect LGBTI rights and to abolish the death penalty" (2016).

When states ratify human rights treaties, groups next mobilize around the goal of ratifying their Optional Protocols. The CRC already achieved the highest level of support of any human rights treaty, with binding agreement from 196 state parties. All 193 UN members committed to the treaty as well as the three nonmembers (the Holy See, Palestine, and the Cook Islands). Given this achievement, the Child Rights International Network (CRIN) campaign focused on increasing state commitment with the objective of ratifying Optional Protocols to the CRC. CRIN launched a campaign in 2010 with the goal of creating a "global campaign for universal ratification of the UN Optional Protocols on children's rights."[6] The campaign included collaboration across NGOs but also relied on networks within the United Nations via the UN special representative of the secretary-general on Violence against Children.

Also, within the United Nations, the Universal Periodic Review serves as a means through which states encourage ratification and highlight states that have yet to ratify human rights treaties. During the 2009 Universal Periodic Review of Afghanistan, Indonesia asked whether Afghanistan planned "to ratify additional core human rights conventions" (7). In the recommendation section, the committee encouraged Afghanistan to ratify the Optional Protocol to the Convention against Torture, the Optional Protocol to the ICCPR, the Optional Protocol to the CEDAW, the International Convention on the Protection of the Rights of All Migrant Workers and Members of Their Families (CMW), the Convention on the Rights of Persons with Disabilities (CRPD), and the International Convention for the Protection of All Persons from Enforced Disappearance. France and Argentina separately called for Afghanistan's support for the Optional Protocol to the CAT

---

[6] https://archive.crin.org/en/home/campaigns/hosted-campaigns/international-treaty-ratification.html

and all of the Optional Protocols to the UN human rights conventions, respectively (2009, 21).

In its 2011 annual country report, the Working Group on the Universal Periodic Review urged the United States thirty-seven times to ratify human rights treaties. Calls for ratification came from individual working group members as well as collectively from the group level. Even Sudan, a country not noted at the United Nations for its human rights pioneering, called on the United States to "ratify the core human rights treaties, particularly the CRC, ICESCR, CEDAW and its Optional Protocol, the OP-CAT and the CMW and the CRPD with its Optional Protocol" (UN 2011). Venezuela, France, Russia, Spain, Canada, Japan, Indonesia, Vietnam, India, Malaysia, Australia, Qatar, Turkey, Haiti, Costa Rica, China, the Netherlands, Slovakia, Republic of Korea, Austria, Trinidad and Tobago, Cyprus, Thailand, Hungary, Iran, Egypt, Guatemala, Democratic People's Republic of Korea, Ghana, Finland, New Zealand, Nicaragua, Bolivia, Algeria, Libya, and the Holy See all separately called on the United States to move beyond signature and ratify core human rights treaties. This activity demonstrates pressure to move from signature to ratification.

Within the policy and activist realm, the United Nations, NGOs, and other states are very interested in pressuring states to ratify human rights treaties. However, the focus on ratification as the goal of state legal signaling makes several foundational assumptions. First is the assumption that legally binding commitment prompts greater compliance than nonlegally binding action. As scholars, we do not know this with certainty, because nonbinding agreements and nonbinding actions have not generated the same degree of research interest and attention. Second, UN and civil society actors tend to assume that ratification is a simple and quick action for a supportive head of state. Within the Universal Periodic Review process, states often express frustration with the United States for taking long periods to ratify after signing human rights treaties. However, they do not fully acknowledge the time-consuming domestic process in the United States of working toward ratification, despite many other states confronting similar processes.

Conclusion

This chapter mapped the existing approaches to the study of international treaty commitment and compliance, noting the parameters placed around the subject that privilege an almost exclusive focus on binding ratification. As I argue here, existing assumptions and conclusions about the (lack of) efficacy of international human rights treaties emanating from the policy and scholarly world are incomplete and can be reassessed through an expanded understanding of commitment. *Committed to Rights* builds on the strengths of the study of international law by expanding the study of commitment beyond ratification. My aim is not to replicate and rerun models of past studies discussed in this review but to inject consideration of other commitment types into future research agendas. In the next chapter, I introduce my argument for analyzing commitment actions separately and for recognizing the different legal commitment paths that states take within the UN human rights treaty framework.

3

Legal Paths for Human Rights Treaty Commitment and Compliance

> By signing multilateral conventions or depositing their instruments of ratification, accession or through other instruments establishing the consent to be bound, the Member States contribute significantly to the advancement of the rule of law in international relations and the cause of peace.
>
> UN Treaty Section Office of Legal Affairs, "Treaty Event 2019"

The UN Action Plan from the Office of Legal Affairs, quoted here, indicates that multiple commitment types warrant celebration. Its goal of celebrating all forms of legal commitment does not align with the ratification centrism found across civil society and academia. Although the research discussed in the preceding sections made important contributions to understanding international human rights law, it falls short for understanding either the range of actions available to states at the point of commitment or how these options affect the range of compliance outcomes. International relations, international law, and sociology scholars miss opportunities to unpack *how* states commit and thus provide more explanation as to *when, why,* and *how* they comply. When considering multilateral treaty law, states have several commitment paths. Concerning UN treaties, there are four primary ways a state can commit to international law: through signature, ratification, accession, and succession. I argue that we must separate out these commitment actions to better understand the legal and domestic political contexts within which states are committing. These contexts, which determined the treaty commitment type, provide insight into states' likelihood of improving their rights practices after commitment and complying with human rights treaties. In this chapter, I move the discussion away from a ratification-centered focus and toward a ratification-comparative focus that allows for a more expanded, nuanced understanding of treaty commitment. I present my conceptual model of legal commitment,

which includes and situates the four primary ways states commit legally
to international human rights law. The important point is not to push
ratification to the side while studying treaty commitment but to incorporate it within a broader context of commitment pathways. I expand on
the descriptive analysis of treaty commitment by type and over time to
lend initial support for calling attention to these actions. This chapter lays
the conceptual and descriptive groundwork for the quantitative and case
analyses in the following chapters.

Ratification is one of four primary ways states commit to international
treaty law at the UN. Through ratification, states commit to be bound by
the terms of the treaty. Accession and succession are similarly binding
action types. Together, states that ratify, accede, or succeed human rights
treaties constitute states party to the treaty – that is, states that are legally
bound to the treaty. However, important differences exist between these
three commitment types. States that succeed to treaties do so as new
states committing to agreements are already committed to by prior
existing states. For example, Czechoslovakia signed and ratified human
rights treaties; when the Czech Republic and Slovakia came into existence, each recommitted to those treaties through succession. Because the
number of new states that emerged to replace old states has been relatively low since the onset of modern human rights regime, the small size
of succession in Figure 3.1 makes sense.

Between 1966 and 2010, states committed via succession fifty-two
times to the core human rights treaties. The UN and the VCLT differentiate between ratification and accession actions. States that commit via

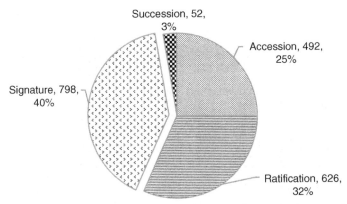

Figure 3.1 Commitment to core UN human rights treaties by commitment type,
1966–2010

accession to treaties did not have a hand in negotiating those treaties and/ or committed to the treaty after its EIF. About 25 percent of all human rights commitment actions were accession actions, meaning about a quarter of state commitment comes from states not involved in designing and negotiating the human rights treaties. Ratification constitutes the largest percentage of binding commitment actions and accounts for about a third of all commitment actions. Ratification commitment comes from states that legally bind themselves to the treaty, participated in treaty negotiations, and had previously signed the treaty. Signature actions make up 40 percent of commitment action; it is striking that nonbinding commitment comprised the largest commitment action activity, given that it is the area that international relations and international legal studies have, overall, focused on the least. Taken together, the descriptive data presented in Figure 3.1 indicate that other commitment types constitute sizable international human rights treaty commitment behavior.

Figure 3.2 plots the different commitment types across the nine core human rights treaties. Across all of the core treaties, commitment via succession is the least frequent type. The gaps between signature, ratification, and accession counts differed a bit across the treaties. The CRC stands out as the treaty with the highest number of ratifications, at 136. The CRPD has the highest number of signatories, 145, but has a large gap between states that signed and those that ratified. Only eighty-six of the 145 signatures ratified the CRPD. Across the CERD and the CAT,

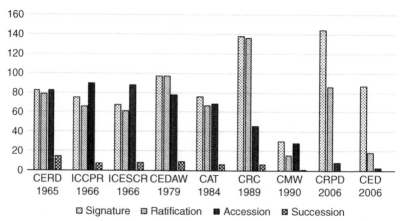

Figure 3.2 Commitment action types by core UN human rights treaty, 1966–2010

commitment via signature, ratification, and accession were very close in numbers. The other recently made treaty, the CED, also had lower numbers of states committing via binding action. While eighty-seven states signed the CED, only eighteen ratified and three acceded. The ICESCR actually had more commitment actions via accession than ratification, at eighty-eight, compared with sixty-one. For the ICESCR, more states bounded themselves without participating in negotiations than those that did participate in negotiations. This trend also holds in the CAT, CERD, ICCPR, and CMW treaties.

Figures 3.3 through 3.11 graph the ratification, accession, succession, and signature of the nine core human rights treaties over time. Three of the treaties, the ICCPR, CERD, and ICESCR, opened for signature in 1966. CEDAW, CAT, CMW, and the CRC opened between 1980 and 1990. The CED and CRPD are the latest human rights treaties to open (2007). The figures reveal separate trends in commitment activity based on commitment type. All treaties except for the CMW had a notable spike in signatures prior to high binding commitment activity (Figure 3.9). ICCPR, ICESCR, and CEDAW all had notable and separate spikes in ratification, accession, and signature behavior. The accession actions around the early 1990s coincide with the introduction of the newly independent former Soviet states in Eastern Europe. All figures reveal a striking gap between high levels of signature actions and lower levels of ratification. While many states may be on board to sign human rights treaties soon after the treaties open, they diverge on when precisely they are able to bind themselves through ratification. For example, 125 states signed the CRC when it opened in 1990, but only about half, fifty-nine were able to advance to ratify that year. Similarly, 120 states signed the CRPD when it opened in 2007, but only fourteen states ratified that year. These early booms in signature commitment are overlooked and disregarded in most

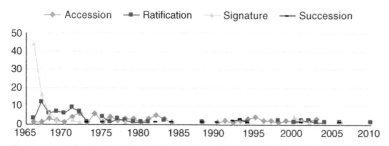

Figure 3.3   CERD commitment, 1965–2010

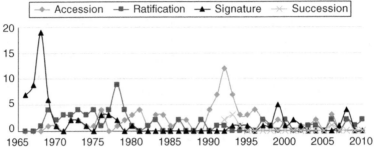

Figure 3.4   ICCPR commitment, 1966–2010

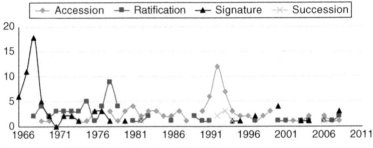

Figure 3.5   ICESCR commitment, 1966–2010

international relations and international legal studies analyses: states are simply coded as non-committers and dismissed as not having ratified the treaties.

Paths to Commitment

States come to international human rights commitment through four distinct paths, which I argue are important to understand how, when, and to what extent they reach compliance. The pathways argument theorizes that states diverge on how and when they enter the treaty-making and commitment process. Institutional standards and norms have established trajectories along the pathway to commitment and compliance, but states differ in how they move along it. Domestic institutions and contexts shape states' legal pathway choices, and international legal regimes limit the available options. The above figures show

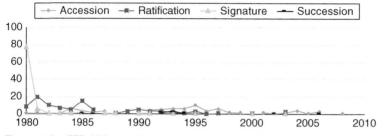

Figure 3.6 CEDAW commitment, 1980–2010

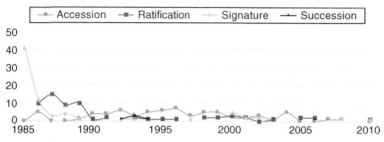

Figure 3.7 CAT commitment, 1985–2010

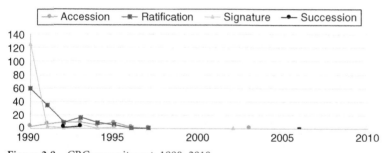

Figure 3.8 CRC commitment, 1990–2010

that types of treaty commitment happen at different times and non-ratification actions make up the majority of human rights treaty commitment actions. Advancing to what these actions mean for compliance, I argue that the four commitment types of signature, ratification, accession, and succession are important to differentiate when studying human rights behavior.

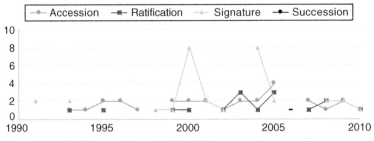

Figure 3.9   CMW commitment, 1990–2010

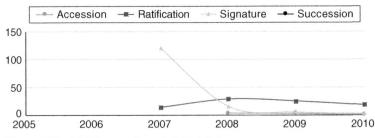

Figure 3.10   CRPD commitment, 2006–2010

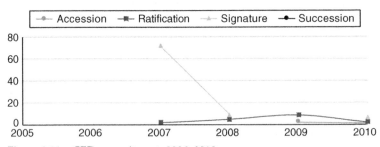

Figure 3.11   CED commitment, 2006–2010

Signature is the only nonbinding way for states to formally commit to treaty law within the UN framework. Even though it is a nonbinding commitment, there are expectations of adherence to the terms of treaty, rooted firmly in the VCLT. Given the expectation of honoring the intent and purpose of the treaty, it is surprising that signature has been generally overlooked within the study of international human rights law.[1] As demonstrated in the descriptive analysis of human rights treaty actions, signature has the highest frequency of action.

Signature is a first step toward ratification and is important to study in its own right. Nonbinding norms have a strong record of invoking change in human rights practices. For many states, treaty signature is an initial commitment action on their legal pathway. Understanding the initial step of consent contributes to the study of international human rights commitment. Treaty signature bridges the legal and normative approaches to international law. I argue that signature is particularly important for states confronting difficult domestic paths to ratification. For these states, signature offers a faster and intuitionally simpler way for heads of state that support international human rights law to commit. Without waiting for the legislature to get on board with treaty ratification, the president, the prime minster, or other head of state can signal to both international and domestic audiences that the executive supports human rights. This has potential reputational benefits for the head of state within the diplomatic world abroad and within the political world at home.

There are also pragmatic benefits of signaling to other parts within the government that the executive office is taking a hard line position against specific human rights violations. For *Legislative Approval States*, signature is a means to signal and commit years, and sometimes decades, in advance of legislative-branch support for ratification, such as the US Congress's stalling ratification of the highly popular CRC, CEDAW, and CRPD treaties. After *Legislative Approval States* sign human rights treaties, I expect that the supportive executive will begin to improve human rights conditions prior to ratification. For these states, the transformative period of human rights practices happens before binding legal commitment. States without domestic legislative barriers to ratification do not expect comparable delays, debates, and difficulties in moving forward with ratification after the executive has expressed support; these *Executive Approval States* approach signature differently.

Ratification has been the "go-to" action and all-encompassing concept which scholars have written about and studied in international

---

[1] As mentioned, while reviewing the literature, I know of only a handful of studies that have included signature and subject to ratification, of human rights treaties in their quantitative analysis: Landman (2005), Comstock (2020), Cole (2012), Simmons (2002), and Cardenas (2007). These works are important for advancing how we think about commitment and how we measure compliances.

commitment and compliance. When using ratification as a universal category for commitment actions, we miss studying about what ratification actually means, constitutes, and motivates. We know from legal definitions and the body of scholarship on human rights law that ratification is a highly sought-after goal. We know that it is a firm, legally binding commitment to treaty law. Conceptualizing ratification uniquely and distinctly from other types of treaty commitment leaves us with a more precise definition and understanding of what ratification is. Ratification is the legally binding form of treaty commitment enacted by states which participated in treaty negotiations and previously signed the treaty. It is the second step in a two-step commitment process. All states that ratify human rights treaties have already signed the treaty. Ratifiers have successfully navigated whatever domestic processes were required following signature and prior to ratification. The processes may be cursory or near nonexistent or they may be institutionally complex and arduous. Ratifying states have been involved through all of these points – negotiations, signing, domestic procedural requirements, and then ratification. Parsing out the other types of legal commitment yields a richer understanding of what ratification entails. States reaching treaty ratification have achieved a high level of commitment and participation within the treaty-making process. Ratification signifies that many steps have been taken on a legal pathway to commitment and compliance. Recognizing all that ratification entails provides additional conceptual depth to the action.

I separate out states that have domestic legislative barriers to ratification (*Legislative Approval States*) from those that do not (*Executive Approval States*) and argue that expected relationships between signature and ratification differ based on how easily ratification comes to the executive. *Legislative Approval States* emphasize on signature because it is a commitment action that executives can authorize without legislative approval. The executive can sign whenever they support and endorse a treaty. For ratification, the executive requires more domestic political maneuvering and enough support to convince the legislature to approve ratification. By the time that happens, at times years or decades later, the supportive executive has already made steps to improve the state's human rights practices. *Executive Approval States* do not place the same importance on signature because when the executive wants to ratify human rights treaties, they can do so without confronting the institutional and time constraints.

Accession is the binding form of treaty commitment available to states that did not negotiate the treaty and/or missed the original window of opportunity to sign the treaty. States that acceded to international human rights law are of several types. Some opted out of participating in treaty negotiations; others did not gain independence until after treaty negotiations or treaty creation and did not have the opportunity to commit to the treaty until a later point, when signing was no longer an option.[2] Because of later commitment, these states were no longer allowed to ratify the treaty. Their formal commitment type was accession. All accession states were late to the treaty in one or more of these ways – late to involvement (missing negotiations), late to commitment (missing the signature window), late to the international stage (missing these early processes altogether). Lateness distinguishes accession states from signature and ratification states. Accession states' legal pathways entered into the treaty-making process later than other states.

I build on earlier studies of international cooperation by differentiating states involved in negotiations from those that were not involved and later committed via accession, I argue and find support for my argument that states that were present but opted out of negotiations (Early Members) had worse practices following commitment than the states that opted in. States that did not exist at the time of negotiations but committed through accession because they missed the timing for signing and ratification (Late Members) did not share the same initial disinterest in the treaty. These states experienced an advantage of having more time to be socialized to the treaty's norms and expectations. For these states, I expect that human rights practices improve following accession.

Succession is the binding form of legal commitment to treaty law by new states that are replacing prior states' ratification. Treaty commitment through succession is an infrequent and unique pathway to treaty commitment. Only a small handful of states qualify to commit this way. A prior state must first have ratified an international treaty; following an emergent independent state's replacing the prior state, the new state must decide whether to keep the existing legal commitments. Instead of starting fresh on the international stage, the new state recommits by renewing the prior ratification and committing through succession. Two periods in the modern era contained waves of new states in the international system. The first was the wave of decolonization in Africa

---

[2] Even when not specifically stipulated that a window of signature has closed, many states maintain the international legal norm of accession following EIF.

during the 1960s. Between 1960 and 1970, forty-two new states joined the UN, almost all of which were in Africa. The second wave was at the end of the Cold War and mostly came from the former Soviet states in Eastern Europe. Between 1990 and 1993, twenty-eight states joined the UN following the fall of the Soviet Union.

Succession commitment status is not a permanent means for former colonies or newly independent states to commit to all future treaties. Succession commitment only applies to treaties that existed and were committed to by the prior state. The new state can commit to new treaties via signature, ratification or accession. Many of the modern human rights treaties were created and opened for signature following the wave of postcolonial independence in Africa. Because of this temporal component, succession commitment rarely applied to postcolonial African states committing to the UN core human rights treaties. For example, the Democratic Republic of the Congo committed to the Genocide Convention, which opened in 1948, through succession in 1962 but through accession to the ICCPR, which opened in 1966.

Succession commitment applies to former Soviet states that gained independence in the 1990s following new states gaining legal identities. New states gaining independence during this wave committed through succession to many UN human rights treaties since they predated independence. Six core human rights treaties opened for signature before 1990. Three additional treaties, the CMW, the CRPD, and the CED, were created in 1990 or after. Figure 3.12 illustrates the timing of core human rights treaties against the number of new states admitted as UN members per year. New states were capable of signing and ratifying or acceding to the later treaties and did adjust their commitment actions accordingly. Slovakia, for instance, committed to the ICCPR via succession in 1993 but signed and ratified the CRPD in 2007 and 2010, respectively. To reiterate, succession commitment reflects a temporal and territorial relationship rather than a blanket future relationship with international law.

Domestic conditions distinguish succession states from other states committing to human rights treaties. States that commit through succession improve human rights practices following commitment, thanks to preexisting support for the treaties. With an underlay of domestic support, succession states are not confronting the same types of challenges as states committing to a treaty for the first time. Uniquely, succession states are recommitting to human rights treaties at a period of potential regime change, new emphasis on human rights recognition, and resituating identity on the world stage. The latter process, in particular, heightens

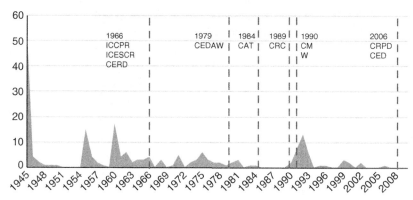

Figure 3.12   Number of new UN member states per year and core human rights, 1945–2010

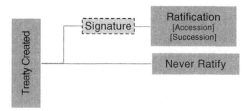

Figure 3.13   Common approaches to human rights treaty commitment

succession states' need for recognition and legitimation within the international system. Human rights treaty succession offers a unique and public means for new states to signal alignment with international human rights norms.

Figure 3.13 depicts the common, traditional approach to the study of human rights treaty commitment, which mostly frames commitment as dichotomous: either states ratify or they do not. Some scholarship has recognized signature but not fully incorporated it into causal explanations. Rather, it depicts signature as an insignificant act on the way to the more important ratification. Existing research considers accession and succession as synonymous with ratification (when, if at all, the additional commitment types are mentioned).

In Figure 3.14, I visualize my alternative model to treaty commitment, incorporating the logic of varied commitment pathways. The four types

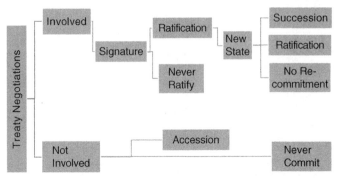

Figure 3.14   Legal paths to committing to human rights treaties

of treaty commitments have clear relationships with time and sequencing; acceding states were not involved in negotiations leading up to treaty creation; signing is a required step before ratification; ratification is a prerequisite for succession. Studies considered time implicitly and explicitly when examining how long it takes a state to ratify (Hathaway 2007; Vreeland 2008; Cole 2009; Haftel and Thompson 2013; Kelley and Pevehouse 2015). Beyond this, however, time is an important consideration for understanding at which point the states joined during the treaty development process. As Figure 3.14 illustrates, there are inherent relationships between commitment actions and temporal ordering. Ratification is not an isolated commitment event but rather encapsulates negotiations and signature. Succession in turn encapsulates ratification along with signature and negotiation involvement. It is also important to note that some states sign but never ratify human rights treaties. The legal pathway to commitment, for these states, is incomplete. Figure 2.1 shows 798 signatures to human rights treaties but only 626 ratifications. That means that there were 172 cases of states signing but not following through with ratification. These 172 cases have, thus far, been underexamined in the study of human rights treaties.

In Table 3.1, I summarize the arguments and expectations associated with the different types of treaty commitments discussed in this chapter. Different states use different types of commitments and respond differently to them. It is clear from the legal definitions and characteristics of signature, ratification, accession, and succession that they are inherently separate actions; it is also clear that there are varying expectations of state human rights practices following commitment. Consistent with much of the research on human rights treaties, I expect contexts wherein ratification does not result in

Table 3.1 *Commitment actions and human rights expectations*

Commitment action	Expected relationship with rights	Mechanisms of change
Signature	None	*Executive Approval States* These states will not view signature as an important point of commitment.
	Positive	*Legislative Approval States* Supportive executives lead to improvement in rights after signature, prior to ratification.
Ratification	Negative	Ratification-centric focus of civil society and other actors relieves pressure once commitment goal is met.
	None	Rights changes happen before ratification.
	Positive	*Negotiation Participants* States are socialized toward rights through the negotiation processes.
Accession	Negative	*Early Members* Opted out of treaty negotiations and have lower investment in the treaty and human rights.
	Positive	*Late Members* These states were not present for the treaty development but had time to be socialized. Without the earlier step of signature, states committing via

Table 3.1 (*cont.*)

Commitment action	Expected relationship with rights	Mechanisms of change
		accession focus action around their one commitment act.
Succession	Positive	These states are undergoing democratization, are seeking international legitimation, and confront extra international pressure to adhere to human rights norms.
No Action	None/Negative	These states have not participated in any of the formal treaty-making processes. Their pathway to commitment has been nonlegal and nonpar-ticipatory within the international human rights regime.
	Positive	Once normative support for treaty and human rights becomes uni-versal, customary international law norms can hold states accountable for adhering to treaties they did not con-sent to.

improved human rights practices. When disaggregated from the effects following signature, ratification will not be expected to elicit substantial changes in human rights behavior. However, I argue that ratification states participatory experiences during treaty negotiations contribute to improved rights. Scholars have theorized that some of the negative findings associated with human rights ratification occur because the civil society backs away from pressuring states once the commitment goal of ratification has been met (e.g., Hafner-Burton and Tsutsui 2005). Given many NGO campaigns' ratification-centric approach, I incorporate this expectation as a result of a false dichotomy of commitment paths.

In contrast with existing research, I expect that ratification's precursor, signature, can be associated with improved human rights practices. I argue that this will be likely for *Legislative Approval States*, which have more difficult and delayed ratification processes. I expect that states recommitting to human rights treaties through succession will have improved human rights practices following commitment, as will states that accede to human rights treaties because of late entry into the international system (rather than due to opting out of treaty negotiations). Determining and situating a state's legal pathway to commitment allow for greater understanding of domestic contexts effecting compliance, for clarifying arguments and a set of expectations of state human rights behavior.

States taking no legal commitment action to human rights treaties maintain a path of sustained nonengagement. I expect that these states will have worse human rights practices overall than participatory states that engage with formal, legal pathways to human rights treaty commitment. Over time, states with no action of treaty commitment may be bound informally through customary international law. Nonparticipatory states have the potential path of nonconsensual "consent" to treaty terms. Given the enforceability of customary international law, nonparticipatory states have the possibility of improving rights practices over time once pressured by the international human rights regime. Disaggregating legal commitment types opens the possibilities to positive paths to compliance.

Conclusion

In this chapter, I introduced the book's central approach, arguing that there are legal pathways to committing and complying with international human rights law that are more complicated and nuanced than the falsely dichotomous approach of treaty ratification. So often when scholars address the question of treaty commitment, they are really asking about ratification. Theoretical drivers of treaty behavior related to regime type, NGO activities, moral obligations, and domestic politics underestimate the differences in commitment types to human rights treaties. The underlying assumption – that nonbinding commitment is insignificant – dismisses signature as potentially meaningful, despite signature actions comprising the largest type of commitment actions. Understanding the timing and conditions leading to types of treaty commitments allows for more accurately predicting a state's relationship with the treaty.

As illustrated through descriptive statistics of treaty commitment, ratification is only one of the four dominant ways states commit to UN treaty law. Each type of commitment (ratification, signature, accession, and succession) has different requirements and contexts under which states commit. When asking why states ratify international law, scholars thus far have overlooked and "over bundled" the other actions into a seemingly universal answer. In fact, this question warrants a more complex approach. Similarly, I call for a study of compliance with international human rights treaties that takes into consideration when, how, and why states committed before using the action as a fulcrum for change. This chapter made the case to move away from a ratification-centered approach; the following chapters examine data and cases across treaties by testing the effects of signature, ratification, accession, and succession on changes in human rights practices. In each chapter, I develop arguments specific to each commitment type that build on the domestic context argument introduced here. I find evidence that states commit differently and comply differently. This is a straight forward statement with significant implications for the study of international human rights law. It is also the cause for optimism.

4

Signature

A First Step in a Two-Step Commitment Process

For nearly a decade, the US has been on the sidelines as new treaties have been developed and existing treaties gained international support . . . By signing the Disabilities Convention, the US is beginning to reassert leadership on international human rights.

Human Rights Watch, "US: Treaty Signing Signals Policy Shift"

"The administration is putting itself on the wrong side of history," said Kenneth Roth, executive director of Human Rights Watch. "'Unsigning' the treaty will not stop the court. It will only throw the US into opposition against the most important new institution for enforcing human rights in fifty years."

Human Rights Watch, "United States 'Unsigning' Treaty on War Crimes Court"

The aforementioned quotes demonstrate strong reactions to US signature behavior. The signing of the Convention on the Rights of Persons with Disabilities (CRPD) and the withdrawal of signature from the Rome Statute of the International Criminal Court evoked vehement support and condemnation. A leading human rights nongovernmental organization (NGO), Human Rights Watch, clearly observed that signing behavior merited attention and commentary. However, ratification is visibly the end goal for human rights groups. When states sign important treaties such as the CRPD, the international community recognizes this as a significant step en route to ratification. Especially for the United States, which distanced itself from international human rights law, signing the CRPD marked an important shift toward re-emphasizing human rights. Though significant, most of the discourse surrounding the United States and the CRPD centers on the United States' inability to ratify the treaty. The United States withdrawal from the Rome Statute through "unsigning" the treaty was met with extreme criticism from rights groups and other governments. This backlash demonstrates the significance placed on signature.

Though signature is nonbinding, signing human rights treaties holds meaning both for signatory states and the international community. Signature presence demonstrates the promise of respect for and commitment to human rights and the endeavor to continue the commitment path toward binding ratification. Signature absence demonstrates a rejection of the international human rights regime and human rights themselves. States signed core human rights treaties more than eight hundred times between 1966 and 2017. The United Nations takes treaty signing seriously and celebrates with pomp and circumstance when heads of state agree to sign. Despite the celebratory tone and full attention paid to signature ceremonies at the United Nations, scholars generally dismiss signature as insignificant and unworthy of analysis in its own right.

This chapter dispels the assumption that nonbinding treaty signature is ineffectual in improving a state's human rights practices. I begin by defining treaty signature and examining trends in human rights treaty signature. Next, I introduce the argument that the softer form of treaty commitment through signature is important. External to the state, NGOs and International Organizations hold states to their signature obligation and increase accountability to rights standards following signing. Internal to the state, signature marks the executive's willingness to commit to international human rights standards. Signature allows supportive leaders to circumvent unsupportive legislatures and continue to advance human rights ideals. International rights networks can mobilize to advance treaty terms around unsupportive executives. I analyze the case of Nigeria to illustrate how rights groups mobilized around signature in the absence of ratification. I then focus on the cases of the United States and Canada, seeking variation across legislative involvement and regime type to illustrate causal mechanisms linking treaty signature and improvements in human rights. I conduct statistical analyses examining the effect of signing the International Covenant on Civil and Political Rights (ICCPR) and Convention on the Elimination of All Forms of Discrimination against Women (CEDAW) on human rights practices over time and find strong support for my argument that signing matters for human rights – especially for states confronting legislative approval mechanisms for ratification. I conclude the chapter by situating signature's importance against existing work in international law and call for reevaluating its general dismissal.

What Is Treaty Signature?

Signature is a first formal step in the treaty commitment process, whereby an original party to the treaty commits to not defeating the treaty's object and purpose (Vienna Convention on the Law of Treaties [VCLT] Articles 10 and 18). Signature is not legally binding.[1] The international community expects states that signed to eventually follow through with ratifying. Ratification is the second step in the commitment process and the international act of commitment through which a state consents to be bound to a treaty (VCLT Articles 2(1) (b), 14(1) and 16).[2] The anticipated two-step pathway to binding commitment intrinsically ties signature and ratification through legal processes and expectations.

Signature is an executive level–driven action. Heads of state typically sign international treaties or authorize ministers of foreign affairs, secretaries of state or other plenipotentiaries to sign on their behalf. If there is no documented authorization approving a representative to sign at the behest of a head of state, the signature ad referendum applies once confirmed by the state (VCLT 12(1) (b)). Treaty signing is an authoritative international-level action signifying a national-level decision committing a state to an international treaty. The act of signature denotes state consent for participation in the commitment process.

Figure 4.1 provides a breakdown of signature and ratification counts across the nine core UN human rights treaties. In all the treaties, more states signed than ratified. Above each count column is the percentage of signatures that culminated in ratifications. The first six of the core treaties created – the Convention on the Elimination of All Forms of Racial Discrimination (CERD), ICCPR, International Covenant on Economic, Social, and Cultural Rights (ICESCR), CEDAW, Convention against Torture and Other Cruel, Inhuman, or Degrading Treatment or Punishment, and Convention on the Rights of the Child (CRC) – all had ratification counts that reached 88 percent or higher as a percentage of all signatures. No human rights treaty had yet to see 100 percent of signatures culminate in ratification. Based on overall participation as well as rate of ratification following signature, the CRC is the most committed to of the

---

[1] This book and this chapter, more specifically, address "simple signature" rather than "definitive signature." In definitive signature, signature is the final act of commitment and is common for bilateral agreements or one between a handful of states rather than open for the global system. See Aust (2007, 96–97) for more discussion about definitive signature.

[2] Definitions of these terms come from the VCLT of 1969.

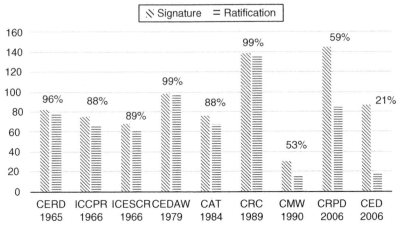

Figure 4.1 Commitment to human rights treaties by type, 1966–2010

core UN human rights treaties, achieving 99 percent ratification with 136 of the 138 signatures leading to ratification. CEDAW similarly resulted in a 99 percent ratification rate (97 ratifications out of 98 signatures). The three most recently created core treaties, the International Convention on the Protection of the Rights of All Migrant Workers and Members of Their Families (CMW), CRPD, and International Convention for the Protection of All Persons from Enforced Disappearance (CED), all had lower percentages of signatures resulting in ratifications. The CMW had the lowest count of commitment engagement overall, with only thirty states signing and sixteen ratifying. The treaty faced heated opposition from many migrant-receiving states. The Migration Policy Institute identified the treaty's extension to undocumented workers as impeding ratification (Yau 2005). The CED had the lowest percentage of signatures result in ratification, with only 21 percent of the 87 signatures leading to ratification. While the most recent treaties have the lowest rate of ratification of signatures, the high levels of signature participation with the CRPD (145) demonstrate that the relative newness of human rights treaties does not bar states from supporting through signature. Nor does time alone account for the rate of signature moving toward ratification.

Nonbinding Obligation

The defining characteristic of signature, which distinguishes it from the other three actions covered in this book, is its explicitly nonbinding nature. Through signature a state does *not* consent to be legally bound to a treaty. Other areas within international law commonly refer to *definitive signature* – that is, signature that expresses full consent to be bound (Aust 2000, 96). However, each core human rights treaty specifies whether further action is required for binding consent. All of the core human rights treaties contain *simple signature*, the nonbinding obligation to act in good faith to avoid acts that would defeat the treaty's object and purpose. The Government of the Netherlands explicitly acknowledged the character of signature thus: "by signing a treaty, a state expresses the intention to comply with the treaty. However, this expression of intent in itself is not binding" (Government of the Netherlands 2019). The nonbinding simple signature does not make a state a party to a treaty, but "it can create benefits and obligations for the signatory State" (Bradley 2012, 208).

Expectation of Continuation

Another term for *simple signature* is *signature subject to ratification*. This language stresses the need for additional action to translate commitment from nonbinding to binding. Treaty signature is not expected to be the final act of treaty commitment. Rather, the first step of nonbinding signature carries with it the expectation that the signatory state continue commitment and fully ratify the treaty. As the United Nations makes clear, "signature does indicate the State's intention to take steps to express its consent to be bound by the treaty at a later date. In other words, signature is a preparatory step on the way to ratification of the treaty by the State" (UN 2019c).

The United Nations encourages states to pursue ratification following signature. In 1998, as part of marking the fiftieth anniversary of the Universal Declaration of Human Rights, the United Nations campaigned for broader CEDAW ratification. CEDAW chairperson Salma Kahn, for example, reported that as part her campaign efforts that "I have also written a letter to Mr. Bill Clinton, President of the United States of America urging him to ratify CEDAW to mark the 50th anniversary of UDHR by giving new impetus to human rights of women" (UN 1997/ 1998). Treaty bodies urge states to move from signature to ratification through treaty committee state reports. The UN Committee on Enforced Disappearance, the treaty body for the Convention for the Protection of All Persons from Enforced Disappearance, urged Slovakia to ratify the treaty's Optional Protocol (UN 2019).

Who Signs International Law?

The following section offers a closer descriptive look at which states sign international human rights treaties. Though some human rights treaties have near-universal support, there is variation in whether states sign treaties. As demonstrated in Chapter 3, not all states follow the two-step commitment path of signature followed by ratification.

Regime Type

Looking closer at state regime types and their behavior, Figure 4.2 presents one empirical measure of regime type: the average state Polity2 scores across ICCPR treaty commitment. Polity2 is a measure ranging from −10, the least democratic annual observations, to 10, the most democratic annual observations from the Polity IV Project. Generally, scores 1–6 are coded as partial democracies and 7–10 as full democracies (Marshall, Gurr, and Jaggers 2017, 35). Figure 4.2 plots country-year observations based on commitment action(s) and democracy score. Signature states, overall, had Polity2 scores comparable to the Polity2 scores of states that had ratified, at 4.1 and 4.7. When only looking at states that signed but did not ratify, the Polity2 score was notably lower, at 1.9. Figure 4.2 illustrates the fact that states that achieved the two-step signing and ratification process had the highest levels of democracy. States without any commitment to the ICCPR had the lowest Polity2 scores of −2.9. It again is worth noting difference in regime characteristics between noncommitters and signatories. Much of the existing scholarship interprets treaty signature as synonymous, either

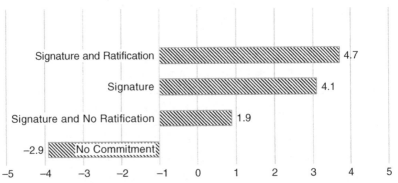

Figure 4.2   Average democracy scores for ICCPR signature and ratification states

by default or intent, with noncommitment. Looking at simple descriptive measures of democracy indicates that state characteristics vary across signature observations and no commitment observations.

Region

Figures 4.3 and 4.4 examine ICCPR signature and ratification by world region. Based on UN definitions of global regions, state committers are graphed across Africa, Oceania, North America, Asia, Europe, and Latin America. European states had the highest count of ICCPR signatures, at 23. Latin America, Africa, and Asia all had close counts of signature, at 17, 15, and 14, respectively. Oceania and North America had the lowest counts at 4 and 1, reflecting the lower number of states in each region.

Figure 4.4 graphs the average count of years between states' signing and ratifying the ICCPR. The count is the period of nonbinding

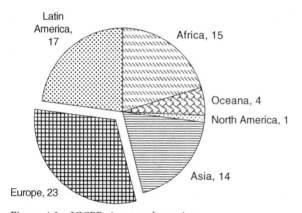

Figure 4.3 ICCPR signature by region

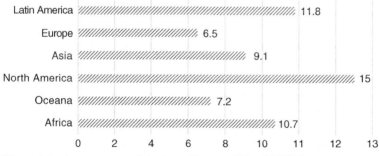

Figure 4.4 Average years of signing without ratifying ICCPR by region

commitment. The region with the most years, on average, was North America, at fifteen years. This value was driven by the US gap between signing and ratifying the treaty. Across all regions, the average number of country-year observations of ICCPR signature without ratification was ten years. When removing the United States, the overall average drops to nine years. European and Oceanic states were below average in the number of country-year observations of signature without ratification. Latin America was above average, at 11.8 years. Overall, Figures 4.3 and 4.4 depict signature as a widespread commitment action that operates for a significant amount of time prior to ratification.

Figure 4.5 graphs the count of years of signature without ratification at the state level. This figure provides a clearer sense of which states have extended periods between signing and ratifying human rights treaties. Although the United States does have one of the longest periods between signing and ratifying the ICCPR (fifteen years, tied with Egypt), Belgium and twelve other states took longer to ratify after signing. Liberia had the longest time at thirty-seven years.

From the descriptive statistics presented in Figures 4.1 to 4.5 it is apparent that (1) human rights treaty signature constitutes the majority of commitment behavior, (2) state commitments exist for years within a nonbinding context leading up to ratification, and (3) important differences in regime type exist between signatories and noncommitters. In the next sections, I argue that the existence and pervasiveness of time between the two commitment actions contribute to treaty signature's importance.

Why Nonbinding Commitment Is Important

Scholars and policymakers have long dismissed treaties as potentially inconsequential and ratification as a cheap signal without substance. Leading up to World War I, the German Chancellor referred to the Treaty of London as merely a "scrap of paper." Much international relations scholarship has pointed to no change in or worse human rights practices following ratification (e.g., Hathaway 2002), leading some to question whether treaty commitment is merely window dressing (e.g., Keith 1999). From this perspective, signature is likely to be an even cheaper signal than binding commitment actions. Within international relations and legal studies, the legalization approach as well as norm diffusion literature informs more positive expectations of nonbinding human rights commitment.

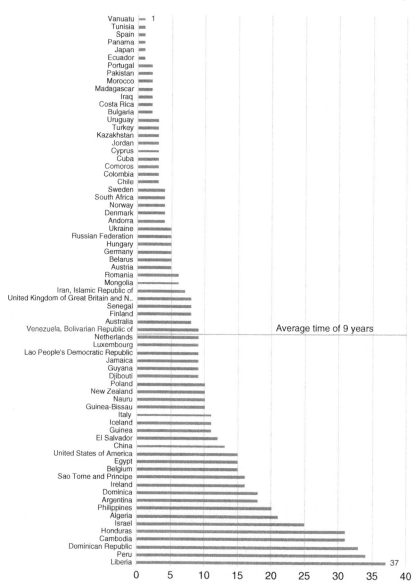

Figure 4.5 Years with ICCPR signature but not ratification, by state

The legalization approach to international law and organization conceptualizes "soft" obligation as one component along the continuum of legalization. Legalization comprises three elements of laws, institutions, or other agreements: obligation, precision, and delegation (Abbott et al. 2000, 401). The most pertinent dimension to the discussion of treaty signature in this chapter is the *obligation* dimension.

> Obligation means that states or other actors are bound by a rule or commitment or by a set of rules or commitments. Specifically, it means that they are *legally* bound by a rule or commitment in the sense that their behavior thereunder is subject to scrutiny under the general rules, procedures, and the discourse of international law, and often of domestic law as well. (401; emphasis in original)

While ratification, or other binding commitment actions, clearly situates on the "hard law" end of the obligation continuum, signature is not necessarily on the far "soft law" end. The authors define the two ends of the obligation continuum as a binding rule/*jus congens* on the hard law end and an "expressly nonlegal norm" on the soft law end (404). From the legalization framework, there is the explicit and implicit expectation that, in general, lower levels of legalization along the three characteristics of law and institutions will result in lower levels of compliance. Even though signature carries with it expected obligation, that obligation is still softer than the formalized binding obligation that comes with ratification. If states are not legally bound, held to precise standards, and have terms implemented through third parties, there simply will be less chance of states adhering to what they have agreed upon.

Counter to prevailing expectations that nonbinding signature is inconsequential, I argue that signature can be a substantial and meaningful signal. Drawing from and building on research emphasizing the role of domestic institutions and the importance of a process-based study to international law, I introduce an argument that human rights treaty signature matters, particularly for states with institutional barriers to ratification. Treaty signature is the only formal yet nonbinding category of international treaty commitment. Yet, there is reason to be optimistic about human rights after treaty signature. Though nonbinding, treaty signature advances commitment beyond recognition of normative expectations. The formality that accompanies treaty signature and the written rights standards elevate signature beyond nonlegal forms of state human rights norms support.

Evidence abounds that human rights laws and norms need not be binding to positively influence rights practices. A rich literature on norms (e.g., Clark 2010; Risse, Ropp, and Sikkink 1999), socialization of international human rights (Goodman and Jinks 2004; Hafner-Burton and Tsutsui 2007; Greenhill 2010; Risse, Ropp, and Sikkink 1999), and soft international law (Abbott and Snidal 2000; Efrat 2016; Schlager 2000) points to the power of nonbinding commitment and standards to result in substantive rights changes. In Shelton's (2000) extensive and wide-ranging edited volume on nonbinding norms in the international legal system across environmental, human rights, security, and other issue areas, Weiss writes in a concluding chapter that nonbinding, "non-contractual relations" are "most successful if there is consensus among the participants on the underlying social norm(s)," though "unanimity is not required" (542).

The core UN human rights treaties enjoy widespread state support. Seven of the nine core human rights treaties currently have over 160 state parties, and participation is ever increasing.[3] By the time a treaty reaches opening for signature, states have already actively participated in creating the treaty, engaged in negotiations, and received information about the treaty through the General Assembly as well as other formal UN channels. Of course, there is qualified support expressed through reservations, understandings, and declarations (RUDs) as well.[4] In general, the international legal community has tolerated these qualifications as part of a broader goal of increasing state participation. The landmark International Court of Justice Advisory Opinion (1951) stated that reservations are accepted "manifestations of a new need for flexibility in the operation of multilateral conventions" and allowed for greater state participation. The global support for established human rights norms contributes to nonbinding signature's ability to hold states to their promises.

Signature, of course, advances beyond normative rhetoric alone. Once states sign human rights treaties, they establish their intention to continue with commitment toward ratification and act in line with the treaty on the international stage. Treaty signature is a public act of commitment witnessed by the global community, which includes other UN member states, NGOs, and the United Nations with all of its auspices. These actors can hold signatory states to their commitment to adhere to the object and purpose of the treaty. With a headline of "It's Official! U.S. Signs U.N. Arms Trade Treaty," Amnesty International recognized the importance of treaty signature and demonstrated keen awareness of state behavior. The article reads:

---

[3] As of July 2019.
[4] See Neumayer 2005 and Comstock 2019.

> In an important step forward for human rights and international law,
> Secretary of State John Kerry signed the Arms Trade Treaty on behalf
> of the U.S. earlier today ... Kerry's signature signals the intention of
> the U.S., the world's largest arms exporter, to abide by the terms of
> the treaty. (n.d.b.)

Though not NGOs' final goal for state commitment, treaty signing is recognized as important along the path to commitment.

Awareness and celebration of treaty signature extend beyond the United States and security-related agreements. Amnesty International similarly heralded the signing of the Escazú Agreement, the first regional environmental treaty in Latin America and the Caribbean, as a "major victory for the environment and human rights." The Americas Director for Amnesty International commended the signatories.

> The leadership of the dozen countries who signed the Escazú Agreement
> today should serve as inspiration for the rest of the region and beyond. We
> urge all other countries in Latin America and the Caribbean to promptly
> follow their example for the survival and wellbeing of current and future
> generations. (Amnesty International 2018b)

Though legal scholarship expresses skepticism about signature's potential influence, and civil society prefers harder commitment, situating signature as a formal step in advancing and codifying norm recognition shows the power of signature to influence states' human rights practices.

When Signature Matters for International Human Rights Law

Signing treaties is an executive-level action, authorized by a head of state and enacted either by the head of state, or more likely, an individual granted authority to act at their behest. Treaty signature will not and cannot happen without such approval. Signature protocol is part of international and domestic policy. The United Nations requires an executive-level representative to sign an Instrument of Full Powers, through which they grant specific individuals the authority to sign international law. Without such authority, an individual cannot legitimately sign for a state. The legal counsel of the United Nations advised member states that

> only heads of States or Government or Ministers for Foreign Affairs,
> or a person acting *ad interim* in one of the above positions may
> execute treaty actions by virtue of their functions. All other individuals
> must be in the possession of appropriate full powers. Proper full

powers are required by all persons seeking to sign a treaty deposited with the Secretary-General. (2010)

In some states, the executive level continues to control the commitment process and maintains authority over ratification. However, in the majority of states in the international system, the executive level does not have full authority to ratify multilateral human rights treaties. In most states, the legislature has the primary authority to decide which treaties will be ratified. I argue domestic ratification requirements and procedures affect the emphasis states place on signature. By understanding the difficulty in achieving ratification, we can theorize signature's significance. I argue that *Legislative Approval States* – states confronting a formal and institutionalized legislative approval process for ratification – will use signature to commit to treaty law when the executive is supportive but the legislature is not yet supportive to the extent of achieving ratification. Positive change toward treaty compliance can occur after signature in these states. *Executive Approval States* – states wherein the executive is capable of ratifying international treaties when they want to – do not confront formal and institutionalized legislative barriers to treaty ratification, and the executive does not need to signal treaty support via early signature.

The Importance of Legislative Approval of Treaty Ratification

The United States is likely the most notable state confronting legislative barriers to treaty ratification but is by no means alone in requiring this type of formalized ratification process. Almost two-thirds of states require legislative approval for treaty ratification. In *Legislative Approval States*, the legislature is required by domestic law to approve treaty ratification before the state can legally consent to be bound by the treaty. The legislature can credibly act as a barrier to ratification even (and at times especially) when the executive supports ratification. The presence of legislative barriers to ratification can result in significant ratification delays (Kelley and Pevehouse 2015). Recent attempts by sitting US presidents to advance treaty ratification through the US Senate record the difficulty of the domestic process. In 2012, the US Senate rejected ratifying the UN CRPD primarily along party lines after President Obama signed and supported the treaty. In 2014, Republicans blocked a second opportunity to ratify the treaty by refusing to send the treaty to the Senate floor. Though widely supported internationally and textually less controversial domestically than other rights treaties, the US president was unable to successfully advance his human rights policy preferences through the domestic ratification process.

Legislative Approval States are known for their ratification delays. Aside from the notoriety of US Senate politics, other states face domestic constraints. Belgium took fifteen years after signing ICESCR to ratify, while Executive Approval State Australia took only three years between signing and ratifying the same treaty. Although generally known as a proponent of human rights, the Netherlands frequently has demonstrated inertia in the area of international human rights. Former UN High Commissioner for Human Rights Mary Robinson called out Dutch Prime Minister Mark Ruttee, criticizing Dutch human rights practices: "more recently, I don't see that voice strongly and I would just like to encourage it very much and encourage the people of this country who I know have a very strong sense of leadership on human rights" (Larson, van Rossum, and Schmidt 2014, 96).

Like the United States, the Netherlands is a Legislative Approval State, confronting a domestic legislative approval process for treaty ratification. These barriers prevent swift ratification of human rights treaties.

Legislative Approval States face a specific hurdle that their counterpart states do not. They incorporate the legislature into decisions of strategy, timing, and content when it comes to successfully advancing treaty ratification. Expanding the number of actors involved in the process increases the difficulty and length of time (but also the likelihood) of achieving a successful end to the ratification process. Increasingly, political science research has pinpointed how legislatures' involvement influences ratification timing and delays, though it has yet to explicitly link legislative veto players to ratification-with-signature dynamics. Kelley and Pevehouse (2015) examined how the institutional interplay between the US Senate and president shaped opportunity costs for introducing and voting on treaty ratification. The more "co-partisans" the president has in Congress, the greater the presidential opportunity costs and the longer it takes to send treaties to the Senate floor for a vote, due to party members' interest in other policy areas (538). This is an important contribution for analyzing how, in the United States, a legislative approval barrier can affect the time to ratification through calculations about bringing the treaty to the Senate floor to vote, including the political costs of the institutional transmission and vote. A logical extension of Kelley and Pevehouse (2015) would be to consider whether US presidents use signature when the odds of ratification are against them since they do not require Senate approval for signature.

Goldsmith and Posner briefly discuss legislative participation in international agreements (2005, 91–94). As the authors correctly state, "In most states, the legislature must consent to most agreements before they can be binding under international law" (91). However, they go on to present a false dichotomy of options available to the executive that overlooks signature as viable: "The executive has a choice ... between making a nonlegal agreement that does not require legislative consent, or a legalized agreement that requires legislative consent" (91). In fact, an executive supportive of advancing an international agreement has another option that marries the two: they can take the first step toward a legalized binding treaty by signing a treaty without legislative involvement. Without abandoning the legalized treaty, the executive can navigate around an unsupportive legislature, sign a treaty, and wait until the legislature becomes supportive enough to ratify the treaty. Just because treaty signature is nonbinding does not make it nonlegal.

Haftel and Thompson (2013) take a deeper look at legislative dynamics and ratification delays. Their research focuses on bilateral investment treaties and finds that when states have greater legal hurdles to ratification, there are greater time delays to reaching ratification. The authors note that "understanding that signature and ratification result from different processes helps explain why they seem to have distinct effects as well" (379). This informative study advanced earlier US-focused works on legislative involvement in treaties by demonstrating that legislative involvement results in delayed ratification globally. The project deliberately excluded multilateral treaties from analysis due to their more complicated commitment procedures. Nonetheless, the findings are important to test across other issues areas and forms of international treaty law.[5]

I take the findings and wisdom from these literatures and advance the study of legislative involvement in international law. I extend the logic of the aforementioned research that argues for the importance of legislative involvement in ratification, apply it to the human rights area, and consider how states that are required to engage the legislature use signature – a commitment form that does not require the legislature. I argue

---

[5] The authors specifically exclude multilateral treaties from their research design due to the more complex commitment procedures that multilateral treaties entail, including the option to accede to the treaty instead of signing and ratifying (363).

Table 4.1 *Human rights changes and signature expectations*

	Legislative Approval State	Executive Approval State
Human rights after signature	Improvement	No or limited change
Human rights after ratification	No change or worsening	Improvement

that signature's importance and use will differ between *Legislative Approval States* and *Executive Approval States* based on how extensively the states rely on the legislatures to advance treaty ratification. Table 4.1 outlines how expected effects of treaty commitment actions differ for each state-group.

In *Executive Approval States*, the executive branch plays a larger role in ratification, with the head of state or other executive branch members, such as cabinet officers, ratifying international treaties. This process removes the legislative hurdle from the ratification process and gives the executive branch greater leeway for choosing the precise time of ratification. While barrier states such as the United States and Belgium confronted delays from their legislature, *Executive Approval States* such as Canada were able to ratify treaties as the executive sees fit.

According to Simmons's (2009) breakdown of ratification procedures, 68 of the 173 states categorized do not have regular legislative approval requirements for treaty ratification. *Executive Approval States* have a slight tendency to be nondemocratic, with 56 percent of the states falling into that category.[6] *Executive Approval States* tend to be from Africa, Asia-Pacific, or the Latin American and the Caribbean regions.

Legislative Approval States are evenly distributed by region (see Figure 4.6).[7] Africa contained the most *Legislative Approval States* with twenty-five, and Latin America had the fewest at eighteen. As scholars of international relations might expect, most of the *Legislative Approval States* are democracies, comprising about 65 percent of the state-group. This percentage is slightly higher than the overall breakdown of democracy to nondemocracies in the sample, which is closer to

---

[6] Based on Polity2 scores.
[7] I use UN Regional Groups of Member States categorization found at un.org/depts/ DGACM/RegionalGroups.shtml.

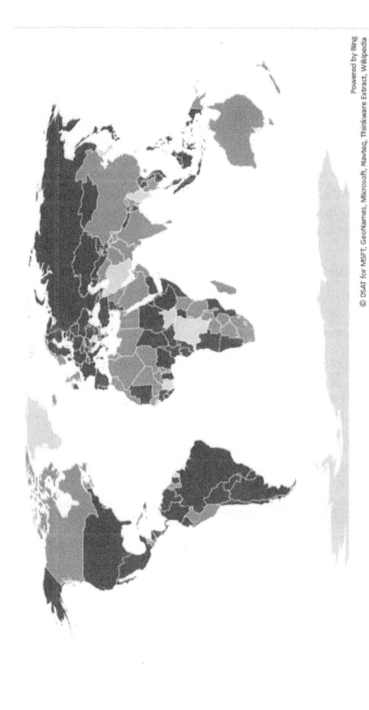

Figure 4.6 Ratification approval process map

60 percent.[8] Figure 4.6 maps states by ratification approval process.[9] States shaded dark gray are *Legislative Approval States* with domestic legislative barriers to ratification. States shaded light gray are *Executive Approval States* without legislative constraints on ratification. States in lightest gray are those for which we lack data on domestic ratification constraints. The map shows that *Legislative Approval States* are distributed around all global regions. Almost all European states, Russia, and some Latin American states have legislative barriers to ratification. Large Asian states such as China and India did not have legislative approval requirements for treaty ratification, nor did most of Northern and Southern Africa. The effect of the English legal system is apparent given the executive-driven ratification processes in the former British colonies of Australia, Canada, and India.

Mechanisms of Improved Rights Following Signature

I argue that two primary mechanisms explain improved human rights following signature of human rights treaties. The first is legal mobilization. Building on existing research that demonstrates legal mobilization around human rights treaty ratification, I show that legal mobilization occurs around the signature step of treaty commitment. The second mechanism is through support from an advocate executive, that is, when the head of state advances human rights standards in a *Legislative Approval State* after treaty signing. Through case analysis of the United States and Canada, I use a diverse case selection approach to examine two democracies that differ along domestic ratification procedures categories. I illustrate how both mechanisms contribute to improved human rights practices following signature. Legal mobilization broadly empowers non-binding signature to translate into meaningful rights changes. More narrowly, the domestic approval process affects which states will be more likely to improve rights following signature.

Treaty Signature and Legal Mobilization

Through legal mobilization, activist groups, other states, NGOs, and even individuals can use the power of law to advance human rights. As a focal

---

[8] States here are bluntly considered as democracies when averaging over 6 on the Polity2 scale.

[9] Data on Ratification Barriers come from Simmons (2009) Ratification Rules data.

point for mobilization, signature offers the promise of the power of law to improve human rights, and sometimes to do this despite an unsupportive executive. Research points to actors' ability to use law to advance rights within a variety of contexts. Legal mobilization is the process by which individuals or groups invoke their legal rights or the rights of others to defend, develop, and expand these rights against the government (see McCann 2008; Zemans 1983). Legal mobilization also describes the processes "by which legal norms are invoked to regulate behavior" (Lempert 1976, 173). As Tam (2013) demonstrates, successful legal mobilization occurs within authoritarian states in addition to the oft-documented cases within democracies. In fact, the lack of democracy can result in a rise in legal mobilization (Cahn 2014). Tam finds that legal mobilization successfully occurred in Hong Kong in a process distinct from the interest-based facilitation of authoritarian rulers (as found in Ginsburg and Moustafa 2008 and Moustafa 2007).

Through signing a human rights treaty, a state is making a public and legal declaration of support. Upon signature, other actors can use a state's treaty commitment to hold it accountable to treaty obligations. Simmons argued that ratifying human rights treaties served "notice that govern-ments are accountable – domestically and externally – for refraining from the abuses proscribed by their own mutual agreements" (2009, 5). Signing human rights treaties serves a similar function by alerting the domestic and international rights communities that the government is accountable for rights. Signing human rights law paves the way for improvement in rights.

States and non-state actors are aware of states' legal commitment and obligations following signature. They use legal commitments to mobilize action around articulated standards. When the executive fails to move from signature to ratification, other actors can step in to advance human rights using the legal weight of signature. A process of rights conscious-ness involves increased awareness of the legal commitment and of the content and rights guarantees provided within the treaty. Once rights consciousness exists, groups can use signature to promote the rights articulated within the treaty. I argue that signature evokes all of these components and leads to improved human rights practices as a result.

Awareness of treaty commitment and awareness of treaty content together create a legal consciousness of what human rights and legal protections exist. Legal consciousness is described, in part, as "both indi-vidual and collective participation in the process of constructing legality" wherein "the law is described and 'played' as a game, a bounded arena in which preexisting rules can be deployed and new rules invented to serve the widest range of interests and arenas" (Ewick and Silbey 2014, 48–49). Merry connects the concepts of legal consciousness with rights consciousness, studying how local communities become aware of "their problems as human rights violations" (2006, 179) and argues that a rights frameworks layers on top of existing frameworks of abuse (181).

Awareness of Treaty Commitment

The international community and domestic communities take note when a state signs an international human rights treaty. Through this awareness, communities above and below the state level can use the legal commitment to advance treaty ideals within a state without the head of state taking initiative.

Guided by Article 102 of the United Nations Charter, which requires states to register treaty actions and the UN Secretariat to publish treaty agreements, the United Nations plays the leading role in disseminating treaty commitment information. The first way that the United Nations makes treaty signatures public is through its annual Treaty Event. The event encourages and celebrates signatures and publicly recognizes those that take place through an end-of-event report detailing which states signed which treaties. The second way the United Nations publicizes treaty signature is through monthly statements of treaties registered with the Secretariat. This publication includes treaty signatures taking place and details which states signed which treaties. The Treaty Section of the UN Office of Legal Affairs also makes these publicly available on its website. Third, the UN depository sends out notifications through a subscription service. Any state, individual, or organization can register for e-mail notifications of treaty activities. Additionally, Members of Permanent Missions to the United Nations can also pick up hard copies of notifications at the UN headquarters.

At the state level, signatory states announce and make public the treaties to which they commit. The Government of the Netherlands publicly lists which human rights treaties it has signed and ratified through its official website and provides links to the UN's website. The Turkish Ministry of Foreign Affairs's website describes its commitment to UN human rights treaties. The US State Department lists the treaties and other international agreements in force on its website and through an annual report.

While primarily geared toward states, all the aforementioned UN notification instruments are publicly available to individuals, groups, and NGOs. Interested domestic activists and groups as well as international NGOs have access to UN member states' treaty-signing records. Beyond these, domestic groups and organizations operating within states have an impressive range of access to information about treaty signing. One factor that greatly varies across and within states is the extent to which the media reports on treaty signing.

Awareness of Treaty Content

The United Nations makes great effort to publicize treaties, their content, and their rights provisions. It makes the full text of treaties available on various websites, including the UN Treaty Collection Status of Treaties, which it updates in real time. The UN distributes monthly treaty-action updates to member states. Specific departments and programs within the UN emphasize public awareness around their respective treaties. For example, UN Women highlights the CEDAW. UNICEF's website writes that its

> work is guided by the Convention on the Rights of the Child (1989). The Convention is the most rapidly and widely ratified international human rights treaty in history. The Convention changed the way children are viewed and treated – i.e., as human beings with a distinct set of rights instead of as passive objects of care and charity. The unprecedented acceptance of the Convention clearly shows a wide global commitment to advancing children's rights. (n.d.)

NGOs and states committed to human rights treaties publicize or link to the UN human rights treaty texts, as mentioned with the Netherlands previously. Prior to the advent of the Internet and its widespread sue for publicizing government and IO policies, the UN used the General Assembly and other bodies to announce and detail new treaties. The UN and other actors within the international human rights regime actively disseminate knowledge about human rights and protective laws. The United Nations launched an innovative campaign in 2020 called "Wiki for Human Rights" to increase human rights knowledge through the website Wikipedia. The campaign tagline was "to claim your rights you must know your rights."

Promotion of Treaty Terms

Once conscious of what rights exist, interested actors must actually mobilize around the law for legal mobilization to occur. For human rights treaties, this means groups, NGOs, IOs, and even individuals must draw from the rights included within treaties specifically and broadly to defend and develop rights. A notable such example is the case of *Toonen v. Australia*, wherein Nicholas Toonen drew specifically from Articles 17 and 26 of the ICCPR treaty and argued that his legal rights were violated by existing Australian law as specified by the Tasmanian Criminal Code, namely, Sections 122(a) and (c) and 123, which criminalized consensual adult homosexual acts. In March of 1994, the Human Rights Committee addressed Toonen's 1991 submission of complaints and ruled that his rights had been violated.[10] As an individual and as the leading member of the Tasmanian Gay Law Reform Group, Mr. Toonen was able to mobilize around the rights guaranteed within the ICCPR.

The importance of legal mobilization is not a contentious proposition within the study of human rights. Conant researched legal mobilization growth at the European Court of Human Rights, which she argued resulted from growth in legal consciousness (2016, 284). Simmons (2009) argues that legal mobilization is a driving means of inducing compliance with human rights treaties. Existing studies focused on legal mobilization and human rights law emphasize mobilization around treaty ratification. However, it is treaty signature that NGOs and other states mobilize around to advance and defend human rights.

Leading human rights NGOs Amnesty International and Human Rights Watch post treaty excerpts linked to the full text, often using the legal texts to anchor critiques of states' human rights violations. In July 2019 testimony before the US House Committee on Oversight and Reform, Subcommittee on Civil Rights and Civil Liberties, Human Rights Watch Senior Researcher on the US Program Clara Long provided testimony on human rights issues concerning US immigration and border practices. In the written testimony, Long notes the importance of the CRC.

> The US has signed but not yet ratified the convention, meaning that it is prohibited from acting contrary to the object and purpose of the treaty ... Although the US has yet to ratify the CRC, the US Supreme Court has recognized its "nearly universal" acceptance. (Human Rights Watch 2019)

Even within a state noted for its reluctance to commit itself to international law, NGOs mobilize around treaty signature in the United

---

[10] Available at University of Minnesota's Human Rights Library, http://hrlibrary.umn.edu /undocs/html/vws488.htm.

States to advance human rights. Though the United States has not ratified the CRC and does not list the treaty in its State Department Report of Multilateral Treaties in Force (2019), signature is a sufficient legal act for the international community to harness through legal mobilization.

Nigeria and the CRPD

In Nigeria, signing the CRPD led the way for domestic disability rights improvements despite the head of state's rejecting treaty ratification and implementation. Nigeria's signing the CRPD increased legal consciousness and rights framing of disability issues as human rights. Even without binding legal commitment, domestic groups and the international community were able to use treaty signature to mobilize around disability rights provided for in the CRPD. Legal mobilization occurred from within the state and outside the state.

Background

The United Nations began working toward recognizing disability rights with the Declaration on the Rights of Mentally Retarded Persons in General Assembly Resolution 2856 (XVI) in 1971, followed in 1975 by the Declaration on the Rights of Disabled Persons in General Assembly Resolution 3447(XXX). The 1980s were declared the UN Decade of Disabled Persons, which concluded with a working group to establish standards for disabled individuals (Economic and Social Council resolution 1990/26). The United Nations did not call for a draft convention on disability rights until 2001. The General Assembly adopted the CRPD in 2006 (UN General Assembly Resolution 61/106). The treaty defines discrimination on the basis of disability as

> any distinction, exclusion or restriction on the basis of disability which has the purpose or effect of impairing or nullifying the recognition, enjoyment or exercise, on an equal basis with others, of all human rights and fundamental freedoms in the political, economic, social, cultural, civil or any other field. It includes all forms of discrimination, including denial of reasonable accommodation. (CRPD Article 2)

Nigeria is a *Legislative Approval State*, with the Nigerian Constitution requiring "a majority of all the Houses of Assembly in the Federation" to ratify treaties (Article 12(3)).

Legal Consciousness

Nigeria signed the CRPD and its Optional Protocol on March 30, 2007. On April 17, 2007, the secretary-general circulated a formal document communicating the signature and depositing the commitment within the United Nations (UN 2007). Upon signing, the CRPD "generated an array of tangible benefits . . . (including) raising the general public's awareness about the human rights of persons with disabilities; highlighting historic and continued abuses of those rights" (Lord and Stein 2008, 476).

Civil society organizations responded to Nigeria's signature. Coalitions for Change formed in 2007, motivated by the view that the Nigerian government had not fulfilled its obligations to disabled persons. Individuals with disabilities established NGOs such as the Hope for the Blind Foundation in Zaria, the Kano Polio Victims Trust Association, the Albino Foundation, and the Comprehensive Empowerment of Nigerians with Disabilities (US State Department 2011, 55).

Because Nigeria signed the CRPD, signaling support, international actors were able to supply training and support in the area of disability rights without noted contestation from the Nigerian government. The United Nations supported and funded local, bottom-up approaches following CRPD signature. For example, the UN Development Program collaborated with local organizations to promote advocacy training and "make people see disability as a human rights issue" (UNDP 2016). In training activists and/or individuals with disabilities, the UNDP realizes an obligation articulated in CRPD Article 4, which calls on states to "promote the training of professionals and staff working with persons with disabilities in the rights recognized in the present Convention so as to better provide the assistance and services guaranteed by those rights" (CRPD Article 4(i)) and to provide "awareness-training programmes" called for in Article 8(d).

Legal Mobilization

The first act of mobilizing rights using CRPD signature occurred when the National Assembly sought implementation of the treaty. The National Assembly presented a bill implementing the provisions of CRPD to President Olusegun Obasanjo for approval and assent, "An Act to Ensure Full Integration of Persons with Disabilities into the Society and to Establish a National Commission for Persons with Disabilities and Vest it with the Responsibilities for Their Education,

Health Care and the Protection of Their Social, Economic, Civil Rights" ("Persons with Disabilities Bill and the Burden of Presidential Assent," The Guardian, March 9, 2015). President Obasanjo refused to sign the bill into law, which would implement the terms of the treaty. No formal statement explained the president's lack of support for the bill. Local sources cited his focus on stabilizing the administration during threats to power during the time.

Following President Obasanjo's removal from office, the Nigerian National Assembly reconsidered the bill and was required to pass it once again after the previous version was rejected. Next, the Nigerian legislature sent the newer version of the bill to President Goodluck Jonathan multiple times. He also refused to assent to the bill.

Disability rights groups and human rights NGOs continued to advocate under the CRPD. Human Rights Watch described this period as "9 years of relentless advocacy by disability rights groups and activists" (Ewang 2019). The legislature repeatedly sent enacting legislation to the president to sign into domestic law. Activism continued following CRPD ratification in 2010. After years of civil society and national legislature attempts at enacting the CRPD, the movement came to a head in early 2019, when President Buhari publicly denied that the bill was sent forward from the legislature: "On January 17, Buhari denied on national television that he had received the bill. Hundreds of people protested, and barely five days later, he signed the bill into law" (Ewang 2019). Rights groups mobilized around the CRPD and Nigeria's signature to advance domestic policy.

Rights Improvements

Despite the unwillingness of two presidents to implement the treaty and the clash of the new human rights disability frame with a traditional frame, the international community has generally observed an overall improvement in disability rights in Nigeria. Although the National Assembly was not able to improve the treatment of persons with disabilities via the implementation of national policy, the public discussions and support of the treaty allowed national groups to advance programs at the state and local levels, effecting some positive degree of change and compliance following treaty signature and prior to treaty ratification. In speaking to the US Committee on Foreign Relations, former executive director of the US National Council on Independent Living Mark Lancaster identified

Nigeria as making strides toward compliance with CRPD: "Nigeria, a country that has a history of serious discrimination against children with albinism, has created a ministerial committee on albinism since their ratification of the treaty." Lang and Upah find that, after signature of CERD, "states have enacted disability legislation" (2008, 28).

There is a "plethora of DPOs [disability people's organizations] in Nigeria that operate at the national, state and local levels" (Lang 2014, 13). Disability advisors have been appointed in nine out of Nigeria's thirty-six states (Asiwe and Omiegbe 2014, 520). The Ministry of Women Affairs and Social Development created a community-based rehabilitation program with centers in twenty-three states. In 2011, the state of Lagos passed the Lagos State Special People's Bill in the State House of Assembly, making Lagos the "first state in Nigeria to promulgate a law specifically aimed at demonstrating the CRPD and similar normative standards" (Asiwe and Omiegbe 2014, 520). Establishing such offices and measures brings these parts of Nigeria in compliance with part of the CRPD that requires government focal points for matters relating to the Convention (Article 33(1)).

NGOs and other domestic groups were able to carry out some CRPD provisions, advancing disability rights prior to Nigeria's 2010 ratification. The Joint National Association of Persons with Disabilities successfully lobbied to amend Section 57 of the 2004 Electoral Act to ensure disabled Nigerians can vote in elections. This revision was reflected in the 2010 Electoral Act (Federal Republic of Nigeria 2010; Policy and Legal Advocacy Centre 2015). In 2006 the Association for Comprehensive Empowerment of Nigerians with Disabilities (ASCEND), another prominent DPO, emerged. ASCEND, along with Mobility Aid and the Appliances Research and Development Centre, presented a disability rights bill to the National Assembly. These and other DPOs remain active. However, they faced organizational, governance, and funding constraints that limit their ability to promote disability rights (Lang and Upah 2008, 20).

Signing the CRPD brought the treaty and Nigerian disability rights issues to the forefront of domestic and international recognition. With signature, the Nigerian government opened itself to support from the United Nations and other programs promoting disability rights. The president could not contest the programs as imposing outside or Western rights on Nigeria because he had already committed through signing the treaty. While signing the treaty did not trigger executive measures to enact the treaty, it allowed for international development measures to send aid and programs into Nigeria and enact parts of the treaty. Signing the CRPD also legitimated the disability rights movement in Nigeria, fueling further domestic support and mobilization. Although the National Assembly was not able to enact the legislation it supported, the national government ended up promoting disability rights through small, funded programs through bureaucracies such as the Ministry of Women Affairs and Social Development. At the state level and community level, leaders were able to see signing the CRPD as a mark of support from the government and proceed with their own implementation independent of national-level implementation.

Legislative Approval States and Treaty Signature: The United States

In addition to the legal mobilization process detailed previously, I argue that a state's ratification process determines the importance that it will place on signature. In states confronting arduous domestic ratification procedures requiring legislative approval, the executive branch can use signature to promote human rights standards. The power to sign treaties gives executives the opportunity to bridge the domestic and international levels to advance human rights. Signing allows executives to support human rights by (1) signaling to the international and domestic communities their pledge to abide by the treaty and (2) entering their state into legal commitment by beginning the two-step process culminating in binding ratification.

Legislative Approval States have clearly defined and legalized ratification processes that require legislative approval before ratification. The domestic process requiring Senate approval of international treaty ratification makes diplomats in the United States and other states keenly aware of ratification difficulties during negotiations. In writing about negotiating in his seminal "Two-Level Games" article, Putnam wrote that "The difficulties of winning congressional ratification are often exploited by American negotiators" (1988, 440). For example, President Carter warned Panamanian politicians that "further concessions by the US would seriously threaten chances for Senate ratification" (Habeeb and Zartman 1986, 42) of the Panama Canal Treaty. During the Second Hague Conference in 1907, much anxiety was expressed on the part of certain powers regarding the difficulty of negotiating treaties with the US, because there is no guarantee that the treaties would be ratified by the Senate or that Congress would pass the legislation which might be necessary to carry them into effect, or that the treaties, if actually ratified and the legislation passed, would be observed by the Government of the US (Carnegie Endowment for International Peace 1917, 130).

The United States and CERD

The US Constitution describes the ratification process thus: the president "shall have power, by and with the Advice and Consent of the Senate, to make treaties, provided two-thirds of the Senators present concur." The requirement of Senate approval makes ratification a rigorous process, earning the Senate the reputation of the "graveyard of treaties" wherein treaties are rejected or fail to make it to the Senate floor.

Technically, the Senate does not ratify international treaty law for the United States but rather recommends or rejects ratification (Crabb, Antizzo, and Sarieddine 2000, 196). An important part of the recommendation process is the advice and consent of the Senate Committee on Foreign Relations, which may "allow and encourage partisan and ideological opponents . . . to engage in dilatory tactics" that delay the process (McCarty and Razaghian 1999, 1122). After a president submits a treaty to the Senate Committee on Foreign Relations, the Committee can reject the treaty for consideration or table it, delaying the treaty from (potentially ever) reaching the Senate floor for vote.

The United States has a simpler procedure for signature, which is entirely controlled by the executive branch: the secretary of state authorizes the negotiation of a treaty; US representatives participate in the negotiation; and following negotiations, as directed by the president, the secretary of state authorizes signature. The separation of signature and ratification between the Executive and Legislative branches allows for the administration in power to advance treaties it supports without the consent of the opposition party in the Senate. This process contributed to the notable delays of human rights treaty ratification. The United States signed the ICESCR in 1977, the CEDAW in 1980, and the CRC in 1995. As 2020, it has yet to ratify any of these treaties. Failure to ratify these core human rights treaties places the United States in the company of other, less democratic states, such as Iran, Somalia, and Sudan.

The CERD treaty offers an example of the United States signing a human rights treaty early, moving toward improved rights, and then ratifying much later. The dominant approach to studying human rights treaties would ignore the twenty-eight years in between US signature in 1966 and ratification in 1994. To do so would overlook significant progress in human rights practices. US CERD signature occurred at a time of changing policy toward racial discrimination. At the time of signature, US Ambassador to the UN Arthur Goldberg described US efforts against racial discrimination as "on the march" (New York Times July 7, 1966).

Per US policy, the executive branch was responsible for negotiating and signing CERD. The executive branch took early interest in creating the UN treaty, being a "leading participant in the long process" (Bitker 1970, 68). During the negotiations, the United States was one of fourteen states that were part of the Sub-Commission on the Prevention of Discrimination and Protection of Minorities to the Commission on Human Rights in 1961. The Sub-Commission was an initial institutional step in the development of CERD at the United Nations. While negotiations and further drafting of CERD took place, the United States expanded antidiscrimination policies at home. The 1964 Voting Rights Act and the 1965 Executive Order 11246, ensuring equal opportunity for minorities in federal contractor employment practices, demonstrated domestic progress. The US Ambassador to the UN Arthur Goldberg was a vocal supporter of the treaty, describing it as "completely with the policy of my Government and the sentiments of the overwhelming majority of our citizens" (New York Times, July 7, 1966). President Johnson quickly authorized treaty signature on September 28, 1966. Goldberg successfully convinced Johnson to sign CERD prior to the start of the 1966 General Assembly to signal US commitment and to "strengthen the U.S.'s standing in the final debates" of the ICESCR and the ICCPR (Jensen 2016, 102).

The US executive branch took steps to fulfill the CERD treaty's intent in the nonbinding commitment period between signature and ratification. President Johnson issued executive orders to support the fundamental rights against discrimination. Executive Order 11375, "Amending EO No 11246, relating to employment opportunity," signed October 13, 1967, expanded on the Civil Rights Act of 1964. Johnson led the campaign for the Civil Rights Act of 1968, known as the Fair Housing Act, to expand nondiscrimination to housing.

Prior to submitting CERD to the Senate, President Carter stated in March 1977 that "Ours is a commitment [to the human rights treaties], and not just a political posture" (450).[11] A longtime supporter of civil rights who promised to strengthen federal provisions, Carter wrote that "ratification of this treaty will attest to our enormous progress in this field in recent decades and our commitment to ending racial discrimination."[12] Carter further pointed out that "the great majority of the substantive provisions of these four treaties are entirely consistent with the US Constitution and laws."[13] President Carter submitted CERD along with the ICCPR and ICESCR to the Senate Committee on Foreign Relations February 23, 1978. The Committee on Foreign Relations held hearings on CERD for four days in November 1979. No further action was taken on CERD in the Senate until June 2, 1994, when the Committee on Foreign Relations recommended ratification with accompanying RUDs. The Senate finally voted in favor of CERD ratification on July 24, 1994. Though the US remains very far from fully implementing CERD, some movement occurred related to treaty signature.

This brief discussion highlights how executives, knowing the difficulty and opposition confronting ratification, advanced implementation of a treaty after signature. Prior to ratification, the US executive branch worked to advance commitment to CERD at the international level via participation in negotiations and signature and in domestic policy terms via expanded antidiscrimination laws.

Counterarguments

The argument I advance in this chapter highlights the potential positive changes associated with treaty signature. There exists, of course, possible alternative arguments with opposite expectations about human rights practices following treaty signature. First, signature can be used as a means of domestic level cheap talk about treaty commitment resulting in no changes in behavior.

> The signing of a convention can "take the heat off" political leaders, allowing symbolic but empty promises to substitute for real improvements.

---

[11] Public Papers of the Presidents of the United States: Jimmy Carter, March 17, 1977 (450).

[12] Public Papers of the Presidents of the United States: Jimmy Carter, February 16, 1977 (164), and Jimmy Carter, "Human Rights Treaties Message to the Senate," February 23, 1978, available at The American Presidency Project, www.presidency.ucsb.edu/ws/?pid=30399.

[13] Ibid.

Nations and leaders that have absolutely no commitment to improving environmental quality can sign a convention and claim credit for "doing something" when, in fact, there will be no improvement.

(Susskind and Ozawa 1992, 147)

This argument suggests the possibility of the "kick the can down the road" executive who signs a treaty to remove pressure from the executive office with the full knowledge that ratification is the legislature's job. If this were the case, we should expect that no change in human rights practices would follow the signing of international human rights law.

Second, a related explanation for why positive changes may not follow signature is that a supportive head of state who signs a human rights treaty is replaced prior to ratification. The next executive may not have the same level of support for the treaty or any interest in continuing the ratification process. The treaty sits as signed but not ratified until another executive advocate or the legislature is able to ratify it without additional executive support.

Examples can be similarly drawn from US politics of presidents who signed human rights treaties followed by administrations taking no steps to advance ratification. While President Carter signed ICCPR along with CERD and ICESCR in 1977 in support of international human rights standards, his successors Presidents Ronald Reagan and George H. W. Bush made no formal effort to advance US commitment to these treaties toward ratification. Ratification was deferred, reflecting domestic conservatives' reluctance to sacrifice sovereignty in favor of international law. But even with successor presidents' reluctance to ratify the treaties, the initial commitment stuck: "certain states, including the US, were reluctant to sign onto the ICCPR because they did not want to be bound to enforce it domestically, not because they disagreed with it as a 'code of civilization'" (McGuinness 2005, 403).

Executive Approval States and Treaty Signature: Canada

As an *Executive Approval State*, the Canadian executive branch controls the signature and ratification of international treaty, taking the place of the Parliament in approving ratification. While no provision of the Canadian Constitution explicitly assigns this role to the executive, it is common practice for the executive branch to take on the role of ratifying treaties (Barnett and Spano 2008). The cabinet, the Department of Foreign Affairs and International Trade, the Minister of Foreign Affairs, and the prime minster are the important actors in treaty ratification in Canada: "this is not to say that the issue of becoming party to the international instrument may not be discussed or even debated on an *ad hoc* basis. There is, however, no requirement for parliamentary approval or study" (Parliament of Canada 2001). Because treaty ratification does not go through Parliament, Canada's approach to ratification is closer to the United Kingdom and Australia. Within these states, ratification approval is decided by the cabinet rather than through legislative approval via the Parliament.

Given the Parliament's limited involvement in the ratification approval process, the executive takes on a stronger role in Canada. The Canadian prime minister has more freedom to act based on party and personal beliefs for human rights treaties than a head of state in a *Legislative Approval State* could. In approaching environmental law, the Canadian prime minister was able to ensure Kyoto Protocol ratification: "with a disciplined majority in the Canadian House of Commons, Prime Minister Chrétien had the institutional capacity to deliver on his personal commitment to the Kyoto Protocol" (Harrison 2007, 97). The executive power during treaty ratification enabled Chrétien to "push through ratification despite significant opposition" (Busby 2010, 134).

Canada requires consultation with the provinces and Aboriginal peoples prior to ratifying treaties that would impact provincial jurisdiction or potentially impact Aboriginal or Aboriginal Treaty rights. Trone goes as far as writing that "the most important formal mechanism for federal-provincial consultation in relation to the making and implementation of treaties is that concerning human rights treaties" (2001, 41). For human rights treaty ratification, Canada seeks the support of all provinces: "provincial and territorial support is sought to ensure effective domestic implementation of Canada's international obligations" (Canadian Department of Justice 2015). According to the senior counsel of the Human Rights Law Section in the Department of Justice Canada, the Canadian government views provincial consultation and support as a "general practice" rather than a legal obligation (Eid 2001, 2). However, guidelines note that "where treaty consultation provisions no not apply to a proposed activity, a 'parallel' duty to consult exists" (Canadian Department of Aboriginal Affairs and Northern Development 2011, 1).

Consultation of Aboriginal groups is generally sought "especially if the treaty being considered involves Aboriginal areas of jurisdiction or authority" (Canadian Department of Justice 2015). The Supreme Court of Canada cemented this requirement in the 2004 rulings of *Haida Nation v. British Columbia* (Minister of Forests), *Taku River Tlingit*

First Nation v. British Columbia (Project Assessment Director), and the 2005 ruling of *Mikisew Cree First Nation v. Canada* (Minister of Canadian Heritage).[14] These consultations are particularly important in the area of human rights, since human rights violations disproportionately influence Canada's Aboriginal groups.[15]

While the United States took twenty-eight years to ratify the CERD treaty, Canada only took four years between signing the treaty in 1966 and ratifying in 1970. This quicker ratification came even with the domestic requirement to consult with the provinces and Aboriginal groups. Without the legislative barrier, Canada's executive branch was able to move more quickly to treaty ratification.

Quicker ratification has been the norm in Canada even when there has been public and/or parliamentary opposition to the treaty. The Foreign Investment Promotion and Protection Agreement (FIPA) with China drew particular criticism. Despite public and parliamentary opposition, the agreement was ratified in 2014, just two years after signature. Because of the lack of parliamentary involvement in the ratification process, the FIPA deal was shrouded in secrecy, with only one hour of public information provided to the parliamentarians ("FIPA agreement with China: What's really in it for Canada?" CBC News, September 19, 2014). Even with the controversy surrounding the FIPA with China, the cabinet ratified the agreement within two years, using its ability to circumvent the Parliament and extensive public debates on the treaty.

Hypotheses

I draw several hypotheses about signature and human rights practices from the aforementioned arguments. Signature acts as an easier-to-access signal of support to both the international community and domestic political community. Because of requirements for legislative approval for ratification, executives in *Legislative Approval States* have incentives and the capability to signal support through signature earlier than the legislatures may allow for signaling via ratification. Supportive executives can initiate some policy changes prior to ratification. By the time

---

[14] Haida Nation v. British Columbia, 2004 SCC73; Taku River Tlingit First Nation v. British Columbia, 2004 SCC74; Mikisew Cree First Nation v. Canada, 2005 SCC 69.

[15] See, for example, the campaigns for Indigenous Peoples rights in Canada by Amnesty International, Human Rights Watch, and numerous United Nations reports citing Canada's poor human rights record pertaining to Aboriginal peoples.

ratification does occur, many *Legislative Approval States* have altered their behavior and improved human rights practices.

H1: *Legislative Approval States will sign human rights treaties earlier than Executive Approval States.*

H2: *When a Legislative Approval State signs a human rights treaty, significant positive changes in human rights practices will result.*

Executive Approval States, by definition, do not confront the same legislative hurdles as *Legislative Approval States.* The executive branch has a much simpler and more straightforward road to treaty ratification. While *Legislative Approval States* can use signature as an earlier signal of support for human rights, *Executive Approval States* do not need to differentiate between the timing of support via signature and ratification. If the executive supports ratification in an *Executive Approval State,* they should be able to ratify soon after signing the treaty. *Executive Approval States* should not, in general, have the same gaps between signing and ratifying as barrier states. For example, in regard to the ICCPR treaty, *Legislative Approval States* had an average gap of about nine years between signing and ratifying, compared with *Executive Approval States'* average gap of about six years.[16] The *Executive Approval State* head of state, knowing that there are no major institutional impediments to ratification, will not see the need to start the engines of change soon after signature when they expect ratification to be just around the corner.

One could argue that *Executive Approval States* use signing human rights treaties for a reputational boost similar to what ratification may provide. If this was the case, we would not expect positive rights changes following signature. Research on ratification and reputational gains does not hypothesize (or find support for) the idea that states follow-through with changes after ratification. Scholars do not find concrete evidence as to what the reputational gains would be (e.g., Nielson and Simmons 2015). In addition, gaining a positive reputation from signature would require broader knowledge of the action beyond that of a diplomatic audience.

H3: *When an Executive Approval State signs a treaty, there should be no significant change in human rights practices.*

---

[16] Calculations come from years of signature and ratification of the ICCPR on the UN Treaty Collection Database.

Statistical Investigation into the Impact of Signing Human Rights Treaties

The aforementioned discussion focused on the legislature's role in the timing of ratification. This section moves the focus to compliance with human rights treaties, looking to the ICCPR to test the effect of commitment actions on compliance between 1966 and 2010. This time frame captures most of the period that ICCPR has been in effect and allows me to include both the independent variables that research on human rights treaty compliance finds to be important and the dependent variables from the Cingranelli and Richards (CIRI) Human Rights Database and Human Rights Protection Scores without interpolating to extend the data to years beyond the existing data.[17]

Measuring Legislative Involvement

Based on the domestic differences in ratification approval, I divide states into two categories. The first consists of states that require legislative approval for treaty ratification. The second consists of states that do not require legislative approval for treaty ratification. This follows from conceptual distinctions found in Haftel and Thompson (2013) and empirical distinctions found in Simmons (2009). Many states require legislative approval before fully committing to treaty law. Of the 173 states examined in Simmons's (2009) data, 105 states required legislative approval for ratification while 68 did not.[18] Sierra Leone's Constitution, for example, stipulates that treaty agreements are "subject to ratification by Parliament by an enactment of Parliament or by a resolution supported by the votes of not less than one-half the Members of Parliament."[19] Other states, such as Australia, rest the power of ratification squarely with the executive. This ratification power is granted by Article 61 of the Australian Constitution, granting executive power for

---

[17] Independent variables: existing available data from Simmons (2009) are 1977–2006; dependent variables: Political Rights and Civil Rights variables from Freedom House begin in 1973.

[18] Simmons (2009) uses a 1 to 3 scale to code the level of domestic institutional hurdle in place for ratification, with 1 being the least and 4 being the highest. This graph adds categories 1 and 1.5 together to graph states that do not require legislative support and 2 and 3 together to graph states that do require legislative approval for ratification. Find Simmons's (2009) data at http://scholar.harvard.edu/files/bsimmons/files/APP_3.2 _Ratification_rules.pdf.

[19] Sierra Leone 1991 Constitution Article 40 (4) h.

"the execution and maintenance of this Constitution, and of the laws of the Commonwealth."[20]

States with legislative requirements for ratification should opt for faster signature of treaties when they want to signal commitment to treaty law. The signature commitment action provides a way of signaling support prior to ratification approval from the legislature. Examining signature along with ratification will help to explain the gap that occurs for some states between signature and ratification.

In this book, I operationalize the concept of legislative involvement in treaty ratification by measuring whether or not domestic policy requires legislative approval for ratification. I use coding from Simmons's Ratification Rules (2009, appendix 3.2), where she codes how states ratify treaties based on descriptions in national constitutions. Covering 173 states, her coding uses the following scale:

1 = individual chief executive or cabinet decision
1.5 = rule or tradition of informing legislative body of signed treaties
2 = majority consent of one legislative body
3 = super-majority in one body or majority in two separate legislative bodies
4 = national plebiscite

I collapse the aforementioned coding scale into two categories based on the extent of legislative involvement. My first category captures states wherein legislative approval is not required for ratification. This concept comprises Simmons's categories of 1 and 1.5. The second concept I operationalize requires legislative approval. Sixty-eight states fall into this category. This corresponds to Simmons's categories of 2 and 3. One hundred and four states fall into this category. None of the states included in coding were listed as Category 4. Dividing the Simmons scale into two distinct categories of legislative involvement offers the conceptual advantage of refining how involvement of domestic processes influences ratification. It also offers the analytical advantage of measuring, graphing, and elucidating the exact significance of legislative barriers' presence or absence.

Model

To account for the endogeneity of treaty commitment to human rights treaties, I utilize instrumental variable regressions. Using instrumental

---

[20] Section 61 of the Australian Constitution.

variable analysis helps to get at the reverse causality between treaty commitment and changes in behavior (Neumayer and Spess 2005). Although the difficulty in finding good instruments is widely recognized, several studies have established good-quality ones for use when testing the effect of treaty commitment. Following from Simmons (2009) and von Stein (2018), I include measures of legal system and regional commitment to instrument treaty commitment. The first instrumental variable is the common law system, which codes whether or not a state operates predominantly within the common law legal system. The second instrumental variable is regional binding legal commitment to the ICCPR treaty. The only notable difference in my treatment of these instruments from the discussed research is that I expand on their consideration of regional ratification to include all binding acts of commitment within a region. This expands the measure to include all ratifications, accessions, and successions within a region, which I theorize affect a state's choice and timing to commit to a treaty.

Results

Across most of the models, signature was associated with better rights practices in *Legislative Approval States* but not in *Executive Approval States*. Models 1 and 3, examining the effect of treaty commitment on *Legislative Approval States* using Freedom House and CIRI measures of human rights, found a significant reduction in human rights violations when *Legislative Approval States* sign the ICCPR. Model 5, using the Human Rights Protection Scores measure of human rights, had no significant finding for signing or ratifying the ICCPR.

Models 1 and 3 point to an interesting relationship between *Legislative Approval States* and treaty ratification. In both models, ratification was found to be a statistically significant indicator of worse human rights (or an increase in violations). While significant improvements in rights practices took place in barrier states following signature, by the time *Legislative Approval States* ratified there were declines in human rights practices. Models 2, 4, and 6 examined the effect of treaty commitment on rights practices in *Executive Approval States*. In none of these three models was signature a significant indicator of improved human rights practices. In Model 4, using the CIRI empowerment index as the dependent variable, signature was associated with worse human rights for *Executive Approval States*. These results point to the finding that

Table 4.2 *ICCPR commitment and Freedom House measures of civil liberties, 1972–2010*

	+ Means more violations	– Means fewer violations
	Model 1	Model 2
	Legislative Approval States	Executive Approval States
Civil liberties lagged one year	0.8004(0.0093)***	0.7708(0.0272)***
Ratification	0.5066(0.2300)**	–2.706(1.985)
Signature	–0.4156(0.1757)***	2.065(1.574)
Polity2	–0.0450(.0027)***	–0.0458(0.0056)***
Durability	–0.0007(0.0004)**	0.0035(0.0031)
GDP	–0.0000(0.0000)	–0.0000(0.0000)
Population	0.0000(0.0000)	–0.0000(0.0000)
Interstate war	0.0619(0.0957)	0.1842(0.1683)
Civil war	0.2207(0.0306)***	0.0570(0.0877)
Constant	0.7704(0.0455)***	0.9113(0.0991)***
Observations	2159	1876

*$p<0.10$, **$p<0.05$, ***$p<0.01$; Stata 14 Instrumental variable regression. Instrumented: ratification. Included instruments: Signature, Polity2, GDP, Durability, Population, Internal War, Interstate War. Excluded instruments: Common Law, Regional Binding Commitment.

signature is not an important turning point for *Executive Approval States* regarding human rights practices.

Discussion of Statistical Findings

The statistical models support my argument that the commitment action of signature is important to examine, particularly for states confronting legislative barriers to ratification. The findings show that signature is an important commitment action but only for *Legislative Approval States*. For these states, the ratification delays (either perceived or actualized) result in the executive placing significance on signature, the commitment action that does not require legislative approval. Separating out commitment into signature and ratification provided insight into which commitment actions mattered for which types of states. While most prior

Table 4.3 *ICCPR commitment CIRI measures, 1981–2010*

	+ Means better rights,	− Means worse rights
	Model 3	Model 4
	Legislative Approval States	Executive Approval States
Empowerment Rights lagged one year	0.7996(0.0171)***	0.6200(0.0241)***
Ratification	−6.612(2.601)***	7.994(2.731)***
Signature	5.591(2.136)***	−6.723(2.336)***
Polity2	0.1080(0.0161)***	0.1880(0.0131)***
Durability	0.0051(0.0019)***	−0.0198(0.0061)***
Internal war	−0.5592(0.1660)***	0.2608(0.2610)
Interstate war	0.0658(0.4749)	−0.6248(0.3710)*
Population	−0.0000(0.0000)	−0.0000(0.0000)
GDP per capita	0.0000(0.0000)	.0000 (.0000)***
Observations	2349	1388
Constant	1.568(.1487)***	3.256(0.2271)***

*p<0.10, **p<0.05, ***p<0.01; Stata 14 Instrumental variable regression. Instrumented: Ratification. Included instruments: Signature, Polity2, GDP, Durability, Population, Internal War, Interstate War. Excluded instruments: Common Law, Regional Binding Commitment.

work examining commitment and compliance with human rights treaties excludes signature from empirical consideration, the aforementioned models demonstrate its importance.

The findings point to the importance of considering how domestic institutions and processes of ratification count and how even nonlegally binding commitment actions can signal engines of change in human rights practices. It is no secret that getting any type of policy through the US Senate can be a long, arduous process. This has especially been the case when approaching international human rights law. For years, the United States had a blanket policy against ratifying human rights treaties. Scholarship has under-engaged the realization that the United States is not the only state facing difficult domestic legislative processes. For example, Argentina requires a majority approval vote of both houses of Congress for ratification, and Denmark requires parliamentary approval with the potential of the additional ratification barrier of public

Table 4.4 *ICCPR commitment human rights protection scores measures,*
1966–2010

	+ Means better rights,	− Means worse rights
	Model 5	Model 6
	Legislative Approval States	Executive Approval States
Human rights protection scores lagged one year	0.8979(0.0066)***	0.9062(0.0256)***
Ratification	0.1084(0.1341)	2.344(2.515)
Signature	−0.0788(0.0956)	−1.720(1.864)
Polity2	0.0117(0.0010)***	0.0070(0.0032)**
Durability	0.0012(0.0002)***	−0.0019(0.0033)
Internal war	−0.1421(0.0168)***	−0.0878(0.0547)*
Interstate war	0.0321(0.0534)	−0.1741(0.2157)
Population	−0.0000(0.0000)***	0.0000(0.0000)
GDP per capita	−0.0000(0.0000)	0.0000(0.0000)
Constant	0.0039(0.0097)	0.0406(0.0513)
Observations	3385	2147

*$p<0.10$, **$p<0.05$, ***$p<0.01$; Stata 14 Instrumental variable regression.
Instrumented: Ratification. Included instruments: Signature, Polity2, GDP,
Durability, Population, Internal War, Interstate War. Excluded instruments:
Common Law, Regional Binding Commitment.

referendum. In this chapter, I explored how the role of the domestic
legislature in ratification of international human rights treaty law
impacted state behavior and trends in compliance.

These findings are consistent with the approach of von Stein's (2005)
and other works positing that states that ratify international law may
select into commitment via changing behavior prior to commitment. In
this study, I find that *Legislative Approval States* did alter behavior prior
to ratification but only after signature. This finding, situated against the
prior works addressing selection effects of ratifying human rights treaties,
demonstrates that some of the time of change leading up to ratification
occurred after signature. Along with considering selection effects to
ratification overall, scholars of international law should consider this
time between signing and ratifying as ripe for studying changes in
behavior.

Robustness Checks

The statistical analysis provided consistent evidence that signature mattered for legislative barrier states; this section further tests the relationship between signature and human rights levels through additional robustness checks. A first robustness check separates out democracies from nondemocracies to test whether the observed effect of legislative barriers is, in fact, only capturing the effect of signing in democracies. One could expect that all democracies, regardless of domestic ratification procedures, take signature seriously (since it is a form of international legal commitment) and would improve rights after signing treaties as an acknowledgment of international law and procedures. This is not the case. When separating out democracies from nondemocracies, I find that *Legislative Approval States*, even when nondemocratic, improve rights practices following signature, not ratification. *Executive Approval States*, even when democracies, do not improve rights following signature. Table 4.5 presents the results of separating out democracies from nondemocracies when modeling the effects of ICCPR commitment on human rights, as measured by CIRI's Empowerment Rights Index. Following from the Polity IV dataset, I code country-years receiving 6 and above as democracies and those 5 and below as nondemocracies. Models 7 and 8 examine the two samples of states that we would expect to be affected by the role of democracy. Model 7 includes *Legislative Approval States* during nondemocratic state-year observations. If level of democracy was driving the relationship between commitment and human rights practices, we would not expect signing to influence nondemocratic states' human rights practices. Similarly, Model 8 includes democratic states that do not face legislative barriers.

If democracy were the prevailing driver of treaty commitment's importance, we would expect signing human rights treaties to have a positive effect on rights practices in these democratic non-barrier states. Instead, I find that the *Legislative Approval State* status remains the important distinction. Democratic states without barriers to ratification had worse rights after signing and improved rights after ratifying. Nondemocratic states with ratification barriers significantly improved rights following signature but not ratification. These findings indicate that states responded to signing relative to their domestic ratification barriers rather than level of democracy.

A second robustness check in Table 4.6 looks to an additional treaty to check the results found for the ICCPR against another human rights treaty,

Table 4.5 *ICCPR and separating out democratic commitment and
ratification approval, 1966–2010*

	Model 7	Model 8
	Legislative Approval States	Executive Approval States
	Nondemocracy	Democracy
Empowerment index lagged one year	$0.6412(0.0450)^{***}$	$0.4941(0.0450)^{***}$
Ratification	$-9.279(3.049)^{***}$	$9.516(5.715)^{*}$
Signature	$6.605(2.158)^{***}$	$-8.342(5.011)^{*}$
Polity2	$0.0845(0.0256)^{***}$	$0.2614(0.1500)^{*}$
Durability	$-0.0030(0.0058)$	$-0.0093(0.0139)$
Internal war	$-0.8031(0.3093)^{***}$	$1.037(1.422)$
Interstate war	$-0.4352(0.6310)$	$-1.230(0.6214)^{**}$
Population	$-0.0000(0.0000)^{*}$	$-0.0000(0.0000)^{*}$
GDP per capita	$0.0000(0.0000)^{*}$	$0.0000(0.0000)$
Constant	$2.712(.3762)^{***}$	$4.017(1.140)^{***}$
Observations	1032	547

$^{*}p<0.10,\ ^{**}p<0.05,\ ^{***}p<0.01$; Stata 14.0 Instrumental variable regression.
Instrumented: ratification. Included instruments: Signature, Polity2, GDP,
Durability, Population, Internal War, Interstate War. Excluded instruments:
Common Law, Regional Binding Commitment.

the CEDAW. This robustness check lends additional support for the argument that signature matters, and it matters most for barrier states. When *Legislative Approval States* signed the CEDAW, human rights practices significantly and positively improved. When *Legislative Approval States* ratified the treaty, human rights practices declined. Neither commitment action was statistically significant for *Executive Approval States*.

Conclusion

This chapter presented the legal distinction between signing and ratifying human rights treaties, arguing for the importance of viewing the actions separately, both conceptually and analytically. I argued that signature translates into human rights improvements via two mechanisms. The first

Table 4.6 *CEDAW and human rights protection scores, 1980–2010*

	Model 9	Model 10
	Legislative Approval States	Executive Approval States
HRPS index lagged one year	0.9700(0.0053)***	0.9793(0.0050)
Ratification	−0.4274(0.2692)*	0.0588(0.1140)
Signature	0.3780(0.2396)*	−0.0495(0.0973)
Polity2	0.0039(0.0007)***	0.0018(0.0008)**
Durability	−0.0004(0.0004)	−0.0000(0.0002)
Internal war	−0.0921(0.0134)***	−0.0726(0.0135)***
Interstate war	0.0148(0.0362)	−0.0009(0.0255)
Population	−0.0000(0.0000)**	−0.0000(0.0000)
GDP per capita	−0.0000(0.0000)*	0.0000(0.0000)
Constant	0.0638(0.0137)***	0.0292(0.0069)***
Observations	2529	1510

*p<0.10, **p<0.05, ***p<0.01; Stata 14.0Instrumental variable regression. Instrumented: Ratification. Included instruments: Signature, Polity2, GDP, Durability, Population, Internal War, Interstate War. Excluded instruments: Common Law, Regional Binding Commitment.

mechanism relies on legal mobilization around treaty signature. In the absence of a supportive executive, domestic and international rights groups along with IOs and states can use state signature as a focal point around which to mobilize rights movements and to open the opportunity to signal international rights support. The second mechanism is through supportive executives who advance treaty ideas within a legislative constraining context. When faced with the prospect or reality of legislative delays to treaty ratification, supportive executives begin treaty implementation prior to ratification.

Using statistical analysis centered on the ICCPR treaty, I found strong support for the importance of signature in explaining future human rights practices. I argued that the timing and extent of domestic legislative involvement in the treaty ratification process was important in understanding when and how states change behavior following commitment. I specifically argued that states confronted with domestic legislative barriers to ratification use signing treaty law as an important juncture of commitment, signaling the support of their executive branches. As a result, signing becomes an important point against which to judge and assess changes in rights behavior.

The findings in this chapter push against using ratification as the only focal point for compliance analysis. Most of the models in this chapter found that ratification was not a significant indicator of human rights practices. In models where ratification was significant, it appeared to be part of a broader commitment and compliance story, since signature was also significant. This finding supports existing international relations and international law scholarship finding a negative or null relationship between ratification and compliance with international human rights law. Together with the existing literature, the findings from this chapter call into question the importance placed on studying compliance tied to ratification as a fixed point and support a call to study ratification as an overall process, which allows for the consideration of compliance occurring before ratification. In an early discussion of Hathaway (2002), which is perhaps the earliest and most expanded quantitative work engaging human rights compliance, Goodman and Jinks critique her work for using ratification to measure acceptance of international law and state that ratification is not a "magic moment"; in fact, they point to signature as an earlier point of treaty obligation (2003, 173). No research has yet followed through on exploring or analyzing the suggestion that signature fully commences the formal acceptance of international treaty law. My analysis contributes to understanding human rights treaty commitment and compliance, focusing on the role of signature in formal commitment to international treaty law, and supports the argument that commitment is a process, not a "magic moment" of ratification (Goodman and Jinks, 2003).

These findings point to a brighter outlook for the relationship between international law, state commitment, and compliance behavior. Based on current studies analyzing compliance with human rights treaties, many scholars have claimed a limited role for international law in state behavior. The findings of earlier, foundational, quantitative work that tested the relationship between human rights treaty ratification and changes in rights behavior led to pessimistic conclusions. Keith, for example, concluded that "overall, this study suggests that perhaps it may be overly optimistic to expect that being a party to this international covenant will produce an observable impact" (1999, 112). Hathaway also concluded that the noncompliance occurred following ratification, writing that "noncompliance with many human rights treaties is commonplace" and "the current treaty system may create opportunities to use treaty ratification to displace pressure for real change in practices" (2002, 2022). Both Keith and Hathaway caution against completely ruling out the role of ratification, offering that it is part of a process, with ratification being "only the final step in a long socialization process" (Keith 1999, 113) and noting that "ratification of human rights treaties has an undetected long-term positive effect on individual ratifying countries" (Hathaway 2002, 2022).

This chapter's findings call the negative assessments into question. Prior scholarship is correct in arguing that ratification is not necessarily a significant, magic moment demarcating compliance shifts and that compliance instead is part of a longer process. We can measure part of that process of change though analyzing timing of signature. Domestic legislative barriers are not the only barriers states face in committing to international treaty law. Some executive branches and heads of state simply do not support human rights or specific human rights treaties. Yet as we saw in the Nigeria case, civil society and international organizations were able to use CRPD signature to mobilize rights when confronted with an unsupportive head of state.

5

Accession

Late Commitment and Treaty Negotiations

> After nineteen weeks of formal meetings to draft a comprehensive statute, the PrepCom sent to Rome a draft convention of 116 articles with 1,700 brackets containing disagreed language.
>
> Washburn on the output of the first preparative round of treaty negotiations for the International Criminal Court Rome Statute Treaty

Introduction

During the International Criminal Court (ICC) negotiations, a like-minded group banded together to advance mutual interests and further development of the Rome Statute. The group "shared and agreed on a set of principles, arrived at in Rome, which expressed a detailed vision of the nature and values of the Court" (Washburn 1999, 367–369). The formal structure of negotiations allowed the like-minded group to share information, expertise, and garner enough votes to advance mutually agreed-upon proposals. Like-minded group members ratified the Rome Statute and became vocal supporters of the ICC mission following its creation. The Rome Statute negotiations began three years before treaty completion in 1995, with a final, focused five-week round to conclude (362–363). This timeline is short compared with human rights treaty negotiations, which can take decades to negotiate and finalize, offering many opportunities for state involvement in treaty creation. While treaty design and international negotiation are frequently studied topics within international relations (e.g., Abbott and Snidal 2000; Koremenos, Lipson, and Snidal 2001; McKibben and Western 2014), thus far state involvement in treaty negotiations has been an overlooked factor in explaining treaty compliance. As the ICC anecdote illustrates, actions during negotiations can have long-term effects after negotiations end.

This chapter builds on existing findings by linking negotiation participation, commitment, and compliance.[1] I ask whether states that contributed to writing a treaty show greater compliance than states that did not. Not only is treaty negotiation an important process to further explore, but negotiation participation also affects how a state commits to a treaty: ratifying states commit to treaties they themselves negotiated, while acceding states commit to treaties that others negotiated. International relations and international legal studies have yet to differentiate binding commitment types. Without doing so, we miss the opportunity to delve deeper into the processes behind commitment that foreshadow compliance practices. Recognizing the differences between ratification and accession allows the opportunity to analyze changes in negotiation participants and nonparticipants' rights practices.

This chapter's central finding is that the distinction between accession and ratification commitment is significant. Whether or not a state participated in negotiating a human rights treaty affected compliance outcomes. I argue that the socialization that occurs during the negotiation process contributes to lasting human rights effects and that states that negotiated the International Covenant on Civil and Political Rights (ICCPR) improved their rights practices following ratification. States that opted out of negotiation participation and acceded to the ICCPR had worse practices following commitment. I account for states that gained independence after negotiations took place and were therefore unable to negotiate the ICCPR. These states did not have the same negative trends in human rights as the opt-out states.

These findings make the legal and analytical distinction between the two principle forms of binding treaty commitment important for two reasons. First, they point to the benefits of participating in treaty negotiations. Second, they flag the distinction between states that opted out of negotiations and those that never had the option to participate in the first place. This chapter thus deepens our understanding of how differences in binding commitment matter and how participation in international organizations and negotiation connects to changes in human rights practices.

---

[1] Baccini and Urpelainen (2014) examine whether the negotiation period (not negotiators vs. nonnegotiators) is a time of significant compliance shifts when examining Preferential Trade Agreements and environmental issues. They find that negotiating states do not increase their compliance shifts during that set time.

What Is Treaty Accession?

Treaty accession is the "act whereby a state accepts the offer or the opportunity to become a party to a treaty already negotiated and signed by other states" (UN Treaty Collection, 2018). In terms of legal effect, accession mirrors ratification in that commitment via accession is a legal act of binding obligation. Political scientists and legal scholars have largely interpreted the two actions as interchangeable (e.g., Hathaway 2002; Keith 1999; Simmons 2009). However, accession has two important characteristics that differentiate it from ratification.

First, accession is unique in that it distinguishes state commitment based on negotiation participation. The United Nations and the Vienna Convention on the Law of Treaties (VCLT) recognize that states that accede to international treaties are committing to a treaty that other states negotiated. Accession offers a form of commitment for states that did not participate in treaty negotiations, setting them apart from those that negotiated and ratified. Some treaties strictly enforce this definitional distinction while others do not codify the norm. In the latter cases, states typically adhere to the norm of distinction between the two commitment types.

Second, the United Nations and VCLT recognize that acceding states enter commitment following formal treaty entry into force (EIF). Unless explicitly noted otherwise within the treaty text, only original parties to the treaty that followed the signature/ratification process can do so prior to EIF. States not committing to the treaty during this period, often an explicit window of commitment opportunity, must wait until EIF has been announced: "1)A treaty enters into force in such manner and upon such date as it may provide or as the negotiating States may agree. 2) Failing any such provision or agreement, a treaty enters into force as soon as consent to be bound by the treaty has been established for all the negotiating states" (VCLT Article 24(1–2)).

Figure 5.1 graphs the ratification and accession commitment count for the core UN human rights treaties. More states acceded to the Convention against Torture and Other Cruel, Inhuman, or Degrading Treatment or Punishment (CAT), the Convention on the Elimination of All Forms of Racial Discrimination (CERD), the International Covenant on Economic, Social, and Cultural Rights (ICESCR), the ICCPR, and the International Convention on the Protection of the Rights of All Migrant Workers and Members of Their Families (CMW). More states ratified the Convention on the Elimination of All Forms of Discrimination against

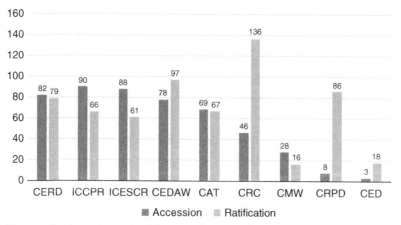

Figure 5.1 Accession and ratification of core UN human rights treaties, 1966–2010

Women (CEDAW), the Convention on the Rights of the Child (CRC), the Convention on the Rights of Persons with Disabilities (CRPD), and the International Convention for the Protection of All Persons from Enforced Disappearance (CED). Overall, more states committed via ratification (626) to the core human rights treaties during this period than acceded (492).

Window of Opportunity

The UN Treaty Handbook states that it is common for multilateral treaties to have a "window of signature." This window opens and closes the opportunity for signature and identification of a state as an original party to the treaty. After window closing and excluding states from designation as an original party, states may no longer *ratify* the treaty. Instead, they can commit through accession. When treaties contain such specific windows of signature, the treaty design privileges states that are already (1) aware of and informed about the treaty content and (2) support the treaty issue area. Both of these components describe states that have actively promoted the treaty in negotiations and other conferences, working groups, and so on. Windows of opportunity for treaty signature are less common for human rights treaties than other issue areas. The Convention on the Non-Applicability of Statutory Limitations to War Crimes and Crimes against Humanity, a chapter IV UN human rights treaty, is an example of a human rights treaty with a signature window. Article 5 of the treaty established a formal end of signature: signing began on December 16, 1968, and "shall, until 31 December 1969, be open for signature." Though the formal signature window is not as common in human rights treaties as other issue areas, the existence of such a window reinforces the distinction of commitment types within the broader practice and study of international treaty law.

Accession and EIF

States that miss signing during the specified window of signature are allowed to join the treaty through accession at a later time, upon treaty EIF. Treaty EIF timing is determined by the terms written within each treaty. Two typical paths specify EIF. It can either be tied to a specified date or based on a threshold of support. Through this approach to EIF, a specified number of ratifications must be met in order for the treaty to go into effect. International human rights treaties at the United Nations have adopted the second approach to EIF. All the core human rights treaties required a particular threshold of ratifications to occur to initiate the treaty entering into effect. Table 5.1 lists information about human rights treaties' creation and EIF. Six of the nine core treaties had a threshold of twenty ratifications, one treaty had a threshold of twenty-seven ratifications, and two treaties required thirty-five ratifications for EIF. The nine core human rights treaties took on average 5.1 years to EIF after opening for signature. The ICCPR, ICESCR, and the CMW stood out as taking the longest with 10, 10, and 13 years, respectively. The CRC had the shortest time between treaty creation and EIF, taking only one year to reach the required threshold of twenty ratifications. The CRC is the most widely accepted and popular of the core human rights treaties, with 196 parties as of July 2019. The CEDAW was close behind, taking only two years to reach the EIF requirement of twenty ratifications. The negotiating and drafting states determined EIF threshold requirements for all of these treaties. The timing of EIF reflects the ratification threshold requirements and global support.

The UN Convention Relating to the Status of Refugees, an important human rights treaty (although not considered a core treaty), also adopted a threshold approach to EIF. The Refugee Convention, as it is commonly referred, only required six ratifications for the treaty to move into force (Article 43(1)). States ratifying or acceding after EIF had nine days following commitment for state EIF (Article 43(2)). Given the smaller threshold requirement for the Refugee Convention, it is not surprising

Table 5.1 *Core UN human rights treaties creation and EIF*

Treaty	Year Created	Entry into Force	Entry into Force Ratification Threshold	Years for EIF
CERD	1966	1969	27	3
ICESCR	1966	1976	35	10
ICCPR	1966	1976	35	10
		1979 Human rights committee	10 declarations	13
CEDAW	1979	1981	20	2
CAT	1984	1987	20	3
CRC	1989	1990	20	1
CMW	1990	2003	20	13
CRPD	2006	2008	20	2
CED	2006	2010	20	4

that the treaty entered into force in 1954, three years following its creation. The differing threshold demonstrates that the treaty designers had the power to significantly alter the legal timeline of the treaty through the EIF specification. EIF timing exhibits one crucial factor negating states shaped.

Patterns of Accession

States acceding to international human rights treaties commit to already-negotiated agreements. An obvious question becomes whether states did not negotiate a human rights treaty because they were not interested in doing so (opting out of negotiations) or because they institutionally could not do so because the state had yet to gain its independence (unable to negotiate). Figure 5.2 graphs the total accessions to the ICCPR treaty and distinguishes between Late and Early UN Members. I consider states that joined the United Nations prior to 1964 Early Members and those after as Late Members. Most of the ICCPR negotiations and drafting occurred by 1964. States that joined the United Nations by that time had the opportunity to participate in at least some of the treaty's negotiations and draft revisions. States that joined after this period were not institutionally allowed or able to be part of the negotiations.

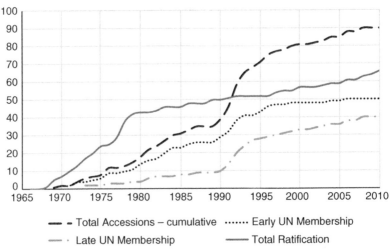

Figure 5.2   Total accessions to the ICCPR by late and early UN membership
compared with ratifications

Figure 5.2 compares accession commitment trends of Early UN
Members and Late UN Members with cumulative ratification counts
over time. Ratification actions dominated the binding commitment
actions to the ICCPR until the early 1990s, when the count of total
cumulative accessions to the ICCPR surpassed the total counts of ratifications of that treaty. The jump in accessions following 1990 represents
an increase in commitment from both Early and Late UN Members and
captures the increased presence of former Soviet states as newly independent states in the international system. After 1990, both states with
Early and Late UN Membership contributed to the total accession
counts.[2]

Although negotiators did not specifically articulate accession restrictions within the ICCPR text, states overall adhered to the international
standards. Most of the commitment to the ICCPR followed the UN and
VCLT guidelines, although the treaty did not explicitly require this. This
commitment behavior demonstrates that states generally adopted the
standards for commitment even when not legally required to do so.
The first Late UN Members to accede to the ICCPR were Barbados and
Mauritius, which both acceded in 1973. The ICCPR entered into force in

---

[2] As detailed more in the discussion of succession in Chapter 6, not all new states followed
succession.

1976, and the Human Rights Committee entered into force in 1979. Only eight of the ninety state accessions occurred prior to the 1976 EIF. The remaining accessions occurred after 1976. All accession states but one followed the protocol of acceding without signing the treaty. Cambodia signed and then later acceded to the ICCPR, adopting a nontraditional commitment path. During that period, Cambodia experienced severe regime instability and widespread violence under the Khmer Rouge, which may have affected its commitment decision and behavior.

Who Accedes to International Law?

Regime Type

Scholarship highlights the importance of regime type in the commitment to and recognition of global human rights. Studies explore whether regime type makes commitment to human rights treaties more or less likely. Generally, human rights scholarship points to a fundamental relationship between democracies and valuing human rights (Davenport and Armstrong 2004; Donnelly 1999; Guilhot 2005; Moravcsik 2000). As Moravcsik argues, "the primary proponents of reciprocally binding human rights obligations were ... the governments of newly established democracies" (2000, 220). The international legal community has echoed the expected relationship between democracies and human rights. The Vienna Declaration and Programme of Action included the statement that "democracy, development and respect for human rights and fundamental freedoms are interdependent and mutually reinforcing" (1993, 608). This research area generally considered human rights law commitment broadly, without the distinction between ratification and accession.

Looking to commitment trends across regime types, Figure 5.3 examines regime type patterns while comparing states that acceded, those that ratified, and those without binding commitment to the ICCPR. Using the Polity2 score measure from the Polity IV Project, I plot states' average democracy score by their commitment to the ICCPR. Polity2 ranges from −10, signifying the least democratic states, to 10, signifying the most democratic states. Partial democracy is coded as a Polity2 value between 1 and 6, and a full democracy between 7 and 10 (Marshall, Gurr, and Jaggers 2017, 35).

By far, states that ratified the ICCPR had the highest average democracy score. States that were Late Members to the United Nations (after 1955) and acceded to the ICCPR had the next highest democracy score

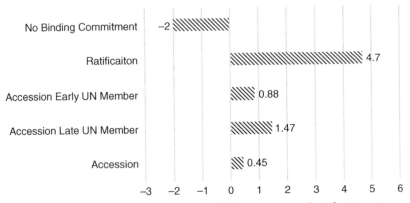

Figure 5.3   Average democracy scores for ICCPR accession and ratification states

(1.47). After that, the next highest average democracy score was for the Early Members that acceded to the ICCPR, with a score of 0.88. Without separating Early and Late UN Members, acceding states had an average score of 0.45. These democracy scores greatly differ from states that had no binding commitment to the ICCPR, with an average Polity2 score of −2. It is important to note that none of the Polity2 score averages reached 6, meeting the threshold of democracy. From Figure 5.3, however, we can see that states that ratified the ICCPR tended to be about three times more democratic than Late UN Member acceding states and about ten times more democratic than acceding states overall.

Region

Scholarship on human rights treaties also underscores the importance of global region. In particular, scholars highlight a divide between Western and non-Western state cultures influencing the perception, interpretation, and implementation of human rights standards (e.g., Donnelly 1984). Whether states within a region value and commit to human rights treaties influences neighboring states in the same region (Hathaway 2007; Simmons 2000). Asian states are argued to have unique human rights approaches (e.g., Bauer and Bell 1999; Kelly and Reid 1998) and to oppose oversight into domestic affairs (Kahler 2001). African state treaty participation and practices have drawn considerable attention (e.g., Udombana 2001; Welch 2001), underlying an expectation that they may differ from other regions in their human rights behavior. Smith-Cannoy places sub-Saharan Africa, the Middle East and Northern Africa, and South Asia on the weak end of a spectrum of "regional support for human rights instruments" (2012, 54). However, Carlson and Listhaug (2007) find stronger support for universal approaches to human rights than regional ones when studying citizens' perceptions of human rights across regions.

Figures 5.4 and 5.5 examine ICCPR ratification and accession by world region. Using the United Nations' regional categorization, I graph the count of accessions (Figure 5.4) and ratifications (Figure 5.5) across Africa, Oceania, North America, Asia, Europe, and Latin America. African states had the highest count of accessions to the ICCPR, with thirty-six states acceding, followed by Asia, with twenty-five states acceding. European states had the highest count of ICCPR ratifications (twenty-three), followed by Latin America (fourteen). Oceania and North America had the lowest counts for both commitment action types, reflecting the smaller number of states that fall within these regional categories.

Legal Tradition

Research tells us that states vary their international legal behavior based on legal tradition (Mitchell, Ring, and Spellman 2013). Common law states, overall, had better human rights practices than civil, Islamic law, and mixed legal traditions. Figure 5.6 graphs accessions and ratifications to the ICCPR and depicts the percentage of states making each commitment action from each of the legal traditions. I plot the composition of each commitment action type against the overall breakdown of state legal traditions. Doing so allows a comparison. Overall, civil law constitutes the largest legal tradition, with 52 percent of states; common law constitutes 25 percent of states; Islamic law, 14 percent; and mixed, 10 percent. Coding of legal traditions comes from Mitchell, Ring, and Spellman (2013). Civil law states made up the largest percentage of Late UN Member accession actions (63 percent). Civil law states comprised Early UN Member accession actions the lowest percentage, comprising 48 percent of the actions.

Common law states comprised 25 percent of the global sample and remained close to that percentage of commitment actions. These states made up the largest percentage of Late UN Member accession actions (23 percent) but only 18 percent of the ratifications and Early UN Member accessions. Islamic law states comprised 14 percent of the global sample. This legal tradition ranged in composition of commitment action with 10 percent of Late UN Member Accessions, at the low end, and

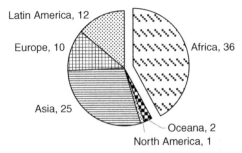

Figure 5.4   Accessions to the ICCPR by region

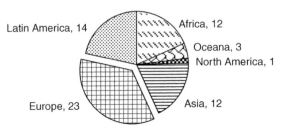

Figure 5.5   Ratifications to the ICCPR by region

18 percent of Early UN Member accessions at the high end. Finally, states with mixed legal traditions constituted 10 percent of the global sample. This percentage held consistent across accessions (11 percent) and ratifications (9 percent). However, when splitting accessions between Early and Late UN Members, states with mixed legal traditions comprised 16 percent of the Early UN Member accessions compared with only 5 percent of the Late UN Member accessions.

Legal tradition composition and trends in accession and ratification reveal that generally no action was overrepresented to the extreme by any legal tradition. The most noticeable shift away from average legal tradition compositions came when dividing accession between Early and Late UN Members. Civil law states were much more likely to comprise Late UN Member accessions than Early Member accessions, with civil law states constituting 11 percent more of the Late UN Member accessions than its baseline composition of the global sample. Alternatively, states with mixed and Islamic law traditions represented more of the Early UN Member accessions than their baseline percentages. This may reflect the growing number of civil law states in the United Nations following 1955 and the decolonization process.

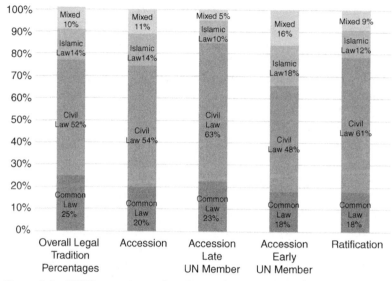

Figure 5.6 ICCPR accession and ratification by state legal tradition

Taken together, the earlier figures describe African and nondemocratic states as comprising the largest groups of states that acceded to the ICCPR treaty. Democracies, European states, and civil law tradition states constituted the largest groups that ratified the ICCPR treaty.

Modeling the Determinants of ICCPR Accession

The aforementioned descriptions reveal three important lines of distinction that international relations and international law scholars consider important when studying international human rights law: regime type, world region, and legal tradition. In this section, I look to quantitative analysis to statistically model the factors that influence state accession to international human rights treaties. States that committed via accession to one human rights treaty tended to do so for other human rights treaties. Of the states that acceded to the CERD, ICCPR, and the ICESCR, sixty-one of ninety-five committed through accession. What factors explain the determinants of treaty accession? I use a ratification model as a comparison model. In doing so, I can compare and contrast how the same explanatory variable can either explain both commitment types or highlight where different factors have larger/different effects for state accession versus ratification.

To model the determinants of accession to UN human rights treaties, I employ a Cox proportional hazards model, which is widely used to model human rights treaty commitment (Haftel and Thompson 2013; Neumayer 2005; Schneider and Urpelainen 2013). Hazard ratios indicate each variable's influence in explaining treaty accession. Values higher than 1 increase and values lower than 1 reduce the likelihood of accession in any given year. Once a state accedes, it leaves the analysis or is a "failure." States do not re-accede to a treaty, so there are no instances of repeated "failures." The unit of analysis is the country-year. The following models cover 1966–2010 (states continued to accede to human rights treaties after 2010, but 2010 is the end of the model).

In Table 5.2, Model 1 examined ICCPR accession. The higher states' Polity2 score and Human Rights Protection Scores, the less likely they are to accede to the ICCPR. A one-point increase on the Human Rights Protection Scores scale lowers the likelihood of a state acceding to ICCPR by 22 percent. A one-point increase on the Polity2 scale decreased the likelihood of acceding by 6 percent. Although not reaching the level of statistical significance, Late Members to the United Nations increased the chances of a state acceding to the ICCPR. Asian states were significantly less likely to accede, and states following Islamic Law were 48 percent less likely to accede. Model 2 focused on explaining ICCPR ratification as a comparison model. Late UN Members were significantly less likely to ratify the treaty, as were civil law states. Being a Late UN Member lowers the likelihood of ratifying the ICCPR by almost 40 percent. Latin American states were more likely to ratify the treaty; states in this region were 300 percent more likely to ratify.

The findings from the models indicate that while regime type did play some role in explaining treaty commitment, there was no substantial difference across ratification and accession. Whether or not a state was an Early or Late Member to the United Nations mattered in determining the likelihood of each commitment type. This finding makes sense given the temporal connection between accession and (1) absence from treaty negotiations and (2) commitment following EIF. Legal tradition mattered across both commitment types, with Islamic law states less likely to accede and civil law states less likely to ratify. Figures 5.7 and 5.8 graph the cumulative hazards of ICCPR accession (from Model 1) and ratification (from Model 2). The cumulative hazard of accession rises steeply in the 1990s. The cumulative hazard of ratification rises leading up to 2010.

Table 5.2 *Determinants of ICCPR accession and ratification*

	Model 1 Accession	Model 2 Ratification
Polity2	0.9410(0.0256)**	1.005(0.0284)
Durability	0.9870(0.0093)	0.9979(0.0047)
GDP	1 (0.0000)	1 (0.0000)
Population	1 (0.0000)	1 (0.0000)
Late Member	1.384(0.3164)	0.3887(0.1672)**
Human rights		
Protection scores lag1	0.7822(0.1074)*	0.9968 (0.1299)
Africa	0.5823(0.2457)	0.9952 (0.8235)
Oceania	0.3749(0.3695)	2.596(2.488)
Asia	0.4897(0.2186)*	1.333(1.204)
Europe	0.7621(0.4389)	3.323(2.836)
Latin America	0.4946(0.2627)	3.213(2.549)*
Common law	0.7925(0.2374)	0.6548(0.3354)
Civil law	0.8192 (0.1974)	0.4327(0.2404)*
Islamic law	0.4285(0.1532)***	1.007(0.5079)
Mixed	1 (dropped)	1 (dropped)
Number of countries	156	156
Number of failures	69	51
Observations	5795	5975
Prob.chi2	0.000	0.077

*p<0.10, **p<0.05, ***p<0.01; run on Stata 14.0

Negotiation Participation and Human Rights Compliance

International human rights treaties have successfully completed negotiations that constitute many compromises by negotiating states. Negotiating states have been involved in drafting, rewriting, and defining terms of international law and have taken ownership over what elements have been included or removed from the final treaty. The negotiating states, together, decide how to develop the treaty and whether or not the treaty is likely to be successful. As Lupu points out, "Some (treaty) negotiations fail, and negotiations for other potential treaties may never even begin because the relevant parties do not expect them to be fruitful" (2016, 1222). And as Lawand notes, the trust, transparency, and ownership over the treaty that happens during negotiations creates a "culture of compliance" (2007, 343). I argue that participating in the negotiation

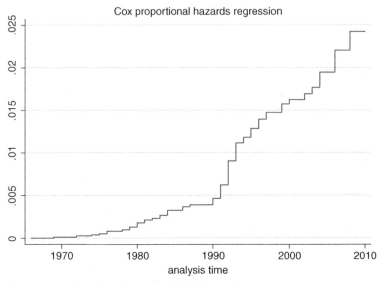

Figure 5.7   Cumulative hazard of ICCPR accession

process has a discernable and positive effect on compliance not seen in nonparticipating states. Socialization of expected rights practices and expected behavior occurs during negotiation participation and contributes to a positive outcome on treaty compliance.

Literature on international human rights points to the significance of socialization of human rights norms, but thus far has overlooked the specific way that negotiation participation can socialize participants to human rights. Research supports activists' role in socializing states to higher standards of human rights through treaty ratification (Simmons 2009) and changes in domestic practices (Keck and Sikkink 1998; Risse, Ropp, and Sikkink 1999). Shared membership in IGOs can socialize states into improved human rights practices (Greenhill 2010) and increased levels of democracy (Pevehouse 2002), especially through the "process of interaction with other states" (129).

These arguments rest on states' repeated interaction over human rights. Treaty negotiation offers an ideal setting and process through which actors repeatedly interact, with the specific intent of discussing and codifying human rights norms. Treaty negotiations at the United Nations offer the same institutional setting as the socialization that occurs within the UN General Assembly and a more authoritative setting than other IGOs. States that are at the negotiating table for human rights treaties

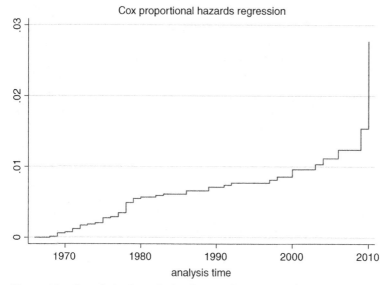

Figure 5.8   Cumulative hazard of ICCPR ratification

have an interest in promoting international human rights. While some are less supportive of universal human rights than others, the interaction with rights-supportive states is beneficial to all states involved. Through repeated interactions during prolonged treaty negotiations, participant states are socialized into endorsing and enacting higher standards of human rights. States that come to the negotiating table with higher human rights values raise the bar and expectations of other states, and over time and through socialization affect the other states' standards and practices. If a state is in the minority view of endorsing one position in the treaty, its delegates will see firsthand the majority of states endorsing another view of human rights. For example, when negotiating the ICCPR, paragraph 5 of the 6th Article – "Sentence of death shall not be carried out on a pregnant woman" – was put to vote. Fourteen states voted in favor of the amendment and one opposed it. After the majority supported the inclusion of this particular sentence, the state against it did not raise the issue again. When the complete paragraph was voted on, no states voted in opposition.[3] Socialization can occur during negotiations

[3] Bossuyt (1987, 142–143). The state in opposition was not identified in the ICCPR Travaux Preparatoire.

since they create a "favourable political climate among participating States, facilitating communication among them" (Maraugh 2007, 243).

Directly related to socialization toward improved human rights, the negotiation process contributes to states' shifting and converging preferences over time. During lengthy negotiations, participants articulate their arguments and ultimately must come to consensus for the negotiations to successfully conclude. The act of negotiation can change how parties approach issues over time. Raiffa notes that the "priorities of the two sides changed during the discussions" of the Panama Canal Negotiations; after negotiating the treaty, the United States placed "much more importance" on defense rights while "the importance of the land and water issue declined" (1982, 179).

Even the hegemonic United States can alter its preferences during treaty negotiations. In looking at voting patterns in the UN General Assembly, Bearce and Bondanella (2007) find that interests converge between states with shared international governmental organization memberships. Having the shared experience and interest in IGOs brought about interest convergence over time for member states. In a similar way, states that participate in negotiations together can see their interests and positions converge over time. Shifting preferences have participants coming away from negotiations believing that elements in the finalized treaty are codifying their preferences, making the states more likely to adhere to the standards. The important difference with negotiation participants is that they get to influence which interests get into the treaty in the first place.

Providing information deters cheating and reassures other states of a state's intent to comply with the treaty (Abbott 1993; Abbott and Snidal 1998). States communicate their interests and preferences during negotiations, signaling to each other where they stand on numerous issues within the treaty. With this signaling, states can map out other states' preferences, get a sense of where the international community is on an issue area, and make informed decisions about how to articulate, argue, and debate their own interests during negotiations. Related, participants learn powerful states' preferences and positions during treaty negotiations. Lupu contends that treaties that have been successfully negotiated "represent bargains to which the most powerful states have already agreed" (2016, 1244). In this vein, Denmark and Hoffmann highlight how many Western states negotiated treaties and presented them to former colonial states to sign (2008, 207). The authors point to the unsurprising fact that most treaties were signed in European cities, setting the stage for a European framing (210). States then can make assessments and calculations about shifting their positions to align with world powers' positions. Although arguments about state power assume that the most powerful state's positions prevail during international negotiations, there is evidence that developing states successfully use the forum of negotiations to bring new issues to the discussion, block settlements, and modify the overall outcome (Page 2004). Negotiations taking place within the United Nations maintain the one country–one vote system that allows less-powerful states to be influential during treaty negotiations.

A clear question following from an emphasis on negotiation is whether the general support for human rights that brings states to negotiate in the first place is what drives future rights practices. In other words, are selection effects driving a positive relationship between treaty negotiations and human rights outcomes? Methodologically, the analyses employ statistical strategies to account for selection effects. It is important to conceptually pause and briefly address how dismissing negotiations as merely a stopping point is problematic. At the very least, it limits the study of negotiations and other factors complicating the proposal that states select into negotiations and that prior interests/approaches/broad commitment to rights are unchanged and therefore explains future rights behavior.

While one concern of studying the effect of negotiation participation on outcomes may be the endogeneity of interest in the subject matter prior to negotiations, it would be over hasty to dismiss the unique role of negotiating in outcome state behavior. A selection-effects counterargument relies on several assumptions: first, that subject-matter interest is the dominant factor bringing states to the negotiating table. Issue-linkage arguments demonstrate one strong alternative, that bringing additional issues to the table increases the likelihood of engagement and settlement for states that otherwise would find the agreement to be of little or no value (Axelrod and Keohane 1985; Morrow 1992; Putnam 1988) and can increase the motivation for extended commitment and compliance (Koremenos et al. 2001; Tomz 2007). Hafner-Burton (2005) explicitly shows that linking human rights with trade, for example, is beneficial for human rights. The second assumption is that subject-matter interest is always associated with respect for human rights. States may, in fact, be drawn to negotiation tables to *limit* global human rights standards. During ICCPR negotiations, there was significant state opposition to include a provision of equality between the sexes out of fear it may "encourage too many women to work outside their homes" (Bossuyt 1987, 77). These states brought with them preferences widely viewed as antithetical to human rights. A third assumption holds that interest translates into completed and successful negotiations. It is not surprising that states negotiating human rights treaties demonstrate an interest in human rights before reaching the negotiation table. But as Holmes and Yarhi-Milo (2017) caution, it is incorrect to assume that participants' prior interests automatically lead to successful negotiations. Many negotiations fail, even when parties are interested in the subject matter. A recent and notable example is the extreme difficulty in drafting a treaty on Business and Human Rights. States generally voice support for improving businesses' human rights practices. However, the specifics of the extent to which corporations are held accountable through international legal mechanisms (and how to hold them accountable in the first place) vary greatly (Fidler 2018). The fourth and final assumption is that interest in human rights seamlessly translates into behavioral shifts. We know from a wealth of scholarship that the relationship is more complex. Posner (2014), for example, writes that liberal democracies participate in drafting human rights treaties not to change their behavior but to change the behavior of *other* states. Existing compliance research with negative relationship findings between ratification and compliance illustrate that there is not an automatic translation into improved rights.

Lasting Divide between Participants and Nonparticipants

States that did not participate in treaty negotiations were not exposed to these processes to the same extent. The divide between negotiating states and nonparticipatory states extends beyond the end of negotiations. States that did not participate in early rounds of Rome Statute negotiations "expressed concerns and raised questions that had been previously debated and, in some cases, even settled" (Bassiouni 1999, 449). While these states have less input and ownership over the treaty, negotiating states have extended positive effects on human rights. States that negotiated the Ottawa Convention played important roles following negotiations, including instrumental "political and financial support" (Lawand 2007, 344). Even when domestic administration changes from one head of state who supported and engaged in negotiations to another, the positive effects of negotiation remain largely intact. Withdrawing from international treaties, and human rights treaties specifically, is extremely rare. Even when negotiating states withdraw, we see lasting and positive effects of the negotiation process. The United States participated in almost every negotiation round of the Rome Statute for the ICC. Despite President Bush's withdrawal from the Rome Statute, the United States still heavily supports and participates in the ICC. President Bush himself took several supportive positions toward the ICC following treaty withdrawal. He walked back several restrictions on funding the ICC in the American Service-members Protection Act and did not veto the first UN Security Council referral to the ICC. The United States has also attended the ICC Assembly of States Parties since 2009.[4] Its participation in treaty creation ensured that the United States would remain committed to the ICC even if it was no longer formally committed to the Rome Statute.

The foundational UN human rights treaties took decades of negotiations. Many of the negotiators remained involved for the duration and participated in other related treaty negotiations as well. The ICCPR and ICESCR negotiations took almost two decades of repeated interaction and debate, concluding in 1966. These two foundational treaties began negotiations as one and split into two after disagreements arose during negotiations. In this case, negotiation participants had the opportunity to influence the framing and content of two treaties.

ICCPR Negotiations

ICCPR negotiations are well noted and documented in legal histories and social science analysis (e.g., Roberts 2015). During the height of the Cold War, the United States and Soviet Union used the medium of human rights treaty negotiations to advance their own interpretations of human rights and exert their political power. The most contentious issue when negotiating the ICCPR was the division between civil and political rights and economic, cultural, and social rights. A brief look at the procedural history of the ICCPR illustrates the time and involvement many states invested in drafting the treaty. Across the years and treaty drafts, many states were involved in finalizing the ICCPR. Drawing on the UN Human Rights Treaties Travaux Préparatoires project at the University of Virginia School of Law, along with the Bossuty's Guide to the Travaux Préparatoires of the ICCPR (1987), I counted and read through 472 meetings and documents related to the ICCPR negotiations. For the

---

[4] American Bar Association-ICC Project, "The US-ICC Relationship," available at www.aba-icc.org/about-the-icc/the-us-icc-relationship/.

purposes of this chapter, these Travaux Préparatoires allow me to code what states were involved in treaty negotiations each year along with whether or not states voted in roll-call votes during negotiations. States had many opportunities to participate between 1947 and 1966. Twenty-nine roll-call votes were held at the Commission on Human Rights between 1949 and 1953, along with sixty additional votes at the Third Commission of the UN General Assembly between 1950 and 1966.

The first session of the Drafting Commission on Human Rights was held in June 1947, and the finished ICCPR treaty was presented to the General Assembly in December 1966 (A/RES/2200/21). In the intervening nineteen years of negotiations, states shaped the direction, focus, length, and other dimensions of the ICCPR treaty. States had numerous opportunities to involve themselves in the negotiations through formal commission roles or through comments and suggestions during more than one hundred formal meetings and committee sessions. Figure 5.9 shows the meetings and reports produced during the extensive ICCPR negotiations. The first meetings took place in 1947. The Commission on Human Rights prepared drafts outlining two conventions on human rights. The Commission, comprising members from Australia, Chile, China, France, Lebanon, the Union of Soviet Socialist Republics (USSR), the United Kingdom, and the United States, decided to split the two draft conventions into a declaration and a convention (Bossuyt 1987, xix). The report of the third session listed the United States, China, France, Lebanon, Australia, Belgium, Chile, Egypt, India, Panama, USSR, United Kingdom, Uruguay, Yugoslavia, and the Byelorussian Soviet Socialist Republic as having members working on the draft covenant. During the second session of the Commission on Human Rights held in December 1947, Commission members discussed a Soviet amendment that did not protect individual expression of political opinion. The Soviet representative expressed that "equal rights could not be granted to those who professed ... opinions which tolerated the advocacy of ... national hatred" (Bossuyt 1987, 405). Representatives from Chile and the United Kingdom spoke against the amendment because it "did not protect the individual against discrimination on the grounds of his political opinions" and questioned whether the Soviet representative approved of an "individual being persecuted for his political opinion." Following this discussion, the Soviet amendment was rejected by a 10–4 vote (Bossuyt 1987, 405–409).

Two years later, a 1950 report of the Commission on Human Rights's sixth session listed members from Australia, Belgium (alternate), Chile,

China, Denmark (alternate), Egypt, France, Greece, India, Lebanon, Philippines (alternate), USSR, United Kingdom, Uruguay, and Yugoslavia as contributors to the Commission (Eleanor Roosevelt served as the US representative and chairperson). The Commission on Human Rights produced a first-draft human rights convention in 1950 and submitted a report to the Economic and Social Council in its sixth session. The seventh session meeting of the Commission in 1951 listed members from Australia, Chile, China, Denmark, Egypt, France, Greece (alternate), Guatemala (alternate), India, Lebanon, Pakistan, Sweden, Ukrainian Soviet Socialist Republic, USSR, United Kingdom, United States, Uruguay (alternate), and Yugoslavia.

Treaty negotiation activity spiked in 1951 with 107 meetings. By 1952, the United Nations General Assembly (UNGA) requested the human rights convention be split into two separate conventions, leading to the development of the ICCPR and the ICESCR. The division into two treaties reflected the division between Western and Eastern conceptualizations of human rights, with the West advocating for civil and political rights while the East incorporated economic, social, and cultural rights into international rights standards. Negotiators addressed the persistent tension by creating two separate treaties: "Negotiators opted for a convention that would achieve broad support, and more divisive issues were organized as optional protocols. By splitting these issues off into two additional protocols, the main document was able to move forward with broad support" (Urlacher 2015, 118).

By 1955 most of the negotiations had taken place. A first completed treaty draft was produced in 1950. Treaty development continued, with annual meetings taking place between 1955 and 1965 fine-tuning the

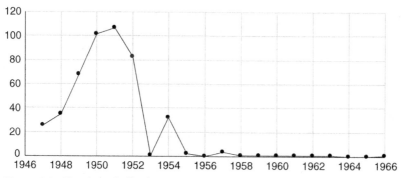

Figure 5.9 Number of official ICCPR meetings and reports, 1947–1966

Covenant. In 1963, a final draft was approved. The UNGA invited "all Governments" to review and comment on the draft convention the same year (UN Audiovisual Library 2020). The ICCPR, along with its Optional Protocol and the ICESCR, were presented to the General Assembly for vote in 1966.

States participating in the negotiations had significant input into the final treaties. During negotiations, participants reconfigured an initial human rights convention. First, states divided the convention into a separate declaration and a subsequent convention. This initial decision shaped the legal "hardness" and resulted in the drafting of the Universal Declaration of Human Rights. Then, states separated the broad human rights convention into two distinct treaties – the ICCPR and ICESCR – due to fundamental disagreements on typologies of human rights. States represented at the negotiation table vitally shaped human rights regime-defining activities in the early years of UN human rights treaty-making.

Measuring Treaty Negotiation Participation with Ratification and Accession

Using the accession/ratification distinction to measure negotiation participation has several clear advantages. First, the distinction is an official and legal one recorded by the United Nations. The source of the data on negotiation comes from the same source as the treaty commitment, offering consistent accounts of a state's treaty participation. Second, through the different commitment actions, the United Nations records a complete and official account of negotiation participants. Third, as a first analysis of negotiation's effect on human rights treaty outcomes, the accession/ratification distinction offers the advantage of being readily and publicly available through the UN Treaty Collection. This makes such measures available across other treaty issue areas for future studies to replicate and test this chapter's argument while examining areas beyond human rights.

Whether or not states participated in treaty negotiations determines how, according to UN guidelines, they can commit to the treaty. International law recognizes states that commit via accession as states that are committing to a treaty they did not negotiate. States that ratify are committing to a treaty they did have a hand in negotiating. Although international relations and international legal scholars have thus far overlooked this distinction, the difference is important. The VCLT situates accession as similarly binding as ratification, listing both as "the international act so named whereby as State establishes on the international plane its consent to be bound by a treaty" (Article 2.1(b)).

After establishing this similarity, international law proceeds to distinguish the two actions' notable characteristics. The UN Office of Legal Affairs specifies that states accede to international treaties after other states first create, negotiate, and sign them. States that commit via accession have not participated in negotiating the treaty. States negotiating the treaty have taken "part in the drawing up and adoption of the text of the treaty" (Article 2.1.e). These states play a role early on in determining the type of commitment the treaty requires. Negotiating states determine whether later accession to the treaty is allowed (Article 15.a and b). Negotiating states also have the option to sign the treaty earlier than other states, prior to its formal opening for signature. States can sign early during negotiation sessions by representatives formally expressing their signature subject to ratification (Article 14.1.d). Negotiating states can impose specific time limits on when states can sign the treaty, adding an accession-specific clause into the treaty. If a signing deadline is included in the treaty, states that missed the window for signature are no longer eligible to ratify the convention. Instead, they must commit through accession.

Though both accession and ratification are legally binding, this chapter advances our understanding through unpacking how the differences across the binding commitment types can matter. As noted in Chapter 2, existing studies on human rights treaties tend to group types of binding commitment together when discussing and analyzing human rights. In short, scholars at most note that accession and ratification are different types of commitment (as in Keith 1999; Neumayer 2008; Simmons 2009).

Measuring negotiation participation through ratification and accession commitment does come with one important disadvantage. This commitment distinction captures presence (whether a state was in the room during negotiations) but not depth (the extent to which states were active within the negotiations). Though the depth of negotiations is an important component to study, my argument focuses on the role that state presence plays in treaty negotiations. Negotiation presence allows states to receive information about human rights standards and facilitates socialization to expected certain outcomes. Measuring presence alone may, in fact, be undercounting the significance of negotiation participation because it is measuring the minimal engagement states had with negotiations rather than the true extent of involvement. As such, using the ratification/accession distinction offers a hard test of whether

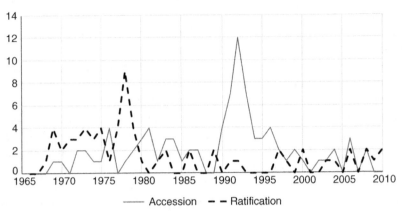

Figure 5.10   Annual count ICCPR accession and ratification, 1966–2010

negotiation participation can matter for rights outcomes. Figure 5.10 graphs ICCPR accession and ratification.

Hypotheses

I expect that states involved in negotiations will have a stronger commitment to the treaty when they ratify. Nonnegotiating states that commit later through accession have not participated in the negotiation process and are expected to have a lower level of commitment to the treaty.

H1: *If a state ratifies (and participated in treaty negotiations), improved human rights will follow commitment.*

Late Commitment: EIF Timing and States Unable to Negotiate

I differentiate between states that were UN members during treaty negotiations (Early Members) and those that joined the United Nations too late to participate in the negotiations (Late Members). This distinction allows me to distinguish states that consciously decided to not participate in treaty negotiations from states that had no opportunity to do so. The ICCPR negotiations took place between 1947 and 1966, predating the independence of many postcolonial states joining the United Nations. Since 1966, the United Nations increased membership from 122 to 193 states.

H2: *If an Early Member opted out of negotiations and later accedes to a human rights treaty, I expect that there will be no improvement in human rights following commitment.*

H3: *If a Late Member had no opportunity to negotiate a human rights treaty and later commits via accession, I expect an improvement in human rights following commitment.*

Possible Counterarguments about Negotiation, Accession, Ratification, and Human Rights

Though scholars have not yet theorized or hypothesized an alternative explanation to my argument discussed previously, I am able to draw on existing literature to outline three possible counterarguments: (1) there is no discernable difference between commitment types (the implicit standing assumption), (2) state interests matter more than negotiation participation, and (3) accession states will have improved human rights practices.

No Difference between Commitment Types

Many scholars group accession together with ratification for the purposes of analysis and conceptual discussions (e.g., Keith 1999; Neumayer 2005; Simmons 2009). The implicit, and sometimes explicit, assumption when combining the commitment actions is that there is no meaningful difference between accession and ratification. We should not expect a state that accedes to treaty law to adjust its behavior any differently than states that ratify. Numerous studies find that ratification is associated with worse human rights practices (e.g., Hathaway 2002; Hafner-Burton and Tsutsui 2005). This counterargument would expect that the same factors contributing to worse human rights following ratification would apply to human rights after accession as well. Whether ratifying as strategic ratifiers (Simmons 2009), being unable to follow through with commitment for other reasons (Chayes and Chayes 1993), or in response to the removal of pressure, states acceding to human rights law will follow suit.

H4: *A state's accession to a human rights treaty will have the same (negative) effect on human rights as ratification.*

State Interest over Socialization

A second counterargument expecting that negotiation participation does not explain human rights practices rests on a state interest–driven argument. This argument would expect that being part of negotiations is not a fundamentally important process, but any changes after negotiating would reflect states' success in embedding their interests into the treaty. This connects into a traditional realist-centric understanding of treaty compliance wherein states are more likely to (or only) comply with treaties when it is in their best interests. As Hafner-Burton and Tsutsui (2005) summarize,

> International treaties result from extended negotiations that reflect the national interests of member states; and those, in turn, reflect domestic bargaining. Because governments only ratify treaties when their national interests are reflected, they are predisposed to comply with the treaties they choose to join. (1381)

Some research points to the finding that most of the time it may not be in a state's interest to comply (e.g., Goldsmith and Posner 2005; Posner 2014); this coincides with the negative relationship found between ratification and human rights practices (Hathaway 2002; Keith 1999).

H5: *State interests, not the negotiation process, are what matter. The more successfully a state embeds its interests into the treaty, the more likely it will be to improve human rights following commitment.*

Accession and Improved Human Rights

A third possible counterargument is that states acceding to international human rights law have additional time to adjust human rights behavior and thus will demonstrate improved rights practices following accession. Acceding to a treaty after missing a window for signature and/or after the treaty has already entered into force allows the acceding states time to adjust behavior prior to committing to the treaty. Many treaties tie accession to treaty EIF, which in turn is typically defined by a threshold of states ratifying the treaty. This threshold of support is a legal actualization of what Finnemore and Sikkink (1998) write about as a tipping point, where a critical number of states agree to a norm. By the time of treaty EIF, many states have already signaled support for the treaty.

Acceding states have longer to take actions to improve human rights. UNICEF suggested that acceding states may begin improving rights prior to committing: "Other States may begin with the domestic approval process and accede to the treaty once their domestic procedures have been completed, without signing the treaty first" (2020). Acceding to a treaty the treaty already has widespread international support and after domestic agents of change have time to mobilize around the treaty. These factors could increase the likelihood that acceding states will have better human rights practices after commitment than their ratifying counterparts.

H6: *If a state accedes to a human rights treaty, improved practices commitment will follow.*

Statistical Investigation into Acceding to Human Rights Treaties

I define "Late Member States" as any state that became a member of the United Nations after 1964, after the final substantive articles of the ICCPR were adopted in 1963. Late Members did not have the same opportunity to opt into negotiations as Early Members. All other states are considered "Early Member States," having UN membership prior to 1964 and ample opportunity to participate in ICCPR negotiations spanning 1947–1966. The United Nations along with Chairperson Eleanor Roosevelt sought expansive participation and global representation during treaty negotiations, with delegates from both Western and non-Western states.[5] There is no reason to expect that there was a "great power" or Western bias for inclusion during the negotiations. Following the tests of accession and ratification on human rights practices, I test a measurement of state interests in the ICCPR in explaining human rights practices.

I use the Fariss (2014) and Schnakenberg and Fariss (2014) Human Rights Latent Human Rights Protection Score measure to model human rights. I use available Human Rights Scores from 1966 to 2010, analyzing forty-four years of state behavior. The latent variable means human

---

[5] For example, India, Indonesia, Costa Rica, Ghana, Nigeria, Saudi Arabia, United Arab Emirates, Brazil, Panama, Chile, Guatemala, Columbia, Uruguay, Peru, Venezuela, and Ecuador all submitted amendments along with the United States and United Kingdom during a 1961 meeting. See Report of the Third Committee. file:///D:/Working%20Projects/Accession%20Paper/ICCPR%20negotiation%20TP%20docs/UNGA%20draft%20ICCP R%20third%20committee%20report.pdf.

rights range from −3.1, capturing lower respect for Human Rights Scores, to 4.7, capturing increased government respect for human rights.

Accession is coded as 1 for the year states accede to treaty law and every year thereafter. Years when a state has not acceded are coded as 0. Ratification is coded as 1 for the year states ratify treaty law and every year thereafter. Years when a state has not ratified are coded as 0. Commitment data come from the UN Treaty Collection. Sixty-six states ratified and ninety-two states acceded to the ICCPR between 1966 and 2010. Figure 5.11 maps accession and ratification states. Grouped Ratification is a dichotomous variable coding binding commitment or no binding commitment to the ICCPR. This variable captures the dominant approach to ratification found within international relations literature and is included as a means to compare the separate effects of accession and ratification against the grouped commitment variable.

Model 1 in Table 5.3 presents the results of a test of the effect of treaty commitment on Early Member States, for whom ratification was significant and positively associated with improved human rights practices. When Early Member States ratified the ICCPR, their Human Rights Protection Score value increased by about 0.8 above the yearly mean value of human rights practices. States that opted out of treaty negotiations and committed via accession had no significant change in human rights practices. Model 2 included Late Member States that joined the United Nations from 1964 onwards, having no opportunity to opt in to ICCPR negotiations. For these states, ratification was not a significant indicator of human rights practices. States that were unable to negotiate the ICCPR and commit via ratification formally committed via accession and had improved human rights practices of about 0.4 above the yearly mean value of human rights practices. Model 3 includes international relations's traditional approach to treaty commitment, grouping ratification and accession together when measuring commitment's effect on future human rights practices. In Model 3, the Group Ratification measure was not a statistically significant indicator of human rights practices.[6]

In Figure 5.12, I visualize the results in Table 5.3 by plotting the coefficients from Models 1 to 3. While accession and ratification both are positive across the models, each is only significant for particular state-groups. The Grouped Ratification variable did not reach statistical significance and did not have a sizable positive effect on human rights. From the statistical analyses and the plotted coefficients, we can conclude that

---

[6] Models 1–3 results held when tested using a fixed-effects regression analysis.

Figure 5.11 Global ratification and accession of the ICCPR, 1966–2010

Table 5.3 *Accession and ratification of the ICCPR, 1966–2010*

	Model 1	Model 2	Model 3
	Early Members	Late Members	All
Accession	1.286(0.7704)	0.3806(0.1761)[**]	
Ratification	0.8368(0.3181)[**]	0.0898(0.1300)	
Grouped ratification	0.0656(0.1317)		
Polity2	0.0526(0.0079)[**]	0.0458(0.0038)[**]	0.0658(0.0034)[**]
Durability	0.0166(0.0012)[**]	0.0049(0.0007)[**]	0.0120(0.0004)[**]
GDP	−0.0000(0.0000)[**]	0.0000(0.0000)[**]	−0.0000(0.0000)[**]
Population	−0.0000(0.0000)[**]	−0.0000(0.0000)[**]	−0.0000(0.0000)[**]
Interstate war	−0.2378(0.1116)[*]	−0.6856(0.2391)[**]	−0.2985(0.0908)[**]
Civil war	−1.465(0.0638)[**]	−1.037(0.0988)[**]	−1.453(0.0349)[*]
Constant	−0.7241(0.3111)[**]	0.5295(0.0692)[**]	0.0654(0.0724)
Observations	4417	1396	5813

*p<0.05, **p<0.01; regular coefficients Stata 14.0
Instrumental regression. Instrumented: Accession. Included instruments:
Ratification, Polity2, Durability, GDP, Population, Interstate War, and Civil War.
Excluded instruments: Regional Treaty Density, Common Law.

the diverging directionalities and significance across ratification and accession are lost when combining the two actions into one measure of treaty commitment.

The difference of means tests for human rights measures are presented in Table 5.4 and support the findings of the aforementioned statistical analyses. The difference in means between Early Members and Late Members held statistically significant for both accession and ratification actions. Ratification had a larger difference in means between the two state-groups, with a change of 0.32 on the Human Rights Protection Score compared with the accession mean difference of 0.04. Whether or not a state opted in to ICCPR negotiations and was able to ratify the treaty had significant impact on the mean Human Rights Scores.

Exploring the State Interests Counterargument

The aforementioned analyses test the effect of negotiation participation on future human rights practices. An obvious critique of the analysis

Table 5.4 *Tests of the differences of means for accession and ratification of the ICCPR for early and late UN members, 1966–2010*

	Mean for Early Member	Mean for Late Member	Mean Difference	Level of Significance
Accession	0.24	0.20	0.04	<0.001
Ratification	0.03	0.35	0.32	<0.001

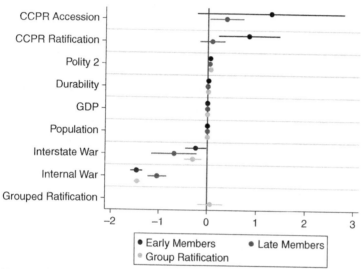

Figure 5.12   Plotted coefficients of Models 1, 2, and 3

could be that it does not test the effect of what happened within negotiations. One might expect states that were able to successfully insert their interests into the treaty to comply differently than states that were less successful in doing so. To explore the depth of negotiations and test the state-interest argument, I analyzed voting data on ICCPR articles, provisions, and amendments from the Third Commission of the UN General Assembly. Votes were open to states beyond those involved in the formal treaty negotiations and concluded before the treaty was opened for signature in 1966. Examining a state's success in actualizing its preferences in the treaty allows me to test the extent to which writing state interest into the treaty affects compliance.

For each of the sixty votes, I coded whether how a state voted aligned with the final vote decision. I then removed the percentage of "unsuccessful votes" from the total number of votes a state participated in to measure the extent to which a state's positions were inserted into the final treaty. The United States tied as the thirteenth-least successful state as measured by how often how it voted against the grain of the majority decision. However, the United States still had its preferences incorporated most of the time. The success rate of the United States was 63 percent. The state with the lowest success rate was Hungary, with its voting preferences reflected in the final decision in 45 percent of its votes. States averaged 77 percent success rates. Of the 117 voting states, sixty-four had at or above-average success rates and fifty-three had below-average success rates.

If a state interest–driven argument about negotiations holds true, we should expect voting alignment to be more informative than negotiation participation when it comes to compliance outcomes. States with above-average rates of vote outcomes would be expected to be more likely to comply with the treaty than states that were less successful in inserting their preferences into the treaty. To test this, I coded states that voted as "successful" (votes aligned with outcomes at/above-average rates) or "unsuccessful" (votes aligned with outcomes at below-average rates). The state coding does not vary over the time analyzed in this study, since these votes concluded prior to the treaty's opening in 1966. Due to the lack of variation in the voting variable over time, I omitted it when testing the voting data as an interaction term with treaty commitment. Instead, I look to the state-group of "successful" states to examine whether they significantly improved human rights practices following treaty commitment. Examining votes more closely allows me to answer whether states that successfully inserted their preferences into the ICCPR complied after committing to it.

In Table 5.5, Models 4 and 5 test the effect of ICCPR commitment on human rights practices by considering whether a state was "successful" or "unsuccessful" in treaty votes. I include the variable Group Ratification, which collapses the accession and ratification variables together to incorporate the general treatment of ratification in the research. I find that "successful" states did not significantly improve human rights practices after commitment. States with above-average rates of success of inserting their preferences into the treaty did not have improved practices following commitment. I find that "unsuccessful" states were significantly likely to have lower Human Rights

Table 5.5 *Fixed-effects analysis of successful and unsuccessful state voting and treaty compliance, 1966–2010*

Human Protection Scores Measure (+ means better rights)

	Model 4 Successful	Model 5 Unsuccessful
Grouped ratification	0.0455(0.0322)	−0.1068(0.0327)[***]
Polity2	0.0496(0.0029)[***]	0.0513(0.0033)[***]
Durability	0.0151(0.0010)[***]	0.0142(0.0013)[***]
GDP	−0.0000(0.0000)	0.0000(0.0000)
Population	0.0000(0.0000)[*]	0.0000(0.0000)[***]
Interstate war	−0.0462(0.0811)	0.0745(0.1005)
Civil war	−0.7142(0.0387)[***]	−0.4274(0.0410)[***]
Constant	−0.3860(0.0265)[***]	−0.1106(0.0410)[***]
Observations	2224	1914
Groups	58	47

Fixed-effects regression run on Stata 14.0 $*p<0.10$, $**p<0.05$, $***p<0.01$; regular coefficients (standard errors)

Scores following commitment. The findings show that successfully inserting their preferences into the treaty was not enough to make states comply with the treaty, but states that were less successful at getting their interests into the treaty may have been sufficiently disgruntled to not work toward improving the rights practices formalized in the treaty. Alternatively, states that were not successful at inserting their preferences into the treaty may demonstrate states against the grain on global human rights norms.

Discussion

This Chapter's findings provide strong support for my argument that involvement in human rights treaty negotiations is an important factor in explaining treaty compliance. States that participated in ICCPR negotiations significantly improved human rights practices following treaty ratification. States that did not avail themselves of the opportunity to negotiate had worse human rights practices when they committed via accession. This pattern did not hold for Late Member States that missed the opportunity to negotiate by joining the United Nations after the fact. For these states, later commitment via accession translated into improved human rights practices. These findings taken together suggest that willingness or unwillingness to participate in human rights negotiations has a real impact on future practices. When testing a state-interest counterargument, I found that above-average success rates in inserting preferences into the ICCPR did not translate into significant improvements in human rights practices. Negotiation participation was a better-supported explanation for human rights improvements than whether states were able to make the final treaty reflect their interests.

Separating out commitment type proved insightful for understanding the likelihood that treaty commitment would result in positive changes. When I separated ratification from accession, I was able to pinpoint the commitment actions' unique effects. This finding pushes back against the general dismissal found in international relations and legal studies of the distinction (and significance) of treaty commitment types. When analyzing the traditional measurement of ratification, which lumped accession with ratification, the statistical significance of commitment disappeared. This null effect of commitment is consistent with other works on human rights treaties that question the merits of treaty commitment for human rights outcomes (e.g., Hathaway 2002; Keith 1999).

Within the broader study of international organizations, these results support prior findings that emphasize socialization's role in human rights, especially the research that points to improved human rights resulting from increased participation in IOs through membership (Greenhill 2010). This chapter demonstrates that engagement through treaty negotiations serves an important role in shaping states' human rights practices.

Evidence of Long-Term Effects of Negotiation Participation

The statistical analyses provided evidence pointing to the important role of participating in treaty negotiations for human rights practices. In this section, I explore negotiation participants' continued rights practices. States negotiating treaties take seriously the terms and obligations they and fellow negotiating states agreed upon. Negotiating states retain interest in preserving and defending the treaty they shaped. I find illustrative evidence that negotiation states continued to support human rights and engage with the international human rights regime long after negotiations concluded. States that negotiated treaties defended the treaties' intent by lodging formal objections when other states issued reservations, seeking to limit their legal obligations to the treaty. Additionally, states that negotiated treaties engaged with treaty body committees.

A first example of positive human rights practices following treaty negotiation is the institutional act of states issuing objections to reserving states. Reservations remove states' legal obligations. Objections are a means for states to question the merit of other states' reservations and defend the object and purpose of treaties (Comstock 2019). If states negotiated and then ratified the ICCPR, they were significantly likely to form objections when other states submitted reservations to the treaty. If states did not participate in ICCPR negotiations and later acceded to the treaty, there was no increased likelihood of forming objections.

Future engagement with the treaty and rights stated within state activity within the Human Rights Committee also illustrates negotiating states' promotion of the treaty they negotiated. As noted earlier, each of the core human rights treaties has a corresponding treaty body, or committee, tasked with monitoring and interpreting its treaty. Committees are tasked with soliciting country reports, monitoring rights practices as they correspond to the treaty, and creating General Comments on the treaty. General Comments "analyze a specific article or general issue in the Covenant in an extended and comprehensive fashion ... as advice to all State parties" (UN OHCHR 2005, 24). Through issuing General Comments, treaty committees offer their interpretation of the obligations and scope of the human rights treaties.

The treaty bodies developed the norm of soliciting responses upon issuing General Comments. The committees seek input and feedback on their interpretations from states parties, NGOs, academia, and other expert groups: "In practice, states rarely put forward their own interpretations of specific rights. They typically base their reports on the interpretations offered by the treaty bodies in General Comments, the reporting guidelines, and the questions provided to them" (Mechlem 2009, 920–922). Despite the overall limited practice of states responding to or contesting the treaty bodies' interpretations of their treaties, I note a pattern of higher response rates from states that negotiated the treaties.

Committee and Responses

Article 28 of the ICCPR established its corresponding treaty body, the Human Rights Committee. With rotating representation from eighteen members, the Human Rights Committee seeks to avoid political bias and aims for diverse representation from state parties to the ICCPR. Article 31 of the ICCPR directs that the Committee "may not include more than one national of the same State" and "consideration should be given to equitable geographical distribution of membership and to the representation of the different forms of civilization and the principal legal systems."

Taking a closer look at the Human Rights Committee's General Comments and states' formal responses to the comments highlights the extended role of negotiating the ICCPR in state behavior. The Human Rights Committee issued its first General Comment in 1981 and as of August 2019 has issued thirty-six in total. The topics of Comments range from general guidance on reporting and states parties' obligations to the treaty to more specific recommendations on the rights of minorities, states of emergency, and torture. States are allowed to submit formal responses to the Committee's General Comments. A pattern emerges in the responses of states that negotiated and ratified the ICCPR of submitting more formal comments than states that did not negotiate and later acceded to the ICCPR.

In 2017, the Human Rights Committee wrote Comment No. 36 on Article 6 of the ICCPR. Article 6 of the treaty covers the "inherent right to life" (ICCPR Article 6(1)). The Article covers capital punishment, the crime of genocide, and the protection of minors and pregnant women from death sentences. The Human Rights Committee applied the right to life to consider enforced disappearances and terminations of pregnancy. The Committee wrote that

> Although State parties may adopt measures designed to regulate terminations of pregnancy, such measures must not result in violation of the right to life of a pregnant woman or her other rights under the Covenant ... parties may not regulate pregnancy or abortion in a manner that runs contrary to their duty to ensure that women do not have to undertake unsafe abortions ... nor introduce humiliating or unreasonably burdensome requirements on women seeking to undergo abortion. (HRC 2017, 2–3)

Following the Human Rights Committee Draft General Comment, twenty-three states submitted formal response comments: eighteen ratified the ICCPR and five acceded. Approximately 80 percent of states that responded had ratified and participated in negotiations. The higher participation rate of negotiating states reveals their tendency to defend the integrity of the treaty's text. Formal responses from negotiating states demonstrate their intent to maintain the wording, scope, and intent of the treaty they had a hand in creating.

The United States argued against what it interpreted as the expansionary interpretation of the ICCPR treaty. The US Congress wrote in a Comment on Draft General Comment No. 36 on Article 6 of the ICCPR that the Human Rights Committee "purport(s) to interpret Article 6 in ways that were proposed and debated by various negotiating delegations, but were excluded from the final text when agreement could not be reached" (US 2017, 3).

> It is a principle of international law that obligations binding sovereign States Parties to a treaty are to be found only within the four corners of the treaty itself, which upon good faith negotiation, signing and due ratification, becomes binding upon them, a principle known as *pacta sunt servanda*. (2)

With the statement, the United States argued against the Human Rights Committee's interpretation of Article 6 of the ICCPR to include the right to abortion. The US Congress argued that the Human Rights Committee sought to "impose obligations beyond what is set forth in the ICCPR" (2).

Australia also negotiated the ICCPR and contested the expansionary interpretation of Comment No. 36 on Article 6 of the ICCPR. Australia's reply to the Comment stated that it "considers that some of the assertions in the draft General Comment do not reflect the legal obligations . . . and, in some cases, extend the obligations of States Parties beyond the law of State responsibility" (UN 2017b). Though illustrative, the aforementioned activities demonstrate the continued presence and engagement of states that negotiated the ICCPR with treaty issues many years after negotiations ended.

Additional Treaty: CEDAW

In Table 5.6 I extend testing the argument that negotiation participation matters for human rights outcomes beyond the ICCPR and look to the CEDAW. The CEDAW offers a treaty comparison across issue areas – from broad rights provisions to more specific targeting of women's rights – and offers examination of a treaty with a shorter negotiation period. While the ICCPR negotiations spanned almost two decades, CEDAW's drafting was closer to five years. The UN Commission on the Status of Women called for a draft convention in 1974, and a draft was completed in 1979. Testing the argument using CEDAW allows me

Table 5.6 *Treaty negotiation and human rights: CEDAW, 1966–2010*

	Human Protection Scores Measure Model 6	(+ Means better rights) Model 7
Human rights lag one year	0.8843(0.0056)***	0.8862(0.0056)***
Ratification	0.1215(0.0668)*	
Accession	−0.1023(0.018)	
Polity2	0.0093(0.0017)***	0.0118(0.0008)***
Durability	0.0019(0.0002)***	0.0018(0.0002)***
GDP	−0.0000(0.0000)***	−0.0000(0.0000)***
Population	−0.0000(0.0000)***	−0.0000(0.0000)***
Interstate war	0.0243(0.0381)	0.0014(0.0380)
Civil war	−0.1771(0.017)***	−0.1659(0.0154)***
Constant	−0.0790(0.0305)***	−0.0018(0.0155)
Number of observations	4238	4238

Instrumental Variable regression *p<0.10, **p<0.05, ***p<0.01; regular coefficients Stata 14.0.Instrumented: CEDAW Ratification, CEDAW Accession. Included instruments: lagged dependent variable Polity2, Durability, GDP, Population, Interstate War, Internal War. Excluded instruments: Ratification, Rules, Regional ICCPR Density, Common law tradition.

to test whether involvement in shorter negotiation periods has a positive effect on rights outcomes similar to the prolonged interaction during extended treaty negotiations.

What I find is strong, positive support for my argument. In Models 6 and 7, I look to treaty commitment types to offer measures of negotiation participation. The commitment distinction between states that ratified and participated in negotiations from states that acceded and did not negotiate held important. When states ratified CEDAW, they had a significant and positive improvement (0.12) on the Human Rights Protection Scores. States that acceded to CEDAW had a negative, non-significant, relationship with the Human Rights Protection Scores. When run without the lagged dependent variable, the results of Models 4–6 held consistent. When the CEDAW models were run with women's rights–focused dependent variables from the CIRI database, the findings also held.

Conclusion

I began this chapter by detailing how commitment though accession differed from ratification and describing what states participated using accession. I then examined substantive and analytical differences between the two commitment types to test the effect of negotiation involvement on human rights behavior. I argued that two elements of accession were important to human rights practices: the relationship between accession and nonparticipation in treaty negotiation and the relationship between accession and later participation in the treaty.

Using data from 1966 to 2010 and focusing on the ICCPR and CEDAW treaties, I demonstrated a significant difference in human rights practices following ratification and accession. This supported my argument that involvement in treaty negotiations mattered for future human rights practices. States that acceded to the ICCPR and CEDAW and opted out of negotiation participation had no significant improvement in human rights following commitment.

The findings are important for scholars of international law, institutional design, and policymakers to consider. The involvement or lack of involvement in treaty-making determined what legal action states could use and affected how they complied with the treaty following commitment. This early involvement and commitment seem to be a key part of understanding what factors influence state behavioral change. States that were not interested in treaty drafting and negotiations demonstrated a lack of interest and investment that carried over after commitment. Despite the noted difficulties that come with more states at the table during negotiations, my findings point to the importance of including states in drafting human rights treaties.

International human rights law scholars' tendency to combine accession with ratification and their explicit assumption that the two actions are indistinguishable obscures the differential effects each commitment action has on human rights practices. This chapter demonstrates the importance of studying accession commitment separately from ratification commitment to understand how the path incorporating negotiation differed in outcome from the path rejecting negotiation.

6

Succession

New States, Old Laws, and Legitimacy

In the Human Rights Committee, General Comment No. 26(61), the Committee referred to human rights agreements as enshrining rights that "belong to the people . . . once the people are accorded the protection of the rights . . . such protection devolves with territory and continues to belong to them, notwithstanding . . . State succession"

UN Human Rights Council

Introduction

At midnight on January 1, 1993, the division of the Czech Republic and Slovakia came into effect. Amid cheering in the Slovak Capital of Bratislava, Slovakian Prime Minister Vladimir Meciar declared, "Two states have been established. Living together in one state is over. Living together in two states continues." ("Czechoslovakia Breaks in Two, To Wide Regret," New York Times, January 1, 1993). Thus, it marked the dissolution of Czechoslovakia after almost seventy-five years as a united country.

Despite warnings from the international community of diplomatic isolation, on December 24, 1990, Slovenes overwhelmingly voted in favor of independence from Yugoslavia with an estimated 94.5 percent supporting independence and 90 percent voter turnout ("Slovenes Vote Decisively for Independence From Yugoslavia," New York Times, December 24, 1990). In 1991, Slovenia and Croatia formally declared independence from Yugoslavia.

On September 1, 1993, the new Government of Bosnia and Herzegovina wrote to the secretary-general of the United Nations to say that it considered itself bound "by virtue of succession to the Socialist Federal Republic of Yugoslavia (SFRY) in respect of the territory of the Republic of Bosnia and Herzegovina" when "Bosnia and

Herzegovina assumed responsibility for its international relations" (UN 1993).

All of the discussed new states confronted political, economic, cultural, and other uncertainty as they embarked on independence. They also faced the legal question of what to do with predecessor state treaty commitments. When new states emerge, what happens to old legal obligations? New states have the option at the United Nations to commit through succession to existing human rights treaties. Upon Slovenia's declaration of independence, its Prime Minister Lojze Peterle promised that "independent Slovenia will uphold all international agreements signed by Yugoslavia and that the new state will erect no barriers to the movement of goods, transport or people."[1] In fact, Slovenia specifically included in its declaration of independence a part pertaining to its international legal responsibilities. Section IV pledges that Slovenia will

> respect all the principles of international law and, in the spirit of legal succession, the provisions of all international contracts signed by Yugoslavia and which apply to the territory of the Republic of Slovenia.

State succession within the international system has significant effects on people's lives, international relations, and international legal systems. However, for the most part, state succession "may not have seemed a topic worthy of detailed analysis" (Tams 2016, 315). Instead, during transition periods, political scientists focused on fundamental changes accompanying regime change, and on democratization in particular. Existing research did not differentiate between ratification and succession commitment types when analyzing commitment timing and influence on human rights treaties.

Research on new states within the international system has long focused on regime transitions, power transitions, and the interconnected relationships between democratization, human rights, conflict, and peace. International relations research has especially been interested in transitions toward democracy. Scholars link economic development with the emergence of democracies (Boix and Stokes 2003) and with sustaining democracy following regime transitions (Przeworski et al. 2000). Democratic Peace Theory scholarship highlights the importance of transitions toward democracy in reducing the likelihood of war (e.g., Ward

---

[1] "Slovenia, Croatia Declare Freedom from Yugoslavia: Balkans: Federal Parliament reacts angrily and orders the army to 'prevent the division' of the nation." June 26, 1991. available www.latimes.com/archives/la-xpm-1991-06-26-mn-1188-story.html.

and Gleditsch 1998) and the relationship between democracy and human rights (e.g., Guilhot 2005).

Human rights scholarship emphasizes the relationship between democratization and human rights in particular. Kim and Sikkink (2010) examine justice in transitional countries, finding that human rights prosecutions after transition contribute to improvements in human rights. Democratizing states are more likely to join international human rights institutions (Hafner-Burton, Mansfield, and Pevehouse 2015) and more have improvements in rights practices following treaty commitment (Hathaway 2002; Hafner-Burton and Tsutsui 2005, 2007; Simmons 2009) than states not democratizing.

The specific and deliberate study of treaty succession has primarily been within monetary issue areas and through qualitative analysis. Scholars focusing on the legal and technical complexities arising when new states enter the global treaty system have predominantly concentrated on the economic and financial fallout of state division, not on human rights practices.

However, the regime-change focus has not specifically considered the lasting legal obligations. Academics and diplomats acknowledge succession is a highly complex issue. Tams, for example, refers to state succession as "one of the more technical and controversial areas of general international law" (2016, 314). International legal and economic scholars examining new-state emergence and replacement focus on tangible and divisible aspects related to state dissolution and replacement: monetary obligations and assets. Williams (1994) examined state succession and international financial institutions, focusing on International Monetary Fund (IMF) and World Bank memberships, payment, obligations, and assets following the dissolution of the former SFRY. Dumberry (2018) examined state succession and bilateral investment treaty (BIT) obligations and found that international tribunals held new states to the predecessor state agreements. For example, a 1989 Canada-Union of Soviet Socialist Republics (USSR) BIT was binding on Kazakhstan (446) after the USSR no longer existed.

This chapter bridges the foundations across the discussed literatures, highlighting the importance of new-state emergence, regime change, and the legal consequences of commitment through succession. In this chapter, I ask whether states that recommit to human rights treaties through succession and have undergone substantial identity-changing transformations improve human rights practices following treaty recommitment. I also compare states that succeeded to international law, replacing a predecessor state's existing legal commitments, to states that are enacting binding commitment to human rights treaties for the first time through ratification. As discussed in Chapter 2, existing quantitative scholarship exploring commitment and compliance trends in international human rights treaties have not disentangled succession from ratification because both are binding commitment types. Without this disentangling, we miss the opportunity to understand how re-emergence within the international arena and the process of reassessing and recommitting to human rights law shapes states' human rights practices. I argue that succession states use the legal act of recommitting to human rights treaties to (1) legitimize new states and (2) re-establish international relationships. I argue that despite substantial overlap between succession states and regime change, the unique dimension of legal-identity shift merits a closer look into succession. This distinction narrows in on variation yet to be examined in either international law scholarship or international relations scholarship focused on democratization: not all regime changes are significant, but new state identities are.

This chapter makes two central contributions. The first is to distinguish extreme regime transitions and state emergence in explanations of human rights behavior. The second is to unpack a rare yet important type of treaty commitment, succession, often overlooked in international legal and international relations research. In so doing, this chapter deepens our understanding of the processes behind legal commitment and the processes underlying regime change and human rights practices.

I begin by detailing the legal definition of treaty succession and differentiate this commitment action from treaty ratification. Next, I argue that succession states use treaty commitment as a means to legitimate a new state and to maintain, repair, and re-establish relationships with international organizations and other states that may have suffered during the conflict period leading up to independence. I draw hypotheses about expected relationships with human rights following succession. I then introduce a possible alternative argument that succession states are likely to have lower levels of compliance and declining human rights practices after commitment through succession due to the instability of their new state. I test the competing arguments by examining the International Covenant on Civil and Political Rights (ICCPR). I find that states committing via succession have significant improvements in human rights practices following commitment, trends that do not consistently hold for other state types. Finally, I take a closer look into the case study of the Czech Republic and Slovakia following dissolution.

The case illustrates how new states understand treaty succession as signaling independence and legitimacy. Focusing on the Czech Republic and Slovakia also follows the divergent commitment and compliance path of new states on democratization. The findings contribute to our understanding about new states, regime change, and the legitimating role of international organizations within the international system.

What Is Treaty Succession?

Treaty succession is arguably one of the more complex concepts and actions within international law. Upon studying succession of postcolonial African states, Maluwa famously wrote of trying to understand the concept and practice of succession that "the international lawyer seeking a way out of this marshland is as likely as ever to be led into the centre of the miry bog itself" (1992, 810). In its simplest form, treaty succession entails a state taking on the obligations of its predecessor state. Legal definitions and directives relating to treaty succession are grounded in the Vienna Convention on Succession of States in Respect of Treaties of 1978 and the Vienna Convention on Succession of States in respect of State Property, Archives and Debts of 1983. The Vienna Convention on Succession of States in Respect of Treaties of 1978 expanded on the earlier Vienna Convention on the Law of Treaties (VCLT) of 1969. The updated treaty devoted an entire agreement to a recognized new phenomenon within international law: succession of states. Situated within the "profound transformation of the international community brought about by the decolonization process" while recognizing that "other factors may lead to cases of succession of states in the future,"[2] the international community codified expectations surrounding state succession. The treaty defines succession of states as "the replacement of one State by another in the responsibility for international relations of territory" (Article 2(b)).

Hafner and Novak (2012) succinctly lay out a taxonomy of state political succession, writing that states arrive at treaty succession through seven paths. Not all of these paths constitute a fundamental shift in a state's legal identity, meaning that some practical cases of political succession do not result in treaty succession. The seven scenarios of political succession are the creation of newly independent

---

[2] Vienna Convention on the Succession of States in Respect of Treaties of 1978 preamble (2), available at http://legal.un.org/ilc/texts/instruments/english/conventions/3_2_1978.pdf.

states, cession of territory, state incorporation into another state, annexation of territory understood as the "forcible acquisition of territory," consensual state merger, separation wherein one group separates from an existing state to form a new state, and dissolution where new states separate and the old state framework ceases to exist (403–406).

In this section, I cover the important fundamentals of treaty succession by (1) underscoring that succession is not an automatic process in international law, (2) explaining the effect of entry into force (EIF) timing on whether commitment will be through succession or accession, (3) addressing the question of continuity of reservations and other post-commitment actions, (4) addressing the relationship between succession and regime change, (5) speaking to the unique relationship between human rights issues and application of succession, and (6) visually depicting patterns of succession over time.

Not an Automatic Process

The two extremes of interpreting new states' legal obligations are the clean-slate doctrine and the universal succession theory. The so-called clean-slate or *tabula rasa* doctrine conceptualizes a succession process wherein a new state is "absolutely free of any of the obligations that bound its predecessor" (Hafner and Novak 2012, 401). On the other end of the spectrum is the theory of universal succession, also referred to as the theory of continuity or complete succession, which assumes that new states "inherited all the treaty rights and obligations of the former power in so far as they had been applicable to the territory before independence" (Aust 2000, 372).

The United Nations has typically leaned toward a clean-slate approach. The standard and expectation concerning multilateral treaty law is that treaty succession is not an automatic process upon a new state attaining power. Rather, the new state must willingly and actively (as opposed to passively) consent to being bound to treaties previously ratified by the predecessor state. However, the United Nations does apply the continuity theory approach to prior treaties stipulating the recognition of physical boundaries. This is not the case concerning bilateral treaties, wherein the norm is for automatic succession commitment upon new state emergence (Hafner and Novak 2012, 423). There are also differing interpretations of human rights treaties, specifically, which will be addressed later.

Concerning multilateral treaties, upon the significant change in legal identity between predecessor and successor state, treaty obligations lapse until commitment via succession occurs. New states must actively take on the previous state's prior international legal obligations, as the following excerpts illustrate.

> The obligations or rights of a predecessor State under treaties in force in respect of a territory at the date of a succession of States do not become the obligations or rights of the successor State towards other States Parties to those treaties by reason only of the fact that the predecessor State and the successor State have concluded an agreement providing that such obligations or rights shall devolve upon the successor State. (Article 8(2))
>
> Treaties of the predecessor State cease to be in force in respect of the territory to which the succession of States relates from the date of succession of States. (Article 15(a))
>
> The operation of the treaty shall be considered as suspended as between the newly independent State and the other parties to the treaty until the date of making of the notification of succession. (Article 23(2))
>
> A newly independent state may also exercise . . . any right provided in the treaty to withdraw or modify any consent expressed. (Article 21(2))

A successor state may "have the option to consider itself a party to the treaty" (Article 10(1)) and choose to recommit, only to be considered as such "if the successor State expressly accepts in writing to be so considered" (Article 10(2)). Multilateral treaties may also be considered as applied provisionally until full consent is given (Article 27(1)).

Once the successor state has decided to recommit to a treaty, it must notify the UN depository in writing of its decision and commitment: "A newly independent State may, by a notification of succession, establish its status as a party to any multilateral treaty which at the date of the succession of States was in force in respect of the territory to which the succession of States relates" (Article 17(1)). The other parties to the treaty are made aware, through notifications sent by the depositary, of the new succession commitment (Article 22(4)).

It is helpful to observe the overall legal trends in treaty succession, given its relative rarity. Figure 6.1 plots all UN succession actions from 1945 to 2010, inclusive of all treaty issue areas, against the annual count of new members to the United Nations. The first notable spikes in treaty succession occurred during the 1960s and early 1970s, coinciding with the decolonization process. The next set of spikes occurred during the

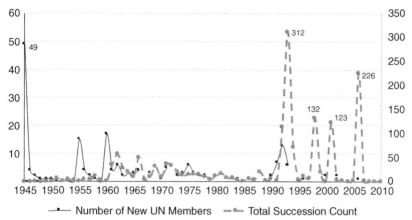

Figure 6.1   Total annual succession counts to all UN treaties, 1945–2010

1990s, coinciding with the end of the Cold War. The largest succession commitment activity occurred in 1993, with 312 successions in that year. The second highest level of succession activity occurred in 2006, with 226. The total annual count of treaty succession roughly corresponds to the annual count of new members added to the United Nations. New member activity tracks with spikes in treaty succession, reflecting the emergence of many new members through state succession circumstances and their interest in quickly addressing issues of international legal obligation.

Entry into Force

A treaty's EIF status may determine whether succession states commit via succession or are considered a contracting state. If a predecessor state signed a multilateral treaty, the newly independent state "may ratify, accept or approve the treaty as if it had signed that treaty and may thereby become a party or a contracting State to it" (Article 19(1)). In both scenarios, the succession state must actualize commitment to the treaty in question and not fall back on the predecessor state's prior commitments.

The question of EIF is of particular interest when addressing human rights treaties. Because UN human rights treaty EIF requires a specified threshold of ratifications, EIF is frequently delayed years beyond treaty creation.

Reservations

An evident legal question when considering the transfer of treaty obligations is this: What happens to the reservations and other legal qualifications made by a predecessor state upon new state succession?
Reservations stand as legal and applicable unless the succession state
actively removes and withdraws existing reservations.

> When a newly independent State establishes its status as a party or as
> a contract State to a multilateral treaty by a notification of succession . . .
> (it) shall be considered as maintaining any reservation to that treaty which
> was applicable at the date of the succession of States. (Article 20(1))

Succession states are afforded the opportunity to submit new reservations
and other treaty actions upon succession, subject to the same restrictions of
original parties articulated within the VCLT (Article 20(2)).

Regime Change

Scholars usually write about treaty succession as accompanying regime
change; many former Soviet states, for example, underwent democratization around the time of treaty succession. However significant the overlap between regime change and succession, regime change alone does not
constitute state succession or set into motion the international legal
norms and expectation of state succession. Tams notes that "state succession needs to be distinguished from changes that do not affect the legal
personality of the State . . . (If) legal personality of the State remains the
same, so do its treaty rights and obligations" (2016, 319). Hathaway
echoes this distinction.

> Changes in government no matter how radical they may be (for
> example, from autocracy to democracy) and no matter how they are
> accomplished (by legal or violent means), do not affect the legal obliga-
> tions of the state. Only the absorption of the state into another or the
> dissolution of the state into separate entities can override the principle of
> continuity. (2008, 128)

Regime transitions to socialism, for example, were "excluded from the
scope of the draft articles problems of succession" and held to prior
obligations in lieu of a "clean slate" within international law (Marek
1968; Hafner and Novak 2012, 401). Looking to human rights, when
the International Court of Justice (ICJ) considered obligations to the UN
Convention on the Elimination of All Forms of Racial Discrimination

(CERD), it referred to Georgia as "the State continuing the legal personality of the Union of Soviet Socialist Republics" (2008, 353).

Human Rights Treaty Succession

Generally, international legal scholars regard the issue area of human rights as distinctive within international law due to the inapplicability of the concept of reciprocity (Posner 2013). Within this distinct fold of international law, treaty succession adds an additional layer of legal complexity. The United Nations has generally taken the approach of allowing new states to decide which treaties to commit to following state succession. There is a fine-grained and important difference to the interpretation of succession states' human rights obligations.

The succession of human rights treaties is of particular interest and importance due to the circumstances through which many cases of state succession occur: political instability, violence, and, often, widespread violation of human rights. Scholars recognize the unique importance of human rights and their capability to transcend political changes in identity. Hafner and Novak note the numerous human rights violations that occurred during the breakup of the SFRY and the legal questions directed at the applicability of treaties during the transition period (2012, 421). Kamminga argued that "individuals residing within a given territory therefore remain entitled to the rights granted to them under a human rights treaty. They cannot be deprived of the protection of these rights by virtue of the fact that another State has assumed responsibility for the territory in which they find themselves" (1996, 481–482).

However elevated the importance of maintaining human rights during difficult transition periods may be, a tension exists between the clean-slate and continuity theories. International tribunals and regional human rights bodies have upheld standards of continuity of rights coverage. Judge Christopher Weeramantry, for example, wrote in an opinion for the ICJ that

> without automatic succession to such as Convention, we would have a situation where the worldwide system of human rights protections continually generates gaps in the most vital part of its framework, which open up and close, depending on the breakup of the old political authorities and the emergence of the new. (1996, 654–655)

While the legal commitment and obligations from the treaty no longer formally obligate the successor state to human rights standards, the human rights standards have, since the predecessor's commitment, become embedded within customary international law. In the UN International Criminal Tribunal for the former Yugoslavia (ICTY) case *Prosecutor v. Delacic et al.* (2001), the ICTY deliberated over whether Bosnian Serbs detained in the Čelebići Camp were protected under the Geneva Conventions. The ICTY Appeals concluded that it was "in no doubt that State succession has no impact on obligations arising out from these fundamental humanitarian conventions" (112–113). The successor states are bound to customary international law human rights standards without, or prior to, new state commitment via treaty succession.

On the interpretive end closer to the clean-slate ideal, the international community recognizes the need for states to actively and willingly adopt new commitment to international human rights law. This legal interpretation recognizes new state autonomy to make international legal decisions and its international legal personality but does not remove expectations of adhering to human rights standards during this transitional period. Gaeta concludes that for litigation purposes, "the consent of new states is required . . . whether they have as a substantive matter succeeded to the responsibility of their predecessor or not" (2009, 493). Rasulov (2003) finds that succession states do not treat humanitarian law succession as automatic.

Taken together, the international community may recognize the continuity of rights connected to individuals but not be able to hold new states accountable for the violation of these rights.

Patterns of Succession

Figures 6.2 to 6.4 visualize patterns of treaty succession across time (Figure 6.2), human rights treaties (Figure 6.3), and as compared with ratification (Figure 6.4). Figure 6.2 reveals several succession spikes since 1966. The largest annual count of human rights treaty succession came in 1993, with thirty-one successions. The next largest spikes came in 2006 with fifteen, and 2001 with nine. Low but sustained treaty succession occurred during the 1970s. Comparing Figure 6.2 with Figure 6.1, which plots succession to all treaty issue areas, makes it clear that because of the later creation of core human rights treaties, the first set of decolonization successions was not as substantial. These states, for the most part, were able to commit to the core human rights treaties as original parties. In Figure 6.3, I compare the counts of succession versus counts of ratification of the core nine UN human rights treaties. Unsurprisingly, the treaties created after 1990 (Convention on the Rights of Persons with Disabilities and the International Convention for the

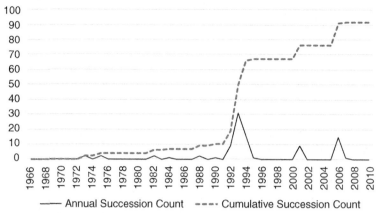

Figure 6.2 Annual and cumulative human rights treaty succession counts, 1966–2010

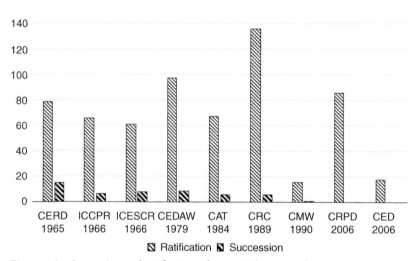

Figure 6.3 Succession and ratification of core UN human rights treaties, 1966–2010

Protection of All Persons from Enforced Disappearance) have the fewest treaty successions. Since these two treaties were created after the largest spike in state succession, new states within the international system were able to commit through signature followed by ratification or accession. The treaty with the highest succession count is the CERD. Figure 6.4 indicates an overall decline in the use of succession by treaty creation timing. The

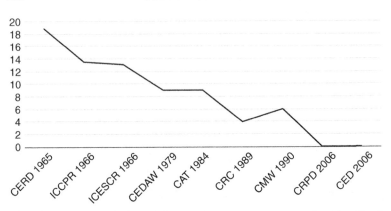

Figure 6.4   Core UN human rights treaty succession as proportion of ratification, 1966–2010

figure tracks the proportion of successions to ratifications across the core human rights treaties.

Who Succeeds to International Law?

The first state to commit to a UN treaty through succession was Cambodia, when it succeeded to the International Opium Convention on October 19, 1951. Since then, states committed to UN treaties through succession 1,543 times across all treaty issue areas and 54 times to the nine core human rights treaties. Although succession is the smallest category of treaty commitment and least frequently used action, succession constitutes hundreds of commitments over time.

In this section, I take a closer look into which states are succeeding to international human rights law. I focus on the phenomena of decolonization and post–Cold War events contributing to the emergence of increased treaty succession. Table 6.1 lists the fourteen states that have succeeded to UN human rights treaties. Montenegro had the highest succession count, with thirteen human rights treaties. Other former Soviet states and former Yugoslav republics topped the list. Island nations constituted the lower bounds of the succession list. St. Lucia and Suriname only succeeded to one human rights treaty each. Table 6.2 lists the human rights treaties that have been committed to through succession. The CERD, Genocide Convention, and the Convention on the Rights of the Child (CRC) had the highest succession counts.

Table 6.1 *UN human rights treaties succession states*

Human rights treaty successor states	Treaty succession count	Core human rights treaties	Core human rights treaty optional protocols
Montenegro	13	6	5
Czech Republic	11	6	1
Bosnia and Herzegovina	10	6	
Croatia	10	6	
Slovakia	10	6	1
The Former Yugoslav Republic of Macedonia	9	6	
Yugoslavia	9	6	
Slovenia	8	5	
Antigua and Barbuda	2	1	
Bahamas	2	1	
Fiji	2	1	
Solomon Islands	2	2	
Saint Lucia	1	1	
Suriname	1	1	

Two prominent processes contributed to state succession trends within the modern international system: (1) decolonization and (2) the end of the Cold War, paired with the collapse of the Soviet Union.

Decolonization

During the 1960s and 1970s a wave of decolonization resulted in newly independent states across Africa and Asia. Nations that had previously been controlled by European colonial powers were now recognized as sovereign states. In 1960, the UN General Assembly adopted the Declaration on the Granting of Independence to Colonial Country and Peoples Between. The Declaration recognized that "all peoples have an inalienable right to complete freedom, the exercise of their sovereignty,

Table 6.2 *Human rights treaties with succession commitments*

Human rights treaty name	Succession count	Core human rights treaty
Convention on the Elimination of All forms of Racial Discrimination	14	X
Convention on the Rights of the Child	11	X
Convention on the Prevention and Punishment of the Crime of Genocide	10	
International Covenant on Economic, Social and Cultural Rights	9	X
International Covenant on Civil and Political Rights	8	X
Convention on the Elimination of All Forms of Discrimination against Women	8	X
Convention on the Non-applicability of Statutory Limitations to War Crimes and Crimes against Humanity	8	
International Convention on the Suppression and Punishment of the Crime of Apartheid	8	
Convention against Torture	7	X
International Convention against Apartheid in Sports	5	

and the integrity of their national territory" and proclaimed the "necessity of bringing to a speedy and unconditional end colonialism in all its forms" (UN 1960).[3]

Between 1950 and 1975, the United Nations admitted eighty-two new members, many of which were newly independent from European colonial powers. There was great diversity across the decolonization experience, with some new states emerging through peaceful transitions (via the UN Trusteeship Agreements) and others emerging through violent conflict (e.g., Algeria, Democratic Republic of the Congo, Kenya, and Zimbabwe), for whom "The forms of violence that characterized colonial rule and the anti-colonial struggles 'haunt' politics and violence . . . even today" (Campbell 2013, 1). Once independent, some new states established stable governments and institutions from the onset (e.g., Ghana) and others underwent state-building amid institutional turmoil (e.g., Mauritania). Freedom House wrote, "Mauritanians have never been permitted to choose their representatives or change their government in open, competitive elections" (1999). The fruits of independence greatly varied for new states.

Through Chapter XII of the United Nations Charter, the United Nations established the International Trusteeship System to "promote the political, economic, social, and educational advancement of the inhabitants of the trust territories, and their progressive development towards self-government or independence" as well as "to encourage respect for human rights and for fundamental freedoms" (United Nations Charter Article 76 (b and c)). After successfully transitioning eleven trustee states to independence or voluntary incorporation within other states, the UN Security Council disbanded the International Trusteeship System. UNSC Resolution 956 declared "that the objectives of the Trusteeship Agreement have been fully attained, and that the applicability of the Trusteeship Agreement has terminated" (S/RES/956(1994)).

Both Micronesia and Palau proclaimed legal autonomy over their treaty commitments upon termination of their Trusteeship Agreements. Each state considered a range of commitment options while reassessing prior commitments. Palau, for example, wrote

> with regard to multilateral treaties previously applied, the Government of the Republic of Palau intends to review each of them individually and to communicate to the depositary in each case what steps it wishes to take,

---

[3] UNGA Resolution 1514(XV) December 14, 1960.

whether by way of confirmation of termination, confirmation of succession or accession. (UN 1994)

According to the UN's website, as of 2019 there are currently seventeen non-self-governing territories (NSGTs) that "remain to be decolonized, home to nearly 2 million people. Therefore, the process of decolonization is not complete." If and when the NSGTs transition to independent states, they will likely undergo the succession process in international affairs, including deciding whether to adopt prior state legal commitments through treaty succession.

In 1988, the UN General Assembly declared 1990 as the beginning of the International Decade for the Eradication of Colonialism. With island nations and African nations in mind, the United Nations marked the upcoming thirtieth anniversary of the 1960 Declaration by recommitting to eliminating colonization. Most member states voiced support for the United Nation's renewed focus on decolonization; former colonial powers, however, were less enthusiastic. The United Kingdom wrote a formal statement in reaction to the General Assembly Declaration:

> As far as Britain and the few remaining British Non-Self-Governing Territories are concerned, the colonial era is over. The peoples of those Territories enjoy a status which conforms to their wishes their choice is to maintain their links with Britain. The proposed International Decade for the Eradication of Colonialism is therefore irrelevant to them. The British Government sees no need for such a Decade, nor for time and resources to be devoted to drawing up an action plan as envisaged in paragraph 2 of resolution 43/47. (UN 1989, 23)

Former British colonies of Egypt, Canada, Australia, India, Solomon Islands, Sudan, and New Zealand all expressed their unwavering support for the 1990 Declaration. Canada remarked that "The eradication of colonialism since the 1950s has been one of the greatest achievements of the UN" (UN 1989, 7). The decolonization process dramatically reshaped the global system by freeing states from colonial powers and reintroducing them as sovereign states.

End of the Cold War and the Collapse of the Soviet Union

The tensions between the United States and Soviet Union during the Cold War, along with the restructuring of the international system following its end, considerably affected treaty succession. The greatest treaty succession activity occurred in the early 1990s following the collapse of the Soviet Union. However, not all of the new states pursued treaty succession, demonstrating that it is not an automatic process for new states.

The dissolution of the Soviet Union resulted in fifteen newly independent states: Armenia, Moldova, Estonia, Latvia, Lithuania, Georgia, Azerbaijan, Tajikistan, Kyrgyzstan, Belarus, Uzbekistan, Turkmenistan, Ukraine, Kazakhstan, and Russia. However, these states did not commit to human rights treaties (or other UN treaties) through succession. Prior to the dissolution of the Soviet Union, these states demonstrated international legal independence. For example, Belarus participated in ICCPR negotiations. Ukraine signed the ICCPR in 1968 and ratified it in 1973. The United Nations recognized many former Soviet states' membership prior to the Soviet Union's dissolution.

Several of the new states that emerged from the Soviet Union that were not previously recognized as independent UN member states took an interesting approach to treaty law by explicitly eschewing succession. Specifically, Estonia, Latvia, and Lithuania did not interpret their treaty obligations or political realities as fitting into the succession designation. The Baltic States "had been annexed unlawfully by the Soviet Union in 1940, when they regained their independence in 1991, they did not regard themselves as successor states to the Soviet Union, but as states which had regained their sovereignty" (Aust 2000, 377).

Estonia, Latvia, and Lithuania all communicated with the United Nations their rejection of treaty succession. The Chairman of the Supreme Council of the Republic of Estonia wrote a letter to the UN secretary-general on October 8, 1991, stating,

> Estonia does not regard itself as party by virtue of the doctrine of treaty succession to any bilateral or multilateral treaties entered into by the U.S.S.R. The Republic of Estonia has begun careful review of multilateral treaties in order to determine those to which it wishes to become a party. In this regard it will act on a case-by-case basis in exercise of its own sovereign right in the name of the Republic of Estonia. (UN Treaty Collection, 2019)[4]

In a letter addressed to the secretary-general on February 26, 1993, the Minister of Foreign Affairs of Latvia wrote that "Latvia does not regard

---

[4] UN Treaty Collection, "Estonia, Note 1," available at https://treaties.un.org/pages/HistoricalInfo.aspx?clang=_en#Estonia

itself as party by virtue of the doctrine of treaty succession to any bilateral or multilateral treaties entered into by the former USSR."[5]

Similarly, Lithuania denounced the idea of succession to USSR treaties. The Permanent Representative of Lithuania to the United Nations sent the following correspondence to the secretary-general on June 23, 1995:

> ... The Republic of Lithuania was occupied by the USSR on the 15th of June 1940. Many Western countries did not recognize the incorporation of the Republic of Lithuania into the USSR. Having restored its independence on the 11th of March 1990, the Republic of Lithuania neither is nor can be the successor state of the former USSR. The Republic of Lithuania cannot take the responsibility for the treaties concluded by the former USSR, for it neither participated in making those treaties nor influenced them. Therefore the Republic of Lithuania cannot take the responsibility for the past treaties concluded by the USSR.[6]

These examples demonstrate that the path through treaty succession is a deliberate and chosen one. Estonia, Latvia, and Lithuania did not view prior USSR treaty commitment as legitimate obligations because they did not view USSR control as legitimate. These states chose not to pursue recommitment through extension, which would have signified legal extension of prior obligations.

Yugoslavia

New states that were once part of the Federal People's Republic of Yugoslavia (FPRY) took the common approach of treaty succession to international treaty commitment. The FPRY fragmented into Bosnia and Herzegovina, Croatia, Macedonia, Montenegro, Serbia, and Slovenia.

Bosnia and Herzegovina, Croatia, Macedonia, Montenegro, and Slovenia all succeeded to treaties previously committed to by the FPRY. Treaty succession was a conscious and deliberate legal decision for each state. Slovenia, for example, performed a review of existing treaty obligations. It notified the United Nations that it "examined 55 multilateral treaties for which [the secretary-General of the UN] ... has assumed the depositary functions .... [T]he Republic of Slovenia considers to be bound by these treaties by virtue of succession to the SFR Yugoslavia in respect of the territory of the Republic of Slovenia ..." Maintaining

---

[5] UN Treaty Collection, "Latvia, Note 1," available at https://treaties.un.org/Pages/HistoricalInfo.aspx?clang=_en#Latvia.

[6] UN Treaty Collection, "Lithuania, Note 1," available at https://treaties.un.org/Pages/HistoricalInfo.aspx?clang=_en#Lithuania.

commitment to international human rights law was so important to Slovenia that the new state wrote international succession into its declaration of independence. Section 4 of the Declaration of Independence asserts Slovenia's commitment to "respect all the principles of international law and, in the spirit of legal succession, the provisions of all international contracts signed by Yugoslavia."[7]

For its part, Montenegro vowed "faithfully to perform and carry out the stipulations" within the treaties it succeeded to (UN 2002, xi), and Serbia wrote to the UN secretary-general on June 16, 2006, that

> the Republic of Serbia continues to exercise its rights and honour its commitments deriving from international treaties concluded by Serbia and Montenegro. Therefore, the Ministry of Foreign Affairs requests that the Republic of Serbia be considered a party to all international agreements in force, instead of Serbia and Montenegro.[8]

Though once all bound by FPRY international legal commitments, the states that emerged as new, independent states formally examined and approached treaty obligations independently. Announcing their succession and human rights commitment was an important action for these states.

Treaty Succession and International Legitimation

I argue that as new states emerge within the global arena, they are inherently interested in gaining international legitimacy. More recent international relations discussion has appraised the legitimacy of international institutions (Buchanan and Keohane 2006) and international law (Bodansky 2008; Wheatley 2010). The most basic international relations understanding of legitimacy is a state's "right to rule" (Buchanan and Keohane 2006, 405). This understanding echoes fundamental conceptions of statehood as maintaining the "monopoly of legitimate force" (Weber 2008, 156).

Treaty succession offers a relatively immediate communication device for new states to signal their commitment to recognized human rights standards as well as their commitment to operating within the established frameworks of international law. Because of new states' desire (and

---

[7] Slovenia Declaration of Independence, available at www.slovenija2001.gov.si/10years/path/documents/declaration/.

[8] UN Treaty Collection, "Serbia, Note 1," available at https://treaties.un.org/Pages/HistoricalInfo.aspx?clang=_en#Serbia.

need) to gain external legitimation and because of the emergence of regimes in the modern era coinciding with democratization, I argue that treaty succession will lead to improvements in human rights practices. Treaty succession culminates in improvements in human rights through the following process: (1) new states seeking international legitimation and aid, (2) use treaty law as a means of demonstrating sovereign power, and thus (3) human rights treaty succession signals to the international community that new states recognize and respect established human rights norms. I discuss these steps later.

IOs and International Law as Legitimators

New states in the international system seek legitimation and recognition of their independence. During this period, they look toward international organizations and international law as legitimizers. Wight defines international legitimacy as "the collective judgement of international society about rightful membership of the family of nations" (1972, 1). He further describes international legitimacy as "moral acceptability ... to the remainder of international society" (1). Early on, scholars recognized international organizations' – and specifically the United Nation's – legitimation function (Claude 1966). Claude wrote of international organizations as "custodians of the seals of international approval and disapproval" (1966, 371–372). States alter their behavior to conform to other states and international organizations' expectations as a means to seek international legitimation.

Finnemore and Sikkink argue that norm adoption during the cascade process is explained by "a combination of pressure for conformity, desire to enhance international legitimation, and the desire of state leaders to enhance their self-esteem" (1998, 896). Hurd (1999) connects the concept of international legitimacy to compliance. Unique from self-interest and coercion-based explanations, states' belief that norms and/or institutions are legitimate compels compliance. The legitimacy that states bestow upon international organizations has spillover effects, transferring legitimacy to states recognized as members of and participants within international organizations. Greenhill (2014) argues that states' human rights practices improve with increased international governmental organization (IGO) membership, converging their practices with their membership partners. This finding holds for IGOs not explicitly connected to human rights, indicating that normative socialization occurs across membership (3). As states identify human rights norms privileged across IGO membership, these international organ-izations themselves become identified as representing shared views and practices of human rights.

New States, Democracy, and Human Rights

Gaining international legitimacy is of particular importance for new states emerging through state succession. The literature recognizes the uniquely important role that new states play in human rights and the unique role that human rights plays for new states. As Moravcsik argues, "the primary proponents of reciprocally binding human rights obligations were . . . the governments of newly established democracies" (2000, 220). Fabry writes that objectives such as human rights and democracy may help new states more than existing states (2010, 223). It is for the new states that gains, improvements, and demonstrations of rights practices matter most. Demonstrated democratic practices often go hand in hand with human rights as important markers of legitimacy and development. However, states transitioning – but not through democratization – also seek legitim-acy. New regimes seek legitimacy to maintain power or access opportun-ities like new trading partners that will benefit their state. Albrecht and Schlumberger (2004) write on the case of Middle Eastern countries, the stability of authoritarian regimes in the region, and strategies of legitim-ation when states were not transitioning toward democracy.

The normative condemnation of colonialism contributed to the necessary and quick recognition of independent states once controlled by colonial powers. As Fabry observes, "The ex-colonies were being acknowledged as sovereign more or less automatically because the new global political climate could not tolerate the continuation of the institution of formal empire, and not as a result of appraisal in terms of some substantive standards. State recognition thus moved from assessing fact to evaluating right" (2010, 148). Buchanan argues that "classic decolonization" offers one of only two scen-arios wherein there is an international legal right to secede and that succes-sion and secession are the "two main circumstances in which 'recognition legitimacy' is typically asserted" (2003, 333 and 263). Visible demonstrations of norm adherence and projections of legitimacy are especially important for new states at the time of independence. Research finds that former colonial states maintain ties to the colonial power and are more likely to have better human rights practices. This relationship is thought to be driven by institutional, policy, and normative vestiges of colonial rule (Mitchell and McCormick 1988; Moravcsik 1995).

Identity and reputation matter for new states. Johnston writes of identity as a social category, with related norms and expectations, which includes the idea that "actors in world politics value image and status as ends in and of themselves" and seek to "maximize status and image" (2008, 75). Channeling Wendt's (1999) scholarship, Kelley writes of the importance of global reputation that "states want social recognition and their governments care about how they are viewed by their own citizens and the global community" (2017, 5). While some recent scholarship questions the role of reputation in human rights compliance (Nielson and Simmons 2015), Downs and Jones conclude in their analysis that "reputation matters, just not so much as some might like" (2002, 113).

As a result, global reputation is something that new states must confront, and it often encompasses their human rights practices. Reputation and global consensus are central to gaining membership into the United Nations. Diplomatic recognition through membership recognizes states and their governments as the legitimate powers in a territory. A new state must apply to the secretary-general affirming acceptance of United Nations Charter obligations. Next, the Security Council votes on the application. At least nine out of fifteen of the Council members must support the membership, including all five Permanent Members. The recognition of a new member state "implies readiness to assume diplomatic relations," and the United Nations checks diplomats' credentialing to ensure that the state "has been accredited by the government actually in power" (UN 2019b). Then, the membership application must obtain at least two-thirds majority vote in the General Assembly for admission into the United Nations. This process requires the acknowledgment of the United Nations Charter tenets of peace, security, and human rights as vital to international participation. In 1947, Western powers opposed the admission of Romania, Bulgaria, and Hungary because "these countries did not meet the requirements . . . in particular (the opponents) referred to their human rights violations" (Conforti 2005, 34).

Treaty Succession

One of the simplest and most important ways for a state to demonstrate its independence and sovereignty is to autonomously conduct international affairs. A state making a treaty commitment signifies the authoritative power to act legally on behalf of a physical territory and government.

Wheatley writes that legitimacy "can be established through deliberate forms of diplomacy and a requirement of consent to international law norms" (2010, 138). By looking to the world of international treaties, new states look to a medium that, as Marshall McLuhan (1964) would say, is the message. Buchanan writes that recognitional legitimacy takes the form of the "power to make treaties, alliances, and trade agreements, thereby altering its juridical relations to other entities" (2003, 263).

Treaty succession serves the purpose of legitimation during times of uncertain international and domestic relations. When a state commits through succession, the international community is notified by the UN depository, which distributes notifications to UN member states when states succeed to international treaty law. Lutz and Sikkink define an international norm cascade as "collections of norm-affirming events." Norm cascades are embodied through "discursive events" that are "verbal or written statements asserting the norm" (2000, 655). Succession communication is the discursive event for new states to assert their commitment to human rights norms. The United Nations provides the legal publicity of membership and norm commitment for the new states committing through succession. The message is delivered to diplomats and lawyers working on behalf of other UN member states and spreads across the globe.

Succession, I argue, is not likely to be a cheap or hollow signal. New states have disincentives to renege on succession commitments, as they are keenly aware that the international spotlight is on them. If states were to succeed to international human rights treaties with no intention of fulfilling their treaty obligations, they soon would be found out. New states violating human rights laws would face shaming from the international organizations and member states whose support and recognition they seek. Additionally, new states in serious violation of international human rights law risk international intervention, either military, humanitarian, economic, or otherwise, limiting their newly established sovereignty. Newly independent states view these risks as too high to systematically violate human rights treaties following succession.

Hypotheses

H1: *If a state commits to a human rights treaty through succession, it will have increased likelihood of improved human rights practices.*

Possible Counterarguments

Documented human rights abuses occur even within established, stable democracies fully committed to human rights treaties. The expectation that new states sincerely commit to treaties and diligently comply is by no means a given within international relations and international law. Several possible counterarguments acknowledge that human rights practices may take divergent paths within new states following treaty succession. A first possible counterargument related to new states and treaty succession focuses on the difficulty and instability inherent to new-state emergence and regime transition. This counterargument expects that new states will have worse human rights following commitment. A second counterargument expects that succession will not result in any change in human rights practices based on an expectation of treaty commitment as "cheap talk."

New States and Worse Human Rights

The breakdown of the SFRY into six new states exemplifies a tumultuous, violent, and destabilizing time. In the late 1980s and early 1990s, the Soviet Union's decline resulted in both political and economic crises. Serbia was the first of the six republics to declare independence from Yugoslavia, in 1991. In 2006, Montenegro and Serbia declared independence from the last configuration of former components of the SFRY. During this period, Yugoslavia experienced extreme levels of violence, including "reports about massacres of thousands of civilians, rape and torture in detention camps, terrible scenes from cities under siege and the suffering of hundreds of thousands expelled from their homes."[9] Actions described by Human Rights Watch as "brutal warfare" (1992) resulted in the creation of the ICTY, with the purpose of investigating and "prosecuting persons responsible for serious violations of international humanitarian law committed in the territory of the former Yugoslavia."[10]

The institutions that often enforce and implement international human rights law domestically may be incapacitated during times of transition toward independence. "This country is disintegrating," Dimitrij Rupel, Slovenia's secretary of foreign affairs, declared at a news conference. "There is great instability, especially from the point

---

[9] United Nations International Criminal Tribunal for the Former Yugoslavia, "The Tribunal—Establishment," available at www.icty.org/en/about/tribunal/establishment.

[10] UNSCR 827, May 25, 1993.

of view of the legal system, so we are forced to search for a new form of coexistence" ("Slovenes Vote Decisively for Independence From Yugoslavia," New York Times, December 24, 1990).

Given the extent of violence and violations of international humanitarian law during the dissolution of the SFRY, one could expect that succession to human rights treaties upon independence would not transform state behavior toward positive human rights practices. If Yugoslavia's experience during transition held true for all succession cases, we would expect a negative relationship between succession and human rights practices.

H2: *If a state commits to a human rights treaty via succession, it will have increased likelihood of worse human rights practices.*

No Changes upon Treaty Succession

Another alternative argument posits no significant changes in rights practices upon succession. Even if the new states' leadership has sincere intentions when succeeding to human rights law, they may lack resources and institutional capabilities to bring their legal promises to fruition. This expected outcome taps into existing literature on human rights that understands treaty commitment to be cheap talk (Goldsmith and Posner 2005) and underscores the lack of enforcement mechanisms attached to human rights law (Guzman 2008, 49). This expected outcome also connects to the possibility that succession states may sincerely want to adhere to international standards of human rights but are unable to commit the resources to do so (Chayes and Chayes 1993). From these various paths, treaty commitment through succession is not expected to result in substantive human rights change.

H3: *If a state commits to a human rights treaty via succession, no significant change in human rights practices will occur.*

Statistical Investigation into Human Rights Treaty Succession

Treaty Succession

Succession is coded as 1 for the year states succeed to treaty law and every year thereafter. Years when a state has not acceded are coded as 0. Ratification is coded as 1 for the year states ratify treaty law and every year thereafter. Years when a state has not ratified are coded as 0. Commitment data come from the UN Treaty Collection. Sixty-six states ratified and seven succeeded to the ICCPR between 1966 and 2010. Grouped Ratification is a dichotomous variable coding binding commitment or no binding commitment to the ICCPR. This variable is a measure capturing the existing approach to ratification found within international relations literature and is included as a means to compare the distinct effects of accession and ratification against the lumped commitment variable.

The statistical results in Table 6.3 lend strong support for my argument that states committing to human rights treaties through succession will improve human rights following commitment. In Model I, succession and ratification variables are both included to test each commitment type's effects on human rights practices. In Figure 6.5, I graph the coefficients of Model I. Figure 6.5 shows us that while both succession and ratification were significant and positive effect on human rights outcomes, the size of the effect differs greatly across the two commitment types. Model 2 included a comparison measure of existing approaches to studying human rights treaty commitment. The variable of Grouped Ratification collapsed all binding commitment types into one variable without disaggregating. When doing so, Grouped Ratification had a negative and significant effect on human rights practices, clouding the direction and relationship of new state commitment and human rights outcomes.

The markedly large value of the succession variable's coefficient in statistical analyses demonstrates the need to look closer at the relationship between treaty succession and human rights practices and likely reflects the small number of cases involved in treaty succession. States that succeeded to the ICCPR had a higher mean Human Rights Score than states that ratified the treaty. The mean value of the Human Rights Protection Scores when states committed via succession was 1.29. The mean value of the Human Rights Protection Scores when states committed via ratification was 0.7448. Figures 6.6 and 6.7 are scatterplots of Human Rights Scores over time of states that ratified the ICCPR with those that succeeded to the ICCPR. In Figure 6.2, succession states trended toward clustering higher on the scale of Human Rights Protection Scores. In Figure 6.3, ratification states clustered more around scores of 0 and 1. Although ratification states had higher maximum Human Rights Protection Scores, on average, succession states had higher rights scores. Figure 6.6 also conveys movement of succession state Human Rights Scores toward higher scores, indicative of the plotted coefficients in Figure 5.5 and the statistical results presented in Table 6.3.

Table 6.3 *Instrumental variable regression of succession and ratification of the ICCPR, 1966–2010.*

	Model I	Model II
Succession	29.19(4.530)***	
Ratification	1.195(0.1816)***	
Grouped ratification	−0.6353(0.1507)***	
Polity2	−0.0008(0.0127)	0090(0.0039)***
GDP	0000(0.0000)**	0000(0.0000)**
Population	−0.0000(0.0000)*	−0.0000(0.0000)**
Interstate war	−0.3019(.3726)	−0.2225(0.1013)**
Civil war	−1.189(0.1418)***	−1.466(0.0389)***
Constant	−0.4036(0.1200)**	6871(0.0825)***
Observations	5818	5813

* p<0.10, **p<0.05, ***p<0.01; Stata 14.0
Instrumental regression. Instrumented: Succession. Included instruments: Ratification, Polity2, GDP, Population, Interstate War, and Civil War. Excluded instruments: Regional Treaty Density, Common Law, Durability.

Robustness Checks

I employ several statistical robustness checks of the treaty succession models. The results point to the positive significance of treaty succession on Human Rights Scores and hold consistent across robustness checks testing alternative dependent variables. When using Freedom House measures of Civil Liberties and Political Rights, treaty succession remains statistically significant and positive. Additionally, when using the Cingranelli and Richards Empowerment Rights Index measures as the dependent variable, treaty succession remains statistically significant and positive. These results also hold when including regional dummy variables to control whether regional effects are driving results.

Additionally, I explored whether the succession finding was merely a function of a state's stability. I tested whether the results were conditional on high *durability* variable measures. Durability is a Polity IV Project variable counting how many years a state has had a stable government. I found that succession remained significant as long as a state had been stable for at least two years. Overall, states that committed through succession were significantly likely to

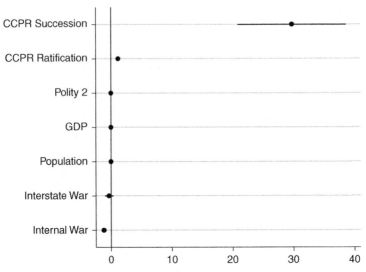

Figure 6.5   Plotted coefficients of Model 1

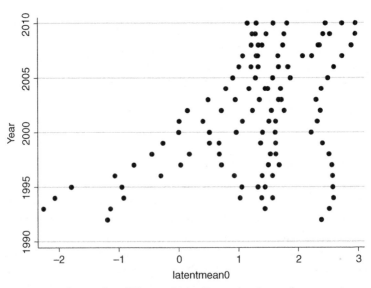

Figure 6.6   Scatterplot of Human Rights Protection Scores for succession states

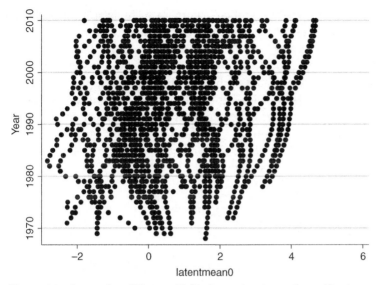

Figure 6.7 Scatterplot of Human Rights Protection Scores for ratification

have higher levels of human rights. Though democracy and stability are undoubtedly part of the story of new states as they work toward improving human rights, recognizing succession as their commitment path indicates the importance of separating out this unique treaty commitment.

Case Focus: Czechoslovakia: Treaty Succession of the Czech Republic and Slovakia

Given the small number of states that utilize succession as a path toward treaty commitment, it is particularly important to delve deeper into the relationship between treaty succession and human rights practices. In this section, I focus on the dissolution of Czechoslovakia into the Czech Republic and Slovakia and each new state's approach to treaty succession. These cases represent a diverse case selection method. As Gerring writes, diverse cases seek "to maximize variance along relevant dimensions" (2008, 650). The goal is to diversify measures of a variable (or combination of variables) of interest along different categorical, theoretical, and/or measures of standard deviation (647). The Czech Republic and Slovakia differed in their democratization timing, which allows me to consider the implicit argument from existing scholarship that democratization is the driving force behind human rights changes in transitional regimes. While the Czech Republic quickly moved toward democracy, Slovakia took longer to move away from Soviet influence.[11] I illustrate how each new state explicitly linked human rights treaty succession with legitimation and recognition from the international community. I then connect the heightened emphasis on legitimation to positive human rights outcomes following succession. Despite variation in democratization, each succession state moved toward human rights improvement.

Background

As of midnight on December 31, 1992, Czechoslovakia ceased to exist. The peaceful succession of the Czech Republic and Slovakia has been dubbed the "Velvet Divorce," following from the "Velvet Revolution" of 1989. Both the separation from the Soviet Union and the separation of the states came peacefully, without a single life lost, earning the "velvet" monikers. Both changes were driven by protests and popular mobilization. Czechoslovakia was itself a relatively modern state, created in 1919 following the collapse of the Austro-Hungarian Empire and brokered by the international community through the Treaty of Versailles, which ended World War I. Article 81 of the Treaty of Versailles established the "complete independence of the Czecho-Slovak State." While Slovak nationalist movements grew during the 1930s, "there was no equivalent of these bodies in the Czech lands" (Young 1994, 3).

Under communist rule, Slovak nationalist movements gained wider acknowledgment, resulting in constitutional recognition of two National Councils, one Czech and one Slovak. With two National Councils, the country recognized two distinct republics with growing institutional separation. The Act of the Slovak National Council 207/1968 and The Act of the Czech National Council 2/1969 established separate national statistical offices for each republic. These legal steps recognized "two independent, sovereign nations" (Article 87(b) Constitutional Act 1968). Among the other democratizing reforms accompanying the Prague Spring, Secretary Alexander Dubcek granted more autonomy to

---

[11] For example, by 1993, the Czech Republic received a 10 out of 10 on the Polity score, but it was not until 2006 that Slovakia reached the same level of democracy.

Slovakia (Kennedy and Russell 2000, 31). Democratization and internal recognition were uneven across the two nations.

Leading up to and upon the collapse of the Soviet Union, anticommunist protests were widespread. To move toward political and economic reforms, "nothing less (was needed) than to reconstruct completely a whole society" (Musil 1992, 178). It was becoming clearer to diplomats that separation would occur. A former US Ambassador to Slovakia recounted, "I guess in the summer of 1992 I started talking to Personnel and said, 'I want to be considered for Ambassador to Slovakia.' They said, 'There isn't a Slovakia.' I replied 'Yes, but there will be'" (Kennedy and Russell 2000, 179).

Succession

Both the Czech Republic and Slovakia opted to succeed to Czechoslovakia's prior treaty commitments. The new states sent separate letters to the UN secretary-general in spring of 1993. In a letter dated February 16, 1993, the Czech Republic wrote that it identified as a "successor State" and "considers itself bound . . . by multilateral international treaties to which the Czech and Slovak Federal Republic was a party . . . including reservations and declarations to their provisions made." Slovakia wrote on May 19, 1993, that

> in accordance with the relevant principles and rules of international law . . . the Slovak Republic, as a successor State . . . considers itself bound by multilateral treaties to which the Czech and Slovak Federal Republic was a party as of 31 December 1992 including reservations and declarations made . . . as well as objections by Czechoslovaks to reservations formulated by other treaty parties.

Both new states recognized January 1, 1993 as the formal date of dissolution. The separate date of succession letters along with the distinct approaches to treaty succession support the assertion that each new state independently assessed and willingly recommitted to treaty obligations through succession. While the Czech Republic took more of a blanket approach to prior obligations, Slovakia submitted a detailed list of treaties affected by the succession process, including notes on the effects on prior treaty signatures. The Czech Republic cited the ICCPR EIF as the point of application was 1976, not 1993, demonstrating its sense of continuous obligation (Human Rights Committee 1995, 5). Such EIF interpretation acknowledged that prior commitments held for the new states.

Legitimation

The Czech Republic and Slovakia recognized the need for a strong reputation, independent identity, and legitimation from the international community. In his official statement, Czechoslovakian ambassador to the UN Moravcik acknowledged the "Czecho-Slovak problem" (UN A/47/PV.12 56). He ceded the high probability that "by January of next year the federation will have ceased to exist. Thus, one of the founding members of the UN will give its place in international politics to the new independent States" (UN 1992, 57). Within this context, Moravcik highlighted the importance Czechoslovakia placed on the United Nations and human rights. The United Nations has a "fundamental role to play" in the development of "democracy and of respect for universal and civilized human rights" (UN A/47/PV.12 47). He also sought immediate inclusion of the new states into the United Nations, noting that "it is my hope that all the current Members of the UN will extend to the Czech Republic and the Slovak Republic the understanding that they have always shown to Czechoslovakia, by admitting them to membership as soon as possible" (57).

Leading up to independence, the Czech Republic sought active engagement within the international community.[12] It sought to reconstruct its identity on the international stage. A large part of the Czech identity reconstruction involved actively distancing the new country from Soviet and communist ties: "they didn't even call themselves Eastern Europeans, in fact; they were now 'Central Europeans' and they were looking West rather than East" (Kennedy and Eicher 2010, 288). Indeed, "the Czech Republic made integration into Western institutions its chief foreign policy objective in the first years after communism" (US Department of State 2020). As an initial and formal act of seeking international legitimacy, both the Czech Republic and Slovakia sought immediate membership into the United Nations.

To gain UN membership, the Czech Republic and Slovakia were required to submit applications to the secretary-general, who then put their membership to the General Assembly for consideration. On January 19, 1993, both new states were admitted to the United Nations without vote (UN 1993, 371). Upon state dissolution, Czechoslovakia no longer maintained international (or any other) political identity, thus

---

[12] www.chicagotribune.com/news/ct-xpm-1992-09-13-9203230370-story.html.

terminating its UN membership. Each new state presented its own member identity within the United Nations. The Czech Republic was one of the members of the Special Committee on the Charter of the United Nations and on the Strengthening of the Role of the Organization (Slovakia was not). Other prominent international organizations were slower to recognize the two new states through membership. The IMF admitted the Czech Republic and Slovakia on January 1, 1993; the General Agreement on Tariffs and Trade on April 15, 1993; and the World Health Organization in 1995.

> In other international organizations, Czechoslovakia, the Czech Republic, and the Slovak Republic came to an official Agreement on Membership in International Governmental Organizations, which formed a position on membership in the ICAO, ILPO, ITU, IMO, INMARSAT, INTELSAT, and the CPI. Czechoslovakia's former membership "will be continued by the Czech Republic," which will "fully support the Slovak Republic in its efforts to become a member of any of these organizations, when the Slovak Republic expresses interest in membership" (Bühler 2001, 275–276). This was unique among the international organization membership transitions as it only allowed one state to assume Czechoslovakia's membership. This avenue again highlights differing and nonautomatic engagement with international law and organizations during the succession process.

On October 6, 1993, in the first speech a representative from the Czech Republic made at the United Nations, Mr. Zieleniec emphasized both democracy and human rights, solidifying the Czech Republic's identity as a rights-valuing international community member.

> The Czech Republic is currently undergoing profound political and economic changes. On the political side, we are constructing a democratic regime in what used to be the communist world. The Government has proven to be a stable one. Meanwhile, we emphasize human rights, and our robust press freedom as well as our human-rights record have been recognized even by very finicky non-partisan international organizations. (UN 1993b)

In the speech, the Czech Republic highlighted its contributions to the United Nations and was "proud of its share in the work" (UN 1993, 14). It immediately ran for one of the rotating seats on the UNSC. The Czech Republic took particular care to distance itself from new states requiring economic aid and its independence processes from the ethnic and religious conflict occurring in Yugoslavia.

The Czech Republic and Slovakia sought diplomatic recognition from other states and quickly received it. The United States readily recognized the Czech Republic and Slovakia, immediately establishing diplomatic relations: "Our position was 'Do it democratically and peacefully and good luck.' After the split, we immediately recognized them both and asked, 'What can we do to help?'" (180). Turkey recognized the states "on the same day" as their independence (Republic of Turkey n.d.).

Slovakia also recognized the need for international recognition and legitimacy. Former Czechoslovakian ambassador to the UN Moravcik became Slovakia's representative to the United Nations upon independence. In his first speech in the new role, he highlighted Slovakia's international embeddedness: "In addition to its membership in the UN, the Slovak Republic today is a member of 53 international organizations" (UN 1993b). Moravcik also restated Slovakia's support for the creation of a UN High Commissioner for Human Rights and reiterated its commitment to human rights by reaffirming that "Slovakia is building its statehood on civic principles based on respect for individual rights" (10).

The increased awareness and desire to obtain international legitimacy contributed to higher levels of accountability for the Czech Republic and Slovakia. After seeking recognition from states and membership into international organizations, the international community was aware of the new states' presence, commitments, and legal obligations.

International Monitoring and Awareness

Through seeking international legitimation and quickly embedding within the international community, new states bring their actions to the center stage. Following Czech and Slovak independence, it is clear that the United Nations, international organizations, human rights organizations, and other states were watching the new states' human rights behavior – they were aware and noting how the states lived up to international norms and their commitments. The ambassador from the United States made clear that support for the new countries was not a rubber stamp approval. Rather, the United States valued human rights and successful steps toward democratization.

> We therefore said to Meciar "we will judge you by your actions; we will help you in any way we can to move Slovakia towards democracy and a free market economy, but we will not support backsliding, including some recent actions against the opposition." Now, if we had gone to Meciar and said, "Look we don't give a damn what you do domestically. If you want to use the security services to intimidate people, if you want

to whack the opposition while they are out of power, be our guest. Just give lots of contracts to American companies and support us in UN votes," he would have happily said, "I agree." But that obviously wasn't our policy. (Kennedy and Russel 2000, 187)

Instead, the United States devoted resources to and valued the human rights outcomes in Slovakia. "We paid a lot of attention to human rights. We spent a lot of time on the yearly human rights reports which for a very small embassy took an awful lot of the time available" (191).

The United Nations quickly embedded the Czech Republic and Slovakia within international human rights law and expected the new states to uphold the same standards as older, more established states. Soon after the new states' admission as members to the United Nations, the international community sought demonstrated and active protection of human rights. The Committee on the Rights of the Child established a 1994 reporting due date for both the Czech Republic and Slovakia on their implementation of the CRC. This was the first human rights treaty body reporting for the new states. The Czech Republic committed through succession to the CRC in February 1993, and Slovakia did so on May 28, 1993. The reports addressed general implementation of the treaty with specific assessments of domestic policy concerning civil rights and freedoms of the child, parental and family environment, health, education, and other special protection (UN 1996). Both states submitted the report late – the Czech Republic in 1996 and Slovakia in 1998 (UN 1998). Late submission of committee reports is common even for established states.

Human Rights Watch included its first separate annual reports on the Czech Republic and Slovakia in 1994. The Czech report made specific mention of domestic policy reform, citizenship requirements, and discrimination against the Roma people. The report on Slovakia addressed issues of censorship against journalism and treatment of the Roma people. Both of the reports provided detailed descriptions of human rights activities within both states, demonstrating Human Rights Watch's awareness and concern.

Observable Rights Practices

Figures 6.8 and 6.9 depict Human Rights Scores over time in the Czech Republic and Slovakia. Both states demonstrated improved human rights over time, with the Czech Republic obtaining and sustaining higher levels of human rights practices than Slovakia. Despite the different levels of improvement, each new state did improve its Human Rights Scores

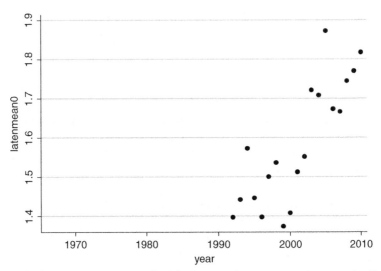

Figure 6.8   Two-way scatterplot of Human Rights Protection Scores in the Czech Republic

following independence and succession to the core UN human rights treaties.

One of the international community's central criticisms of the Czech Republic and Slovakia's human rights records was of their treatment of the Roma people. Targeting the Roma affected their rights ranging from citizenship to increased police brutality. Freedom House recognized that the Czech Republic made strides in improving their treatment of the Roma: "in July the parliament passed legislation that restored citizenship to all those, including Roma groups, who had lost their citizenship between 1948 and 1990" (1999). Although instances of discrimination against Roma and Slovaks remained constant throughout the 1990s, the Czech Republic created an amnesty plan in 1998 available to individuals with criminal sentences with prison terms under five years (US Department of State 2000).

Slovakia did not improve its treatment of the Roma people upon independence. Quite the opposite. Human Rights Watch noted that Prime Minister Vladimir Meciar described Roma children as "mentally and social unadaptable" (Human Rights Watch 1994a). However, after Meciar was defeated by a pro-democratic party in September 1994, the change in leadership resulted in human rights abuses toward ethnic

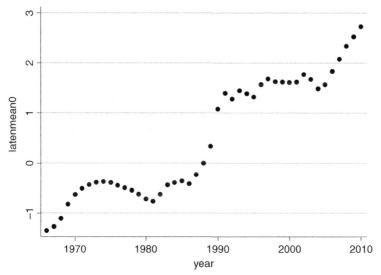

Figure 6.9   Two-way scatterplot of Human Rights Protection Scores in Slovakia

minorities "subsid(ing) substantially" (Human Rights Watch 1995). The varied pattern in Slovakia's human rights levels documented in Figure 6.9 indicate the power struggle between pro-democracy leaders and Meciar. Human Rights Watch (1996a) assessed that the "political in-fighting . . . had a decidedly negative impact on respect for human rights and the rule of law in Slovakia."

Another noted human rights and political issue in both states was the process of "de-communizing." The Czech Republic took action to correct some of the unjust prosecutions under the communist government.

> By the end of 1993, over 96 percent of all those unjustly convicted under the communist regime had been rehabilitated by the Czech courts. In another attempt to deal with past abuses, in March 1993 the parliament established a commission to investigate repressive actions taken by the Czechoslovak security police against dissidents. The commission will work closely with the Prosecutor General's Office, as well as other government agencies. (Human Rights Watch 1994b)

Human Rights Watch (1996b) questioned whether some de-communizing policies, such as the "lustration law," which barred

Communist Party officials from holding certain jobs until 2000, targeted individuals "not for acts that were criminal at the time they were committed, but for having belonged to a now-discredited group"; however, overall, the Czech Republic "demonstrated its commitment to human rights." By 1999, the United States commented that the Czech government "generally respects the human rights of its citizens" and noted the creation of a national Human Rights Council tasked with drafting human rights legislation (US Department of State 2000). At the same time, the United States considered that Slovakia "continued to make progress" and "generally respected the human rights of its citizens" while "problems remained in some areas" (US Department of State 2000).

Both the Czech Republic and Slovakia sought international legitimacy and quickly embedded within international organizations following Czechoslovakia's dissolution. The international community welcomed the new states and promptly held them accountable to international human rights standards. With embeddedness and active accountability measures, both new states improved their human rights practices. For the Czech Republic and Slovakia, treaty succession contributed to the path toward human rights compliance.

Conclusion

In this chapter, I examined and unpacked the treaty commitment action of succession. Through descriptive analysis I detailed what states use this commitment type and how it compares with the dominant form of treaty commitment type, ratification. I argued that succession states will use treaty commitment as a means to legitimate new state regimes and to signal to the international community their support for established human rights norms and established mediums of diplomacy. Through statistical analysis of state succession to the ICCPR treaty, I found strong support for this argument, finding that when states succeeded to the ICCPR, they significantly improved their human rights practices. This finding held through numerous robustness checks.

Importantly, disaggregating succession from ratification mattered. While throughout the chapter I argued for recognizing conceptual and legal differences between the two commitment types, the statistical findings offered empirical support that separating the two measures had implications for measuring and observing human rights outcomes. When separating out ratification from succession actions, I found that treaty succession and ratification separately led to improved human rights practices, with a more sizable effect following succession. However, when I coded treaty commitment as the dominant international relations and international legal studies do (grouped together) the different relationships between commitment types and human rights practices were lost. The chapter's findings reinforce the need for scholars to delve deeper into what legal distinctions mean for the study of human rights law.

When considered more broadly, the chapter's findings offer hope. As many new states emerge from conflict and accompanying institutional contention and general confusion, we may well have expected that new states' commitment to human rights treaties would be hollow and unlikely to result in positive changes in human rights practices. However, the findings point to the will of new states to establish themselves as adhering members of the international human rights community. Given the potential for additional new states emerging from the seventeen NSGTs that remain, along with the Scottish and Basque independence movements (among others), these findings bode well for future new states.

7

Conclusion

This book's motivation was to unpack the ways that states commit to and comply with international human rights treaties. In doing so, I challenged the dominant ratification-centered approach that much of the international human rights scholarship has taken. I focused on three commitment paths states take to commit to treaty law in addition to ratification. I described and explored the contexts from which states committed through signature, accession, and succession and tested how committing using these actions (1) differed from ratification and (2) affected treaty compliance. In this concluding chapter, I review the main findings from the empirical and legal analyses presented in this book and discuss their broader implications for international relations, international legal studies theory, policy, and other areas of international law. I also revisit the project's call to move away from a ratification-centered view of international human rights law.

Summary of Findings

The first half of the book provides straightforward but important descriptive numbers about the types and frequency of commitment to human rights treaties. How are they different? How do they situate against the most studied type of commitment, ratification? I critiqued the dominant approach taken by international relations and international legal scholars, which lumps binding commitment actions together and mostly ignores nonbinding signature commitment. All of the analyses in this book together confirm that it is important to recognize and distinguish types of treaty commitment when studying commitment timing and effects. I showed when commitment actions are disentangled, positive relationships emerge between committing to and complying with international human rights treaties.

In Chapter 4, I focused on treaty signature, the only formal but nonbinding commitment action in UN treaty law. Despite most scholars' dismissal of signature in quantitative or qualitative analysis of human rights treaties, I find that signing human rights treaties is associated with significant improvements in human rights practices. Through quantitative analysis of International Covenant on Civil and Political Rights (ICCPR) and Convention on the Elimination of All Forms of Discrimination against Women (CEDAW) commitment, I find that after states sign, they are significantly likely to improve multiple measures of human rights. I argue that domestic ratification procedures make signature particularly important for states confronting arduous legislative barriers to ratification. Descriptively, signature occurs more frequently than any other commitment type, so these findings are a call for optimism about commitment.

In Chapter 5, I focused on treaty accession, through which nonnegotiating states or states committing following entry into force (EIF) commit to international treaty law. Traditionally, scholars include commitment via accession as indistinguishable from commitment via ratification. Through descriptive, legal, and quantitative analysis, I demonstrate that both legal definitional characteristics of accession prove important. States that negotiated the ICCPR and CEDAW significantly improved human rights practices following commitment, while those that did not negotiate the treaty did not significantly change their human rights practices.

In Chapter 6, I focused on treaty succession, through which new states adopt a prior state's commitments. Though scholars had studied human rights practices relative to regime change (and democratization, in particular), I find that during the emergence of new legal identities, states significantly improved human rights practices following treaty commitment. I argued that new states use treaty succession to legitimate their existence and human rights reputation using international law. When looking closer at the Czech Republic and Slovakia case studies, I demonstrate that new states prioritized establishing international reputations as law-abiding, human rights–norm adopting states and quickly used treaty succession as a means to do so. Given increased scrutiny from the United Nations, member states, as well as specific human rights treaty bodies, succession states were held to higher standards of accountability than stable states. Table 7.1 summarizes the book's main findings.

Using the percentage breakdown of the four commitment actions, Figure 7.1 visually depicts the revealed relationships between each action

Table 7.1 *Summary of findings*

Commitment Action	Finding	Chapter	Treaties
Signature	Positive for states with Legislative Approval procedures	4	ICCPR CEDAW
Ratification	Negative or Null when included against signature commitment (earlier/later steps)		ICCPR CEDAW ICCPR CEDAW
	Positive when included against accession (negotiation context)	5	
Accession	Negative for states that opted out of negotiations		ICCPR CEDAW ICCPR
	Positive for states that joined the United Nations later and were unable to negotiate	5	CEDAW
Succession	Positive	6	ICCPR

and human rights practices. Signature and succession had significant and positive relationships with human rights practices. I found ratification to have a positive relationship when separated out from accession but a negative relationship when distinguished from signature. I also found accession to have both positive and negative relationships with human rights practices. When examining states that opted out of negotiating treaties, I found accession to have either no or a negative relationship with human rights practices. However, when examining states that missed the window of signature prior to EIF, the later accession states had significant and positive relationships with human rights practices.

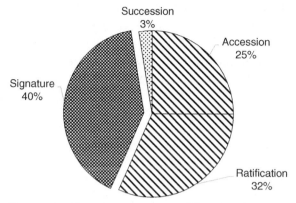

Figure 7.1 Commitment actions and human rights outcomes

Finally, I found that each of the four actions, in some circumstances, have a significant and positive relationship with human rights practices. This finding seems to support the often-quoted Louis Henkin line, that "Almost all nations observe almost all principles of international law and almost all of their obligations almost all of the time" (Henkin 1979, 47).

Revisiting Ratification

Though this project aimed to disentangle treaty commitment from ratification, through separating commitment types we are left with a better understanding of what ratification is and is not. Treaty commitment proved to be more complex and nuanced than a simple coding of whether or not states ratified treaties.

Disaggregating commitment paths from the umbrella of ratification identifies ratification's unique traits. Ratifying states are predominantly those that participated in negotiating and creating the treaty and already signed it. When conceptualizing ratifiers as negotiation participants, I find ingrained interest among states that participated in shaping treaty parameters and rights standards. Participation in creating and constructing rights resulted in states being more likely to adhere to treaty commitment. The first step of signing human rights treaties contributed to a positive relationship with human rights practices. These path characteristics set ratification states apart from accession states that generally did not participate in treaty negotiations and did not sign, or act in any precursor commitment, in advance of acceding to the treaty. Ratification, then, describes states that participated in and engaged more with human rights law than states following other paths to committing to human rights treaties. Overall, I found positive outcomes for these states. More legal participation resulted in more respect for human rights.

However, when looking at the steps negotiating participants took to commit to treaties, I find that the positive effects at the first stage of signature were often followed up by rights backslide upon ratification. So, do states improve human rights practices after ratifying? Not necessarily. But they do improve human rights practices after some types of treaty commitment. Therefore, the deeper question that much international relations and international legal scholarship has been asking for the past few decades has a positive answer: human rights treaties matter. The international legal promises that states make often yield positive results in terms of behavioral changes.

Upon finding this statistical relationship, prior research has concluded that treaty commitment contributed to worsening rights. Through dis-aggregating the types of treaty commitment, this project demonstrated that this isn't always the case. Many paths to committing contributed to positive compliance outcomes. The finding of a negative relationship between ratification and human rights, when studied in the inclusive light of incorporating the earlier relationship between signing and human rights practices, becomes more perplexing. Why do states improve human rights practices upon nonbinding signature and then sometimes backslide upon binding ratification? This does not appear to occur in the context of the other binding commitment acts of accession and succession. The question of backsliding upon ratification is an important one for future research to grapple with.

Implications for International Relations and International Legal Theory

A central takeaway from this book is that treaty commitment and compli-ance is a complicated and messy set of interactions at the domestic and international levels. The paths states take to commit to and comply with international human rights treaties are often winding and nonlinear. How do we interpret this as we move forward with the study of international cooperation and international law, more specifically? We need to under-stand that there are different pieces and paths to committing to and complying with international law. Through disaggregating commitment type, I found very different human rights outcomes. The path is important.

Domestic politics proved extremely important in understanding states' commitment paths. States confronting legislative approval requirements for ratification were bound domestically to act internationally. Binding commitment timing did not reflect heads' of state interest in and commitment to human rights. Rather, for these states, ratification timing reflected a lack of domestic consensus on international obligations. This resulted in extreme ratification delays or acceding to treaties after EIF. Both types of delays have been largely interpreted as revealing a state's overall view of human rights.

New states entering the global system by replacing old states used international human rights law to establish international legal identity. The domestic context of new legal identity with accompanying regime changes proved extremely important in understanding the weight that states placed on committing and complying with international human rights law.

Perhaps the most optimistic takeaway from the book's findings is that creating and participating in treaty drafting was a pathway towards compliance. Such a buy-in and socialization questions some of the bleaker findings about treaty commitment and compliance.

Policy Implications

The study of international human rights has natural and obvious policy importance. Amnesty International estimated that 82 percent of the countries it surveyed tortured or otherwise ill-treated people, 58 percent conducted unfair trials, and 75 percent arbitrarily restricted freedom of expression (2018a). There are international treaties, or parts of international treaties, devoted to each of these human rights violations. Learning more about how to get states to agree to human rights law and motivate compliance with global rights standards has real-life meaning for the millions of individuals suffering from human rights violations every day.

Several encouraging conclusions emerge from this book's analyses. State participation in the creation, negotiation, and continued participation of international policy matters. International organizations, human rights nongovernmental organizations (NGOs), and states can encourage other states to participate in creating new laws or work to keep participatory states from leaving negotiations. States' feelings of ownership and connection with the standards to which they are bound increased the chances that they would actually follow the laws. It can be difficult to arrive at agreement across a multitude of preferences, interests, and cultural and political perspectives, but the evidence in *Committed to Rights* points to the importance of eliciting state participation in human rights law. Even in disagreement, participating increases states' awareness of what the international community considers important for human rights and socializes them toward human rights practices. Emergent international agreements on human rights and business, the environment, and LGBT policies are currently in the fledgling stages of development or under contentious negotiation. My findings point to the importance of increasing and maintaining state engagement with shaping new human rights laws in these and other emerging areas.

It is of striking importance for new states in the international arena to recommit to international law through succession. The policy relevance of this finding points to the significance of quickly incorporating new states into not only international organizations but directly into the international human rights regime. This is an area where representatives from the United Nations or bilaterally from other states could contribute institutional aid to support new states in international legal literacy and participatory importance as they enter the world stage. This offers an important opportunity for the international community to positively intervene, given the high levels of conflict and human rights violations that frequently accompany regime transitions and state independence.

To reinforce and support extant compliance with human rights treaties, it could be fruitful for the United Nations and human rights NGOs monitoring violations to acknowledge the positive advances in human rights that states make following treaty signature in the lead-up to ratification. In examining UN bodies and NGOs, *Committed to Rights* demonstrated that these components of the international human rights regime hold states to account for standards during periods of nonbinding commitment. Less evident was positive recognition for advances in rights practices during this period. Articulating support for states complying with human rights treaties along the path to full commitment may positively reinforce that behavior and encourage other states to follow suit.

Other Areas of International Law

Committed to Rights focused squarely on the area of international human rights law. In the beginning of this book, I acknowledged that this focus came with important contributions as well as limitations, given the breadth of topics within international law.

The themes, findings, and contexts herein transcend various international legal issue areas. New states entering the global system consider and evaluate all areas of international legal commitments. While prominence is given to human rights and peace, demonstrating commitment to international economic and environmental norms also establishes new states' legitimacy within the global community. Indeed, participating in shaping treaties carries importance across issue areas. Though human rights are arguably more religiously and culturally variable across countries, which increases controversy and tension during negotiations, other issue areas also evoke high levels of debate and tension when crafting international agreements. Law making in these areas, too, shapes participatory states' expectations of global norms and resituates their own preferences and interests as negotiations proceed.

Conclusion

Committed to Rights maps the legal commitment and compliance paths to UN human rights laws. Dominant international relations studies of human rights law, and international law more broadly, have unpacked many processes of human rights behavior, but this book is the first to unpack how the nuts and bolts of international law matter for important concepts of commitment and compliance. Descriptions and analyses of signature, ratification, accession, and succession make clear that legal distinctions matter and that behind these nuts and bolts are important domestic political contexts shaping how states can and do commit and comply with international human rights law. Given this mapping, there is much opportunity for future works to carry these ideas, concepts, and hypotheses across other areas of international law.

Variables in Statistical Analyses

Commitment Action Variables

Commitment data for signature, ratification, succession, and accession come from the UN Treaty Collection data. This is publicly available data on the exact date of state treaty commitment.

Dependent Variables

To measure human rights practices, I use the Human Rights Protection Scores, Freedom House Political Rights and Civil Liberties measures, and the Empowerment Rights Index from the CIRI Human Rights Database to test compliance with the ICCPR. These measures capture the political and civil rights covered by the ICCPR. These measures (as with many other human rights measures) suffer from the problem of missing information and selection bias. Only reported rights are included; many human rights violations, of course, are not reported. The Freedom House measures, in particular, are blunt measures of human rights. However, their broad nature is advantageous when examining a treaty like the ICCPR, which covers a broad scope of human rights. Both the Freedom House and CIRI measures are discussed later.

Human Rights Protection Scores

The Fariss (2014) and Schnakenberg and Fariss (2014) Human Rights Latent Human Rights Protection Score measure accounts for systemic change that has resulted in biased coding of Amnesty International and US State Department human rights reports. The resulting data offer latent variables of repression that draw from Amnesty International and US State Department reports but corrects for systematic bias in coding over time, which Fariss (2014) argues resulted in higher coding of physical integrity rights abuses in more recent years. A higher latent Human Rights Protection Score captures increased recognition of human rights. These data are available from 1945 to 2010. For the purposes of this study, I use available mean latent human rights scores from 1966 to 2010, analyzing forty-four years of state behavior. The latent variable mean human rights ranges from −3.1, capturing lower respect for human rights scores, to 4.7, capturing increased government respect for human rights.

Political and Civil Rights

The Political Rights and Civil Liberty variables both consist of a scale of 1 to 7, with 1 as the highest level of rights and 7 the lowest. Freedom House describes a 1 on the Political Rights scale as states that enjoy "a wide range of political rights, including free and fair elections," while a score of 7 represents states that have "few or no political rights because of severe government oppression." A score of 1 on the Civil Liberties scale describes states that enjoy a "wide range of civil liberties including freedom of expression, assembly, association, education, and religion . . . a generally fair system of the rule of law." A score of 7 denotes states that allow "virtually no freedom of expression or association, do not protect the rights of detainees and prisoners, and often control or dominate most economic activity." Between 1981 and 2006, 761 country-year observations had a score of 1, marking few or no oppression, and 634 country-year observations had a score of 7, marking high levels of repression.

Empowerment Rights Index

The Empowerment Rights Index from the CIRI Human Rights Database is an index adding the rights variables of domestic movement, foreign movement, freedom of speech, freedom of assembly and association, workers' rights, electoral self-determination, and freedom of religion measures. The index measure ranges from a score of 0, signifying no government respect for these rights, to 14, signifying full government respect across these rights categories.[1] Between 1981 and 2006, there were 155 country-year observations with a score of 0 and 389 country-year observations with a score of 14.

Lagged Dependent Variables

Following from prior works' modeling of human rights levels, I lag the dependent variable human rights one year (e.g., Keith 1999; Hathaway 2002;

---

[1] CIRI variables short descriptions.

Hafner-Burton and Tsutsui 2005; Neumayer 2005). Inclusion helps to control for endogenous effect of prior human rights practices on state decisions to join onto human rights laws and future human rights practices. Including the prior year's measure allows me to model changes against the previous year's practices.

To control for general state capabilities and characteristics, I include several variables. Following from many studies on human rights (e.g., Fariss and Schnakenberg 2014), I include the Polity2 measure from the Polity IV Database to capture a state's democracy level. This variable ranges from −10 to 10, with the least democratic observations at −10 and highest level of democracy at 10. I also include the durability variable from the Polity IV Database. This variable is a count of the number of years that a state has had a stable regime in place.

Gross domestic product is measured in 2,000 US dollars and is taken from UNDATA. It is important to control for economic capabilities determining compliance levels, as some authors posit that state noncompliance of treaty law is based on adjustment periods and some states' inability to implement changes is based on limited funds. Economic capabilities could also limit how much funding is available for the state government to spend on institutions and personnel to handle issues of international law. Controlling for GDP allows the model to control for the possibility that a state's economic capabilities may be driving its focus and engagement with international law as well as its ability to comply.

Similarly, a state's population is included in models to control for state size influencing a state's ability to comply with treaty terms and any mitigating effects state size has on state capability to engage with international law. Scholars posit that small states engage differently with the international system than larger states do. Population is measured as total population, in thousands, from the UN Data. I include two conflict variables, civil war and interstate war. These come from the PRIO Data on Armed Conflict. These are dichotomous variables coded 0 when there was not conflict and 1 when there was.

*Additional statistical results, descriptive statistics, and supplemental material available on the author's website: [https://audreylcomstock .weebly.com/].

WORKS CITED

Abbott, Kenneth W. 1993. "Trust but Verify: The Production of Information in Arms Control Treaties and Other International Agreements." *Cornell International Law Journal* 26: 1.

Abbott, Kenneth W. and Duncan Snidal. 1998. "Why States Act through Formal International Organizations." *Journal of Conflict Resolution* 42(1): 3–32.

Abbott, Kenneth W. and Duncan Snidal. 2000. "Hard and Soft Law in International Governance." *International Organization* 54(3): 421–456.

Abbott, Kenneth W., Robert O. Keohane, Andrew Moravcsik, Anne-Marie Slaughter, and Duncan Snidal. 2000. "The Concept of Legalization." *International Organization* 43(3): 401–419.

Albrecht, Holger and Oliver Schlumberger. 2004. "Waiting for Godot: Regime Change without Democratization in the Middle East." *International Political Science Review* 25(4): 371–392.

Alston, Philip and Ryan Goodman. 2013. *International Human Rights.* Oxford: Oxford University Press.

Amnesty International. n.d.a. "Arms Control." March 29, 2020. www.amnesty.org /en/what-we-do/arms-control/.

Amnesty International. n.d.b. "It's Official! United States Signs U.N. Arms Trade Treaty." March 29, 2020. www.amnestyusa.org/its-official-united-states-signs -u-n-arms-trade-treaty/.

Amnesty International. 1998. "Economic, Social and Cultural Rights: Questions and Answers." www.amnestyusa.org/pdfs/escr_qa.pdf.

Amnesty International. 2016. "HRC31 Amnesty International Public Statement on the UPR Outcome on Saint Lucia March 2016." www.amnesty.org/en/docu ments/amr56/3735/2016/en/.

Amnesty International. 2018a. "Amnesty International Report 2017/18: The State of the World's Human Rights." February 22, 2018. www.amnesty.org/en/docu ments/pol10/6700/2018/en/.

Amnesty International. 2018b. "Americas: Historic Environmental and Human Rights Treaty Gains Momentum as 12 Countries Sign." www.amnesty.org/en/ latest/news/2018/09/americas-12-countries-sign-historic-environmental-treaty/.

Apodaca, Clair. 2001. "Global Economic Patterns and Personal Integrity Rights after the Cold War." *International Studies Quarterly* 45: 587–602.

Aust, Anthony. 2000. *Modern Treaty Law and Practice.* Cambridge: Cambridge University Press.

Aust, Anthony. 2007. *Modern Treaty Law and Practice.* 2nd edition. Cambridge: Cambridge University Press.

Asiwe, C. C. and Odirin Omiegbe. 2014. "Legal and Ethical Issues of Persons with Special Needs in Nigeria." *Educational Research and Reviews* 9(15): 516–22.

Axelrod, Robert and Robert O. Keohane. 1985. "Achieving Cooperation under Anarchy: Strategies and Institutions." *World Politics* 38(1): 226–54.

Baccini, Leonardo and Johannes Urpelainen. 2014. "Before Ratification: Understanding the Timing of International Treaty Effects on Domestic Politics." *International Studies Quarterly* 58(1): 29–43.

Barnett, Laura and Sebastian Spano. 2008. *Canada's Approach to the Treaty-Making Process.* Ottawa, Canada: Library of Parliament.

Bassiouni, M. Cherif. 1999. "Negotiating the Treaty of Rome on the Establishment of an International Criminal Court." *Cornell International Law Journal* 32(3): 443–469.

Bauer, Joanne and Daniel A. Bell. 1999. "Introduction." In *The East Asian Challenge for Human Rights,* edited by Joanne Bauer and Daniel A. Bell, 3–23. Cambridge: Cambridge University Press.

Bearcem David H. and Stacy Bondanella. 2007. "Intergovernmental Organizations, Socialization, and Member-state Interest Convergence." *International Organization* 61(4): 703–733.

Bitker, Bruno V. 1970. "The International Treaty against Racial Discrimination." *Marquette Law Review* 53(1): 68–93.

Bodansky, Daniel. 2008. "The Concept of Legitimacy in International Law." In *Legitimacy in International Law,* edited by Rudiger Wolfrum and Volker Roeben, 321–341. Berlin: Springer.

Bodansky, Daniel. 2015. "Legally Binding Versus Non-Legally Binding Instrument." In *Toward a Workable and Effective Climate Regime,* edited by Scott Barrett, Carlo Carraro, and Jaime de Melo, 155–165. London, UK: Centre for Economic Policy Research (CEPR) Press.

Boix, Carles and Susan C. Stokes. 2003. "Endogenous Democratization." *World Politics* 55(4): 517–549.

Bossuyt, Marc J. 1987. *Guide to the "Travaux Préparatoires" of the International Covenant on Civil and Political Rights.* Leiden: Martinus Nijhoff Publishers.

Boyle, Alan. 2006. "Human Rights or Environmental Rights? A Reassessment." *Fordham Environmental Law Review* 18(3): 471–511.

Bradley, Curtis A. 2012. "Treaty Signature." In *The Oxford Guide to Treaties,* edited by Duncan Hollis, 208–219. Oxford: Oxford University Press.

Brownlee, J. 2007. *Authoritarianism in an Age of Democratization*. New York: Cambridge University Press.

Buchanan, Allen. 2003. *Justice, Legitimacy, and Self-Determination: Moral Foundations for International Law*. Oxford: Oxford University Press.

Buchanan, Allen and Robert O. Keohane. 2006. "The Legitimacy of Global Governance Institutions." *Ethics & International Affairs* 20(4): 405–37.

Bueno de Mesquita, Bruce, George W. Downs, Alastair Smith, and Feryal Marie Cherif. 2005. "Thinking inside the Box: A Closer Look at Democracy and Human Rights." *International Studies Quarterly* 49(3): 439–457.

Bühler, Konrad G. 2001. *State Succession and Membership in International Organizations: Legal Theories Versus Political Pragmatism*. The Hague: Kluwer Law International.

Busby, Joshua W. 2010. *Moral Movements and Foreign Policy*. Cambridge: Cambridge University Press.

Cahn, Claude. 2014. *Human Rights, State Sovereignty, and Medical Ethics: Examining Struggles around Coercive Sterilisation of Romani Women*. Leiden: Martinus Nijhoff Publishers.

Campbell. 2013. "Africa: Kenya, Zimbabwe, and South Africa: Violence and Transition in Post Settler-Colonial States." *African in Transition* (blog), *Council on Foreign Relations*. July 25, 2013. www.cfr.org/blog/africa-kenya-zimbabwe-and-south-africa-violence-and-transition-post-settler-colonial-states.

Canadian Department of Aboriginal Affairs and Northern Development. 2011. "Aboriginal Consultation and Accommodation: Updated Guidelines for Federal Officials to Fulfill the Duty to Consult." www.aadnc-aandc.gc.ca/.

Canadian Department of Justice. 2015. "International Human Rights Treaty Adherence Process in Canada." www.justice.gc.ca/eng/abt-apd/icg-gci/ihrl-didp/ta-pa.html, accessed on March 26, 2020.

Cardenas, Sonia. 2007. *Conflict and Compliance: State Reponses to International Human Rights Pressure*. Philadelphia: University of Pennsylvania Press.

Carlson, Matthew and Ola Listhaug. 2007. "Citizens' Perceptions of Human Rights Practices: an Analysis of 55 Countries." *Journal of Peace Research* 44(4): 465–483.

Carnegie Endowment for International Peace. 1917. Yearbook: 1917. Washington, D.C.

Chayes, Abram and Antonia Handler Chayes. 1993. "On Compliance." *International Organization* 47(2): 175–205.

Clark, Ann Marie. 2001. *Diplomacy of Conscience: Amnesty International and Changing Human Rights Norms*. Princeton: Princeton University Press.

Clark, Ann Marie. 2010. *Diplomacy of Conscience: Amnesty International and Changing Human Rights Norms*. Princeton: Princeton University Press.

Clark, Ann Marie. 2013. "The Normative Contest of Human Rights Criticism: Treaty Ratification and UN Mechanisms." In *The Persistent Power of Human*

Rights: From Commitment to Compliance, edited by Thomas Risse, Stephen C. Ropp, and Kathryn Sikkink, 125–144. Cambridge: Cambridge University Press.

Claude, Inis L. 1966. "Collective Legitimization as a Political Function of the UN." *International Organization* 20(3): 367–379.

Cole, Wade. 2012. "Human Rights as Myth and Ceremony? Re-Evaluating the Effectiveness of Human Rights Treaties, 1981 to 2007." *American Journal of Sociology* 117(4): 1131–1171.

Comstock, Audrey L. 2019. "Adjusted Ratification: Post-Commitment Actions to UN Human Rights Treaties." *Human Rights Review* 20(1): 23–45.

Conant, Lisa. 2016. "Who Files Suit: Legal Mobilization and Torture Violations in Europe." *Law & Policy* 38(4): 280–303.

Conforti, Benedetto. 2005. *The Law and Practice of the UN*. Third Revised Edition. Leiden: Martinus Nijoff Publishers.

Conrad, Courtenay R. 2014. "Divergent Incentives for Dictators: Domestic Institutions and (International Promises Not to) Torture". *Journal of Conflict Resolution* 58(1): 34–67.

Gerring, John. 2008. "Case Selection for Case-Study Analysis: Qualitative and Quantitative Techniques" in *The Oxford Handbook of Political Methodology*, edited by Janet M. Box-Steffensmeier, Henry E. Brady, and David Collier, 645–684. Oxford: Oxford University Press.

Crabb, Jr. Cecil V., Glenn J. Antizzo, and Leila S. Sarieddine. 2000. *Congress and the Foreign Policy Process: Modes of Legislative Behavior*. Louisiana State University Press.

D'Amato, Anthony A. 1971. *The Concept of Custom in International Law*. Ithaca: Cornell University Press.

D'Amato, Anthony A. 2010. Is International Law Really "Law"? Faculty Working Papers. 103. https://scholarlycommons.law.northwestern.edu/facultyworkingpapers/103

Dai, Xinyuan. 2013. "The 'Compliance Gap' and the Efficacy of International Human Rights Institutions." In *The Persistent Power of Human Rights: From Commitment to Compliance*, edited by Thomas Risse, and Stephen C. Ropp, and Kathryn Sikkink, 85–124. Cambridge: Cambridge University Press.

Davenport, Christian. 1995. "Multi-Dimensional Threat Perception and State Repression: An Inquiry into Why States Apply Negative Sanction." *American Journal of Political Science* 39(3): 683–713.

Davenport, Christian. 1999. "Human Rights and the Democratic Proposition." *Journal of Conflict Resolution* 43(1): 92–116.

Davenport, Christian and David A. Armstrong II. 2004. "Democracy and the Violation of Human Rights: A Statistical Analysis from 1976–1996." *American Journal of Political Science* 48(3): 538–554.

Denemarl, Robert A. and Matthew J. Hoffman. 2008. "Just Scraps of Paper?: The Dynamics of Multilateral Treaty-Making." *Cooperation and Conflict* 43(2): 185–219.

Donnelly, Jack. 1984. "Cultural Relativism and Universal Human Rights." *Human Rights Quarterly* 6(4): 400–419.

Donnelly, Jack. 1999. "Human Rights, Democracy, and Development." *Human Rights Quarterly* 21(3): 608–632.

Downs, George W., David M. Rocke, and Peter N. Barsoom. 1996. "Is the Good News about Compliance Good News about Cooperation?" *International Organization* 50(3): 379–406.

Downs, George W. and Michael A. Jones. 2002. "Reputation, Compliance, and International Law." *Journal of Legal Studies* 32: 95–114.

Dumberry, Patrick. 2018. "State Succession to BITs: Analysis of Case Law in the Context of Dissolution and Secession." *Arbitration International* 34: 445–462.

Dunoff, Jeffrey L., Steven R. Ratner, David Wippman. 2010. *International Law: Norms, Actors, Process*. New York: Aspen Publishers.

Efrat, Asif. 2016. "Legal Traditions and Nonbinding Commitments: Evidence from the United Nations' Model Commercial Legislation." *International Studies Quarterly* 60(4): 624–635.

Eid, Elizabeth. 2001. Interaction between International and Domestic Human Rights Law: A Canadian Perspective. The International Centre for Criminal Law Reform and Criminal Justice Policy. Vancouver, B.C. Canada.

Elkins, Zachary, Tom Ginsburg, and Beth Simmons. 2013. "Getting to Rights: Treaty Ratification, Constitutional Convergence, and Human Rights Practice." *Harvard International Law Journal* 54(1): 61–95.

Elsig, Manfred, Karolina Milewicz, and Nikolas Stürchler. 2011. "Who Is in Love with Multilateralism? Treaty Commitment in the Post–Cold War Era." *European Union Politics* 12(4): 529–550.

Ewang, Anietie. 2019. "Nigeria Passes Disability Rights Law." Human Rights Watch Report. www.hrw.org/news/2019/01/25/nigeria-passes-disability-rights-law.

Fabry, Mikulas. 2010. *Recognizing States: International Society and the Establishment of New States since 1776*. Oxford: Oxford University Press.

Fariss, Christopher J. 2014. "Respect for Human Rights Has Improved over Time: Modeling the Changing Standard of Accountability." *American Political Science Review* 108(2): 297–318.

Fidler, David P. 2018. "UN Treaty Talks and Human Rights Accountability for Corporate Digital Activities," (blog), *Council on Foreign Relations* www.cfr.org/blog/un-treaty-talks-and-human-rights-accountability-corporate-digital-activities.

Finnemore, Martha and Kathryn Sikkink. 1998. "International Norm Dynamics and Political Change." *International Organization* 52(4): 887–917.

Finnemore, Martha and Stephen J. Toope. 2001. "Alternatives to 'Legalization': Richer Views of Law and Politics." *International Organization* 55(3): 743–758.

Fikfak, Veronika. 2014. "Domestic Courts' Enforcement of Decisions and Opinions of the International Court of Justice." In *A Farewell to Fragmentation: Reassertion and Convergence in International Law,* edited by Mads Andenas and Eirik Bjorge, 343–370. Cambridge: Cambridge University Press.

Freedom House. 1998. "Freedom in the World 1998: Cambodia." https://freedom house.org/report/freedom-world/1998/cambodia.

Freedom House. 1999. "Mauritania: Freedom in the World 1999." https://freedom house.org/report/freedom-world/1999/mauritania.

Gaeta, Paola. 2009. *The UN Genocide Convention: A Commentary.* Oxford: Oxford University Press.

Gandhi, Jennifer. 2008. *Political Institutions under Dictatorship.* New York: Cambridge University Press.

Gandhi, Jennifer and Ellen Lust-Okar. 2009. "Elections under Authoritarianism." *Annual Review of Political Science* 12: 403–422.

Ginsburg, Tom and Tamir Moustafa. 2008. *Rule by Law: The Politics of Courts in Authoritarian Regimes.* Cambridge: Cambridge University Press.

Goldsmith, Jack L. and Eric A. Posner. 2005. *The Limits of International Law.* Oxford: Oxford University Press.

Goldstein, Judith, Miles Kahler, Robert O. Keohane, and Anne-Marie Slaughter. 2000. "Introduction: Legalization and World Politics." *International Organization* 54(3): 385–399.

Goodliffe, Jay and Darren Hawkins. 2006. "Explaining Commitment: States and the Convention against Torture." *Journal of Politics* 68(2): 358–371.

Goodman, Ryan and Derek Jinks. 2003. "Measuring the Effects of Human Rights Treaties." *European Journal of International Law* 14(1): 171–183.

Goodman, Ryan and Derek Jinks. 2004. How to Influence States: Socialization and International Human Rights Law. *Duke Law Journal* 54(3): 621–703.

Goodman, Ryan and Thomas Pegram. 2011. "Introduction: National Human Rights Institutions, State Conformity and Social Change." In *Human Rights, State Compliance, and Social Change: Assessing National Human Rights Institutions,* edited by Ryan Goodman and Thomas Pegram, 1–26. Cambridge, UK: Cambridge University Press.

Government of the Netherlands. 2019. "The Difference between Signing and Ratification." www.government.nl/.

Greenhill, Brian. 2010. "The Company You Keep: International Socialization and the Diffusion of Human Rights Norms." *International Studies Quarterly* 54(1): 127–145.

Greenhill, Brian. 2014. "Explaining Nonratification of the Genocide Convention: A Nested Analysis." *Foreign Policy Analysis* 10(4): 371–391.

Greenhill, Brian. 2016. *Transmitting Rights: International Organizations and the Diffusion of Human Rights Practices.* Oxford: Oxford University Press.

Grewal, Sharanbir and Erik Voeten. 2015. "Are New Democracies Better Human Rights Compliers?" *International Organization* 69(2): 497–518.

Guilhot, Nicolas. 2005. *The Democracy Makers: Human Rights and International Order.* New York: Columbia University Press.

Guzman, Andrew T. 2008. *How International Law Works: A Rational Choice Theory.* Oxford: Oxford University Press.

Habeeb, I. William and Mark Zartman. 1986. *The Panama Canal Negotiations.* Baltimore: Foreign Policy Institute Johns Hopkins University.

Hafner, Gerhard and Gregor Novak. 2012. "State Succession in Respect of Treaties." In *The Oxford Guide to Treaties*, edited by Duncan B. Hollis, 396–427. Oxford: Oxford University Press.

Hafner-Burton, Emilie M. 2005. "Trading Human Rights: How Preferential Trade Agreements Influence Government Repression." *International Organization* 59(3): 593–629.

Hafner-Burton, Emilie M. and Kiyoteru Tsutsui. 2005. "Human Rights in a Globalizing World: The Paradox of Empty Promises." *American Journal of Sociology* 110(5): 1373–1411.

Hafner-Burton, Emilie M. and Kiyoteru Tsutsui. 2007. "Justice Lost! The Failure of International Human Rights Law to Matter Where Needed Most." *Journal of Peace Research* 44(4): 407–425.

Hafner-Burton, Emilie M. and James Ron. 2009. "Seeing Double: Human Rights through Qualitative and Quantitative Eyes." *World Politics* 61(2): 360–401.

Hafner-Burton, Emilie M., Edward D. Mansfield, and Jon C. W. Pevehouse. 2015. "Human Rights Institutions, Sovereignty Costs and Democratization." *British Journal of Political Science* 45(1): 1–27.

Haftel, Yoram Z. and Alexander Thompson. 2013. "Delayed Ratification: The Domestic Fate of Bilateral Investment Treaties." *International Organization* 67(2): 355–387.

Haglund, LaDawn and Rimjhim Aggarwal. 2011. "Test of Our Progress: The Translation of Economic and Social Rights Norms into Practice." *Journal of Human Rights* 10(4): 494–520.

Harrison, Kathryn. 2007. "The Road Not Taken: Climate Change Policy in Canada and the United States." *Global Environmental Politics* 7(4): 92–117.

Hathaway, Oona A. 2002. "Do Human Rights Treaties Make a Difference?" *The Yale Law Journal* 111: 1935–2042.

Hathaway, Oona A. 2003. "The Cost of Commitment." *Stanford Law Review* 55(5): 1821–1862.

Hathaway, Oona A. 2007. "Why Do Countries Commit to Human Rights Treaties?" *Journal of Conflict Resolution* 51(4): 588–621.

Hathaway, Oona A. 2008. "International Delegation and State Sovereignty." *Law and Contemporary Problems* 71(1): 115–149.

Henkin, Louis. 1979. *How Nations Behave: Law and Foreign Policy.* Columbia University Press.

Henkin, Louis. 1995. "U.S. Ratification of Human Rights Conventions: The Ghost of Senator Bricker." *The American Journal of International Law* 89(2): 341–350.

Hill, Daniel W. Hill, Jr. 2010. "Estimating the Effects of Human Rights Treaties on State Behavior." *The Journal of Politics* 72(4): 1161–1174.

Hillebrecht, Courtney. 2012. "The Domestic Mechanisms of Compliance with International Human Rights Law: Case Studies from the Inter-American Human Rights System." *Human Rights Quarterly* 34(4): 959–985.

Hillebrecht, Courtney. 2014. *Domestic Politics and International Human Rights Tribunals: The Problem of Compliance.* Cambridge: Cambridge University Press.

Hillebrecht, Courtney. 2016. "Compliance: Actors, Context and Causal Processes." In *Research Handbook on the Politics of International Law,* edited by Wayne Sandholtz and Christopher A. Whytock, 27–54. Cheltenham: Edward Elgar Publishing.

Hollis, Duncan. 2012. *The Oxford Guide to Treaties.* Oxford: Oxford University Press.

Holmes, Marcus and Keren Yarhi-Milo. 2017. "The Psychological Logic of Peace Summits: How Empathy Shapes Outcomes of Diplomatic Negotiations." *International Studies Quarterly* 61(1): 107–122.

Human Rights Watch 1992. "Yugoslavia: Human Rights Abuses in Kosovo 1990–1992." www.hrw.org/legacy/reports/1992/yugoslavia/.

Human Rights Watch. 1994a. "The Slovak Republic." www.hrw.org/reports/1994/WR94/Helsinki-19.htm#P605_186764.

Human Rights Watch. 1994b. "The Czech Republic." www.hrw.org/reports/1994/WR94/Helsinki-07.htm#P257_94812.

Human Rights Watch. 1995. "The Slovak Republic." www.hrw.org/reports/1995/WR95/HELSINKI-14.htm#P579_177632.

Human Rights Watch. 1996a. "The Slovak Republic." www.hrw.org/reports/1996/WR96/Helsinki-17.htm#P883_178739.

Human Rights Watch. 1996b. "The Czech Republic." www.hrw.org/reports/1996/WR96/Helsinki-07.htm#P435_97083.

Human Rights Watch. 2019. "Written Testimony: 'Kids in Cages: Inhumane Treatment at the Border.'" Testimony of Clara Long Before the U.S. House Committee on Oversight and Reform, Subcommittee on Civil Rights and Civil Liberties. July 11, 2019. www.hrw.org/news/2019/07/11/written-testimony-kids-cages-inhumane-treatment-border.

Huneeus, Alexandra. 2014. "Compliance with Judgements and Decisions." In *The Oxford Handbook of International Adjudication,* edited by Cesare Romano, Karen Alter, and Yuval Shany, 437–463. Oxford: Oxford University Press.

Hurd, Ian. 1999. "Legitimacy and Authority in International Politics." *International Organization*. 53(2): 379–408.

International Court of Justice. 2008. Application of the International Convention on the Elimination of All Forms Racial Discrimination (Georgia v. Russian Federation) Request for the Indication of Provisional Measures. October 15, 2008.

Jensen, Steven L. B. 2016. *The Making of International Human Rights: The 1960s, Decolonization, and the Reconstruction of Global Values.* Cambridge University Press.

Johnston, Alastair, Iain. 2008. *Social States: China in International* Relations, *1980-2000.* Princeton University Press.

Kahler, Miles. 2001. "Legalization as Strategy: The Asia-Pacific Case." In *Legalization and World Politics*, edited by Judith Goldstein, Miles Kahler, Robert Keohane, and Anne- Marie Slaughter, 165–187. Cambridge, MA: The MIT Press.

Kamminga, Menno T. 1996. "State Succession in Respect of Human Rights Treaties." *European Journal of International Law* 7(4): 469–484.

Kaye, David. 2011. "Who's Afraid of the International Criminal Court? Finding the Prosecutor Who Can Set It Straight." *Foreign Affairs* 90(3): 118–129.

Keck, Margaret and Kathryn Sikkink. 1998. *Activists without Borders: Transnational Advocacy Networks in International Politics.* Ithaca: Cornell University Press.

Keith, Linda Camp. 1999. "The UN International Covenant on Civil and Political Rights: Does It Make a Difference in Human Rights Behavior?" *Journal of Peace Studies* 36(1): 95–118.

Kelly, David and Anthony Reid, eds. 1998. *Asian Freedoms: The Idea of Freedom in East and Southeast Asia.* Cambridge: Cambridge University Press.

Kelley, Judith G. 2017. *Scorecard Diplomacy: Grading States to Influence Their Reputation and Behavior.* Cambridge: Cambridge University Press.

Kelley, Judith G. and Jon C. W. Pevehouse. 2015. "An Opportunity Cost Theory of US Treaty Behavior." *International Studies Quarterly* 59(3): 531–543.

Kennedy, Charles Stuart and Peter D. Eicher. 2010. Interview with Peter D. Eicher. [Manuscript/Mixed Material] Retrieved from the Library of Congress, www .loc.gov/item/mfdipbib001547/.

Kennedy, Charles Stuart and Theodore E. Russell. 2000. Interview with Theodore E. Russell. [Manuscript/Mixed Material] Retrieved from the Library of Congress, www.loc.gov/item/mfdipbib001445/.

Kim, Hunjoon and Kathryn Sikkink. 2010. "Explaining the Deterrence Effect of Human Rights Prosecutions for Transitional Countries." *International Studies Quarterly* 54(4): 939–963.

Koremenos, Barbara, Charles Lipson, and Duncal Snidal. 2001. "The Rational Design of International Institutions." *International Organization* 55(4): 761–799.

Koskenniemi, Martti. 2010. "International Law and Hegemony: A Reconfiguration." *Cambridge Review of International Affairs* 17(2): 197–218.

Kratochvíl, Jan. 2009. "Realizing a Promise: A Case for Ratification of the Optional Protocol to the Covenant on Economic, Social, and Cultural Rights." *Human Rights Brief* 16: 30–35.

Krommendijk, Jasper. 2015. "The Domestic Effectiveness of International Human Rights Monitoring in Established Democracies: The Case of the UN Human Rights Treaties Bodies." *The Review of International Organizations* 10(4): 489–512.

Landman, Todd. 2005. *Protecting Human Rights: A Comparative Study.* Washington, DC: Georgetown University Press.

Lang, Raymond Lucy Upah. 2008. "Disability Scoping Study in Nigeria." *Commissioned by British Department for International Development [DFID].* www.ucl.ac.uk/lc-ccr/downloads/dfid_nigeriareport

Larson, Eric, Wibo van Rossum, and Patrick Schmidt. 2014. "The Dutch Confession: Compliance, Leadership and National Identity in the Human Rights Order." *Utrecht Law Review* 10(1): 96–112.

Lawand, Kathleen. 2007. "The Convention on the Prohibition of the Use, Stockpiling, Production and Transfer of Anti-Personnel Mines and on their Destruction (Ottawa Convention)" In *Making Treaties Work: Human Rights, Environment, and Arms Control edited by Geir Ulfstein in collaboration with Thilo Marauhn and Andreas Zimmerman,* P324–350. Cambridge: Cambridge University Press.

Lempert, Robert O. 1976. "Mobilizing Private Law: An Introductory Essay." *Law and Society Review* 11(2): 173–189.

Lepard, Brian D. 2010. *Customary International Law: A New Theory with Practical Applications.* Cambridge: Cambridge University Press.

Lord, Janet E. and Michael Ashley Stein. 2008. "The Domestic Incorporation of Human Rights Law and the UN Convention on the Rights of Persons with Disabilities." *Washington Law Review* 83(4): 449–480.

Lupu, Yonatan. 2013a. "Best Evidence: The Role of Information in Domestic Judicial Enforcement of International Human Rights Agreements." *International Organization* 67(3): 469–503.

Lupu, Yonatan. 2013b. "The Informative Power of Treaty Commitment: Using the Spatial Model to Address Selection Effects." *American Journal of Political Science* 57(4): 912–925.

Lupu, Yonatan. 2016. "Why Do States Join Some Universal Treaties but Not Others? An Analysis of Treaty Commitment Preferences." *Journal of Conflict Resolution* 60(7): 1219–1250.

Lutz, Ellen L. and Kathryn Sikkink. 2000. "International Human Rights Law and Practice in Latin America." *International Organization* 54(3): 633–659.

Maluwa, Tiyanjana. 1992. "Succession to Treaties in Post-Independence Africa: A Retrospective Consideration of Some Theoretical and Practical Issues with

Special Reference to Malawi." *African Journal of International and Comparative Law* 4(4): 791–815.

Maraugh, Thilo. 2007. "Dispute Resolution, Compliance Control and Enforcement of International Arms Control Law." In *Making Treaties Work: Human Rights, Environment, and Arms Control Edited by Geir Ulfstein in Collaboration with Thilo Marauhn and Andreas Zimmerman*, 243–272. Cambridge: Cambridge University Press

Marek, Krystyna. 1968. *Identity and Continuity of States in Public International Law*. Geneva: Librarie Droz.

Marshall, Monty G., Ted Robert Gurr, and Keith Jaggers. 2017. "PolityIV Project: Political Regime Characteristics and Transitions, 1800–2016." Dataset Users' Manual. Center for Systemic Peace. www.systemicpeace.org/inscr/p4manualv2016.pdf.

Mayerfeld, Jamie. 2007. "Playing by Our Own Rules: How U.S. Marginalization of International Human Rights Law Led to Torture." *Harvard Human Rights Journal* 20(1): 89–140.

McCann, Michael. 2008. "Litigation and Legal Mobilization." In *The Oxford Handbook of Law and Politics*, edited by Keith E. Whittington, R. Daniel Kelemen, and Gregory A. Caldera, 522–540. Oxford: Oxford University Press.

McCarty, Nolan and Rose Razaghian. 1999. "Advice and Consent: Senate Responses to Executive Branch Nomination 1856–1996." *American Journal of Political Science* 43(4): 1122–1143.

McGuinness, Margaret E. 2005. "Exploring the Limits of International Human Rights Law." *Georgia Journal of International and Comparative Law* 34: 393–421.

McKibben, Heather Elko and Shaina D. Western. 2014. "Levels of Linkage: Across-Agreement versus Within-Agreement Explanations of Consensus Formation among States." *International Studies Quarterly* 58(1): 44–54.

McLuhan, Marshall. 1964. *Understanding Media: The Extensions of Man*. Cambridge, MA: MIT Press.

Mechlem, Kerstin. 2009. "Treaty Bodies and the Interpretation of Human Rights." *Vanderbilt Journal of Transnational Law* 42(3): 905–947.

Merry, Sally Engle. 2006. *Human Rights and Gender Violence: Translating International Law into Local Justice*. Chicago: University of Chicago Press.

Merry, Sally Engle. 2009. *Human Rights and Gender Violence: Translating International Law into Local Justice*. Chicago: University of Chicago Press.

Mitchell, Neil J. and James M. McCormick. 1988. "Economic and Political Explanations of Human Rights Violations." *World Politics* 40(4): 476–498.

Mitchell, Ronald. 1994. "Regime Design Matters: Intentional Oil Pollution and Treaty Compliance." *International Organization* 48(3): 425–458.

Mitchell, Sara McLaughlin and Emilia Justyna Powell. 2011. *Domestic Law Goes Global: Legal Traditions and International Courts*. Cambridge, UK: Cambridge University Press.

Mitchell, Sara McLaughlin, Jonathan J. Ring, and Mary K. Spellman. 2013. "Domestic Legal Traditions and States' Human Rights Practices." *Journal of Peace Research* 50(2): 189–202.

Moravcsik, Andrew. 1995. Explaining International Human Rights Regimes: Liberal Theory and Western Europe. *European Journal of International Relations* 1(2): 157–189.

Moravcsik, Andrew. 2000. "The Origins of Human Rights Regimes: Democratic Delegation in Postwar Europe." *International Organization* 54(2): 217–252.

Morgenthau, Hans J. (1948) 1993. *Politics among Nations: The Struggle for Power and Peace*. Revised by Kenneth W. Thompson. New York: McGraw Hill.

Morgenthau, Hans J., and Kenneth W. Thompson. *Politics Among Nations: The Struggle for Power and Peace*. New York: Knopf, 1985.

Morrow, James. 1992. "Signaling Difficulties with Linkage in Crisis Bargaining." *International Studies Quarterly* 36(2): 153–172.

Morsink, Johannes. 1999. *The Universal Declaration of Human Rights: Origins, Drafting, and Intent*. Philadelphia: University of Pennsylvania Press.

Moustafa, Tamir. 2007. *The Struggle for Constitutional Power: Law, Politics, and Economic Development in Egypt*. Cambridge: Cambridge University Press.

Musil, Jifi. 1992. "Czechoslovakia in the Middle of Transition." *Czechoslovak Sociological Review* 28: 5–21.

Neumayer, Eric. 2005. "Do International Human Rights Treaties Improve Respect for Human Rights?" *Journal of Conflict Resolution* 49(6): 925–953.

Neumayer, Eric and Laura Spess. 2005. "Do Bilateral Investment Treaties Increase Foreign Direct Investment to Developing Countries?" *World Development* 33(10): 1567–1585.

Nielson, Richard A. and Beth A. Simmons. 2015. "Rewards for Ratification: Payoffs for Participating in the International Human Rights Regime?" *International Studies Quarterly* 59(2): 197–208.

Page, Sheila. 2004. Developing Countries in International Negotiations: How they Influence Trade and Climate Change Negotiations. *IDS Bulletin* 35(1): 71–82.

Parliament of Canada. 2001. "Promises to Keep: Implementing Canada's Human Rights Obligations: Report of the Standing Senate Committee on Human Rights." https://sencanada.ca/Content/SEN/Committee/371/huma/rep/rep02dec01-e.htm.

Pevehouse, Jon C. 2002. "With a Little Help from My Friends? Regional Organizations and the Consolidation of Democracy." *American Journal of Political Science* 46(3): 611–626.

Pillay, Navanethem. 2012. "Strengthening the United Nations Human Rights Treaty Body System: A Report by the United Nations High Commissioner for Human Rights." www2.ohchr.org/.

Poe, Steven C. and Neal C. Tate. 1994. "Repression of Human Rights to Personal Integrity in the 1980s: A Global Analysis." *American Political Science Review* 88(4): 853–872.

Poe Steven C., Neal C. Tate, and Linda Camp Keith. 1999. "Repression of the Human Right to Personal Integrity Revisited: A Global Cross-National Study Covering the Years 1976–1993." *International Studies Quarterly* 43(2): 291–313.

Posner, Eric A. 2013. "Human Rights, the Laws of War, and Reciprocity." *The Law & Ethics of Human Rights* 6(2): 147–171.

Posner, Eric A. 2014. *The Twilight of Human Rights Law.* Oxford: Oxford University Press.

Posner, Eric A. and Jack L. Goldsmith. 1999. "A Theory of Customary International Law." *University of Chicago Law Review* 66: 1113–1177.

Posner, Eric A. and Miguel F. P. de Figueiredo. 2005. "Is the International Court of Justice Biased?" *Journal of Legal Studies* 34: 599–630.

Powell, Emilia Justyna and Jeffrey K. Staton. 2009. "Domestic Judicial Institutions and Human Rights Treaty Violation." *International Studies Quarterly* 53(1): 149–174.

Powell, Emilia Justyna and Sara McLaughlin Mitchell. 2007. The International Court of Justice and the World's Three Legal Systems. *Journal of Politics* 69(2): 397–415.

Przeworski, Adam, Michael E. Alvarez, José Antonio Cheibub, and Fernando Limongi. 2000. *Democracy and Development: Political Institutions and Well-Being in the World, 1950–1990.* New York: Cambridge University Press.

"Proceedings in the U.N." *New York Times,* July 7, 1966.

Putnam, Robert D. 1988. "Diplomacy and Domestic Politics: The Logic of Two-Level Game." *International Organization* 42(3): 427–460.

Raiffa, Howard. 1982. *The Art and Science of Negotiation.* Harvard University Press.

Rasulov, Akbar. 2003. "Revisiting State Succession to Humanitarian Treaties: Is There a Case for Automaticity?" *European Journal of International Law* 14(1): 141–170.

Republic of Turkey. n.d. "Relations between Turkey and the Czech Republic." www .mfa.gov.tr/relations-between-turkey-and-the-czech-republic.en.mfa.

Risse, Thomas. 2000. "'Let's Argue!': Communicative Action in World Politics." *International Organization* 54(1): 1–39.

Risse, Thomas, Stephen C. Ropp, and Kathryn Sikkink, eds. 1999. *The Power of Human Rights: International Norms and Domestic Change.* Cambridge: Cambridge University Press.

Risse, Thomas, Stephen C. Ropp, and Kathryn Sikkink, eds. 2013. *The Persistent Power of Human Rights: From Commitment to Compliance.* Cambridge: Cambridge University Press.

Roberts, Anthea. 2011. Comparative International Law? The Role of National Courts in Creating and Enforcing International Law. *International & Comparative Law Quarterly* 60(1): 57–92.

Roberts, Christopher N. 2015. *The Contentious History of the International Bill of Rights*. Cambridge: Cambridge University Press.

Sandholtz, Wayne. 2017. "Domestic Law and Human Rights Treaty Commitments: The Convention against Torture." *Journal of Human Rights.* 16(1): 25–43.

Schlager, Erika. 2000. "A Hard Look at Compliance with 'Soft' Law: The Case of the OSCE," In *Commitment and Compliance: The Role of Non-Binding Norms in the International Legal System*, edited by Dinah Shelton, 346–371. Oxford: Oxford University Press

Schnakenberg, Keith E. and Christopher J. Fariss. 2014. Dynamic Patterns of Human Rights Practices. *Political Science Research and Methods* 2(1): 1–31.

Schneider, Christina J. and Johannes Urpelainen. 2013. "Distributional Conflict between Powerful States and International Treaty Ratification." *International Studies Quarterly* 57(1): 13–27.

Shamsi, Nadia. 2016. "The ICC: A Political Tool? How the Rome Statute is Susceptible to the Pressures of More Powerful States." *Willamette Journal of International Law and Dispute Resolution* 24(1): 35–104.

Shelton, Dinah. 2000. *Commitment and Compliance: The Role of Non-Binding Norms in the International Legal System*. Oxford:Oxford University Press.

Sikkink, Kathryn. 2017. *Evidence for Hope: Making Human Rights Work in the 21st Century*. Princeton: Princeton University Press.

Simmons, Beth A. 2000. "International Law and State Behavior: Commitment and Compliance in International Monetary Affairs." *The American Political Science Review* 94(4): 819–835.

Simmons, Beth A. 2002. "Why Commit? Explaining State Acceptance of International Human Rights Obligations." Berkeley Law Working Paper Series 02–05, 2002. Retrieved from https://wcfia.harvard.edu/files/wcfia/files/752_simmonswhycommit.pdf.

Simmons, Beth A. 2009. *Mobilizing for Human Rights: International Law in Domestic Politics*. Cambridge: Cambridge University Press.

Simmons, Beth A. 2013. "From Ratification to Compliance: Quantitative Evidence on the Spiral Model." In *The Persistent Power of Human Rights: From Commitment to Compliance*, edited by Thomas Risse, Stephen C. Ropp, and Kathryn Sikkink, 43–60. Cambridge: Cambridge University Press.

Simmons, Beth A. 2015. "What's Right with Human Rights." Review of *The Twilight of Human Rights Law*, by Eric A. Posner. *Democracy: Journal of Ideas*, 35 (Winter 2015), 99–106.

Simmons, Beth A. and Daniel J. Hopkins. 2005. "The Constraining Power of International Treaties: Theories and Methods." *American Political Science Review* 99(4): 623–631.

"Slovenia, Croatia Declare Freedom from Yugoslavia: Balkans: Federal Parliament reacts angrily and orders the army to 'prevent the division' of the nation." 1991.

June 26, 1991. Accessed on 3 29 2020 available at www.latimes.com/archives/la-xpm-1991–06-26-mn-1188-story.html

Smith-Cannoy, Heather. 2012. *Insincere Commitments: Human Rights Treaties, Abusive States, and Citizen Activism.* Washington, DC: Georgetown University Press.

Sofer, Sasson, 2013. *The Courtiers of Civilization: A Study of Diplomacy.* Albany: SUNY Press.

Spar, Debora L. 1998. "The Spotlight and the Bottom Line: How Multinationals Export Human Rights." *Foreign Affairs* 77(2): 7–12.

Spilker, Gabriele and Tobias Böhmelt. 2013. "The Impact of Preferential Trade Agreements on Governmental Repression Revisited." *The Review of International Organizations* 8(3): 343–361.

Susskind, Lawrence and Connie Ozawa. 1992. "Negotiating More Effective International Environmental Agreements." In *The International Politics of the Environment: Actors, Interests, and Institutions,* edited by Andrew Hurrell and Benedict Kingsbury, 142–165. New York: Oxford University Press.

Swain, Edward T. 2006. "Reserving." *Yale Journal of International Law* 31(2): 307–366.

Tam, Waikenurg. 2013. *Legal Mobilization under Authoritarianism: The Case of Post-Colonial Hong Kong.* Cambridge: Cambridge University Press.

Tams, Christian J. 2016. "State Succession to Investment Treaties: Mapping the Issues." *ICSID Review: Foreign Investment Law Journal* 31(2): 314–343.

Tomuschat, Christian. 2008. "International Covenant on Civil and Political Rights." United Nations Audiovisual Library of International Law. https://legal.un.org/avl/pdf/ha/iccpr/iccpr_e.pdf.

Tomz, Michael. 2007. "Domestic Audience Costs in International Relations: An Experimental Approach." *International Organization* 61(4): 821–840.

Trone, John. 2001. *Federal Constitutions and International Relations.* Macmillan.

Udombana, Nsongurua J. 2001. "Can the Leopard Change Its Spots? The African Union Treaty and Human Rights." *American University International Law Review* 17(6): 1177–1262.

UN. n.d. "Children." Accessed July 22, 2019. www.un.org/en/sections/issues-depth/children/.

UN. 1945. Charter of the United Nations, October 24, 1945. 1 UNTS XVI.

UN. 1960. UNGA Resolution 1514(XV) December 14, 1960.

UN. 1989. "International Decade for the Eradication of Colonialism: Report of the Secretary General, A/44/800." November 27, 1989. https://undocs.org/.

UN. 1992. "General Assembly: Forty-Seventh Session: Provisional Verbatim Record of the 12th Meeting." October 2, 1992. https://undocs.org/en/A/47/PV.12.

UN. 1993. "Multilateral Treaties Deposited with the Secretary-General: Succession by Bosnia and Herzegovina. C.N.323.1994.Treaties." https://treaties.un.org/doc/Publication/CN/1993/CN.323.1993-Eng.pdf.

UN. 1993b. "General Assembly Forty-Eighth Session: 18th Plenary Meeting." October 6, 1993. https://undocs.org/en/A/48/PV.18

UN. 1994. "Declaration of the Government of the Republic of Palau of 10 November 1994." Accessed on March 29, 2020 at https://2009-2017 .state.gov/documents/organization/65854.pdf.

UN. 1996. "Committee on the Rights of the Child: Czech Republic Report CRC/C/ aa/Add.11 17." June 17, 1996. https://tbinternet.ohchr.org/_layouts/15/treaty bodyexternal/Download.aspx?symbolno=C RC%2fC%2f11%2fAdd.11 &Lang=en.

UN. 1997/1998. "Report on the Activities of the Chairperson between the Nineteenth and Twentieth Sessions of CEDAW." www.un.org/womenwatch/ daw/cedaw/cedaw20/salma.htm.

UN. 1998. "Committee on the Rights of the Child: Slovak Republic." April 6, 1998. https://tbinternet.ohchr.org/_layouts/15/treatybodyexternal/Download.aspx? symbolno=C RC%2fC%2f11%2fAdd.17&Lang=en.

UN. 2001. "General Assembly Human Rights Council: Sixteenth Session, Agenda Item 6: Report of the Working Group on the Universal Period Review: United States of America." https://documents-dds-ny.un.org/doc/UNDOC/GEN/G11/ 100/69/PDF/ G1110069.pdf?OpenElement.

UN. 2002. "Multilateral Treaties Deposited with the Secretary General."

UN. 2005. "Civil and Political Rights: The Human Rights Committee." www .ohchr.org/Documents/Publications/FactSheet15rev.1en.pdf.

UN. 2007. "Convention on the Rights of Persons with Disabilities: Nigeria: Signature." Reference CN407.2007.Treaties-54. https://treaties.un.org/doc/ Publication/CN/2007/CN.407.2007-Eng.pdf.

UN. 2009. "General Assembly Human Rights Council: Twelfth Session, Agenda Item 6: Report of the Working Group on the Universal Period Review: Afghanistan." https://documents-dds-ny.un.org/doc/UNDOC/GEN/G09/146/ 14/PDF/ G0914614.pdf?OpenElement.

UN. 2010. "LA41TR/221/Full Powers Guidelines/2010." https://treaties.un.org /doc/source/publications/NV/2010/Full_Powers-2010.pdf.

UN. 2016. "New Record: Translations of Universal Declaration of Human Rights Pass 500." November 2, 2016. www.ohchr.org/EN/NewsEvents/

UN. 2017a. "Human Rights Committee: General Comment No. 36 on Article 6 of the International Covenant on Civil and Political Rights, on the Right to Life. Advance Unedited Version." https://tbinternet.ohchr.org/Treaties/CCPR/ Shared%20Documents/1_Global/CCPR_C_G C_36_8785_E.pdf.

UN. 2017b. Human Rights Committee, 'General Comment No. 36 on Article 6 of the International Covenant on Civil and Political Rights, on the Right to Life', adopted on First Reading during the 120th Session (draft General Comment).

UN. 2018. United Nations Treaty Collection Glossary.

UN. 2019a. "Committee on Enforced Disappearances: List of Issues in Relation to the Report Submitted by Slovakia." https://tbinternet.ohchr.org/_layouts/15/treatybodyexternal/Download.aspx?symbolno=CED%2fC%2fSVK%2fQ%2f1&Lang=en.

UN. 2019b. "About UN Membership." www.un.org/en/sections/member-states/about-un- membership/index.html.

UN. 2019c. "Treaty Collection: Glossary of Treaty Body Terminology." www2.ohchr.org/english/bodies/treaty/glossary.htm.

UNDP. 2016. Human Development Annual Report: Nigeria. http://hdr.undp.org/sites/default/files/2016_human_development_report.pdf

UNICEF. n.d. "Introduction to the Convention on the Rights of the Child: Definition of Key Terms." [March 30, 2020]. www.unicef.org/french/crc/files/Definitions.pdf.

UNHRC. 1995. Communication No. 670/1995. Ruediger Schlosser v. Czech Republic. CCPR/C/64/D/670/1995.

UNICEF. 2020. "How the Convention on the Rights of the Child Works: Joining, Implementing and Monitoring the World's Most Widely Ratified Human Rights Treaty." www.unicef.org/child-rights-convention/how-convention-works.

Urlacher, Brian R. 2015. International Relations as Negotiations. London: Routledge.

US 2017. "Observations of the US of America On the Human Rights Committee's Draft General Comment No. 36 On Article 6—Right to Life. The UN Office of the High Commissioner of Human Rights. www.ohchr.org/en/hrbodies/ccpr/pages/gc36-article6righttolife.aspx.

US Department of State. 2000. "1999 Country Reports on Human Rights Practices." February 2, 2000. https://2009–2017.state.gov/j/drl/rls/hrrpt/1999//index.htm.

US Department of State. 2011. "2010 Country Reports on Human Rights Practices."

US Department of State. 2017. "Promoting the Rights of Persons with Disabilities." Bureau of Democracy, Human Rights, and Labor. www.state.gov/promoting-the-rights-of- persons-with-disabilities/.

US Department of State. 2019. "Multilateral Treaties in Force as of January 1, 2019: Section 2: Multilateral Treaties and Other Agreements." www.state.gov/wp-content/uploads/2019/07/2019-Treaties-in-Force-Multilaterals-7.23.2019.pdf.

US Department of State. 2020. "U.S. Relations with the Czech Republic: Bilateral Relations Fact Sheet." January 14, 2020. www.state.gov/u-s-relations-with-the-czech- republic/.

Vienna Convention on the Law of Treaties. 1969. UN Treaty Series, 1155, 331.

Vienna Declaration and Programme of Action, U.N. GAOR, World Conf. on Hum. Rts., 48th Sess., 22d plen. mtg., part I, ¶ 8, U.N. Doc. A/CONF.157/24

(1993), reprinted in 32 I. L. M. 1661 (1993). www.ohchr.org/EN/ProfessionalInterest/Pages/Vienna.aspx.

von Stein, Jana. 2005. "Do Treaties Constrain or Screen? Selection Bias and Treaty Compliance." *American Political Science Review.* 99(4): 611–622.

von Stein, Jana. 2008. "The International Law and Politics of Climate Change: Ratification of the UN Framework Convention and the Kyoto Protocol." *Journal of Conflict Resolution* 52(2): 243–268.

von Stein, Jana. 2016. "Making Promises, Keeping Promises: Democracy, Ratification and Compliance in International Human Rights Law." *British Journal of Political Science* 46(3): 655–679.

von Stein, Jana. 2018. Exploring the Universe of UN Human Rights Agreements. *Journal of Conflict Resolution* 62(4): 871–899.

Vreeland, James Raymond. 2008. "Political Institutions and Human Rights: Why Dictatorships Enter into the UN Convention against Torture." *International Organization* 62(1): 65–101.

Ward, Michael D. and Kristian S. Gleditsch. 1998. Democratizing for Peace. *American Political Science Review* 92(1): 51–61.

Washburn, John. 1999. "The Negotiation of the Rome Statute for the International Criminal Court and International Lawmaking in the 21st Century." *Pace International Law Review* (11): 361.

Weber, Max. 2008. *Complete Writings on Academic and Political Vocations.* Edited by John Dreijmanis. Translated by Gordon C. Wells. New York: Algora Publishing.

Weeramantry, Christopher Gregory. 1996. "Application of the Convention on the Prevention and Punishment of the Crime of Genocide (Bosnia Herzegovina v. Yugoslavia), Judgment on Preliminary Objections." *ICJ Reports* www.icj-cij.org/en/case/91/judgments.

Welch, Claude E. Jr. 2001. *Protecting Human Rights in Africa: Roles and Strategies of Nongovernmental Organizations.* Philadelphia: University of Pennsylvania Press.

Welch, Ryan M. 2017. "National Human Rights Institutions: Domestic Implementation of International Human Rights Law." *Journal of Human Rights* 16(1): 96–116.

Wendt, Alexander. 1999. *Social Theory of International Politics.* Cambridge: Cambridge University Press.

Wheatley, Steven. 2010. *The Democratic Legitimacy of International Law.* London: Bloomsbury Publishing.

Wight, Martin. 1972. "International Legitimacy." *International Relations* 4(1): 1–28.

Williams, Paul R. 1994. "State Succession and the International Financial Institutions: Political Criteria v. Protection of Outstanding Financial Obligations." *The International and Comparative Law Quarterly* 43(4): 776–808.

Wood, Michael. 2015. "International Organizations and Customary International Law." *Vanderbilt Journal of Transnational Law* 48(3): 609–620.

Wotipka, Christine Min and Kiyoteru Tsutsui. 2008. "Global Human Rights and State Sovereignty: State Ratification of International Human Rights Treaties, 1965–2001." *Sociological Forum* 23(4): 724–754.

Yau, Jennifer. 2005. "Promise and Prospects of the UN's Convention on Migrant Workers." Migration Policy Institute Report. www.migrationpolicy.org/article/promise-and-prospects-uns-convention-migrant-workers.

Young, Oran and Marc Levy. 1998. "The Effectiveness of International Environmental Regimes." In *The Effectiveness of International Environmental Regimes*, edited by Oran Young, 1–32. Cambridge, MA: MIT Press.

Young, Robert A. 1994. "The Breakup of Czechoslovakia." Research Paper No. 32, Institute of Intergovernmental Relations. Kingston: Queen's University.

Zemans, Frances Kahn. 1983. "Legal Mobilization: The Neglected Role of the Law in the Political System." *The American Political Science Review* 77(3): 690–703.

Zhou, Min. 2014. "Signaling Commitments, Making Concessions: Democratization and State Ratification of International Human Rights Treaties, 1966–2006." *Rationality and Society* 26(4): 475–508.

INDEX

Printed in Great Britain
by Amazon

43846811R00137